Cry of the Human

"... to be alone, to eat and sleep alone,
to adventure alone: cry of the human ..."
—David Ignatow

Cry of the Human

Essays on Contemporary
American Poetry
Ralph J. Mills, Jr.

University of Illinois Press
Urbana Chicago London

LIBRARY OF CONGRESS CATALOGING IN PUBLICATION DATA

Mills, Ralph J.   1931–
    Cry of the human.

    Bibliography: p.
    1.   American poetry—20th century—History and
criticism.   I.   Title.
PS325.M54   1975   811'.5'409   74-14507
ISBN 0-252-00459-0

Acknowledgments are gratefully extended to the following authors, publishers, and agents for their kind permission to quote from copyrighted poetry.

To Atheneum Publishers, for excerpts from THEY FEED THEY LION, by Philip Levine, 1972; and for an excerpt from "A Scale in May" in THE LICE, by W. S. Merwin, 1963. Copyright © 1960, 1961, 1962, 1963 by W. S. Merwin.

To City Lights Books, for "The Day Lady Died" from LUNCH POEMS, by Frank O'Hara. Copyright © 1964 by Frank O'Hara.

To Corinth Books, for an excerpt from THE MAXIMUS POEMS, by Charles Olson, 1960.

To Curtis Brown, Ltd., for excerpts from "At Thirty-five," by Donald Hall. Reprinted by permission of Curtis Brown, Ltd. © 1964 by Donald Hall.

To Doubleday and Company, Inc., for excerpts from THE COLLECTED POEMS OF THEODORE ROETHKE, copyright © 1937, 1954, 1958, 1959, 1960, 1961, 1962, 1963, 1964, 1965, 1966 by Beatrice Roethke as administratrix of the estate of Theodore Roethke. Copyright © 1932, 1934, 1935, 1936, 1937, 1938, 1939, 1940, 1941, 1942, 1946, 1947, 1948, 1949, 1950, 1951, 1952, 1953, 1954, 1955, 1956, 1957, 1958, 1961 by Theodore Roethke.

To Farrar, Straus & Giroux, Inc., for "Grandparents" and excerpts from "Waking in the Blue" in LIFE STUDIES, by Robert Lowell, copyright © 1956, 1959 by Robert Lowell; for excerpts from "Waking Sunday Morning" in NEAR THE OCEAN, by Robert Lowell, copyright © 1963, 1965, 1966, 1967 by Robert Lowell. For "Dream Song #8" and "Dream Song #29" from THE DREAM SONGS by John Berryman, copyright © 1959, 1962, 1963, 1964, 1965, 1966, 1967, 1968, 1969 by John Berryman.

To Donald Hall, for excerpts from THE DARK HOUSES, 1958.

To Harcourt Brace Jovanovich, Inc., for an excerpt from "The Love Song of J. Alfred Prufrock" in COLLECTED POEMS 1909–1962, by T. S. Eliot.

To Harper and Row, Publishers, Inc., for excerpts from THE ALLIGATOR BRIDE and THE YELLOW ROOM by Donald Hall; for excerpts from "Getting There" in ARIEL, by Sylvia Plath.

To Houghton Mifflin Company, for excerpts from WHAT A KINGDOM IT WAS, FLOWER HERDING ON MOUNT MONADNOCK, and BODY RAGS, by Galway Kinnell; for an excerpt from LIVE OR DIE, by Anne Sexton.

To George Hitchcock and Kayak Books, for excerpts from RED DUST, by Philip Levine.

To Philip Levine, for excerpts from ON THE EDGE, 1963.

To Little, Brown and Company, for lines from "Open the Gates" from SELECTED POEMS by Stanley Kunitz. Copyright © 1958 by Stanley Kunitz. Reprinted with the permission of Atlantic–Little, Brown.

To the Macmillan Company, for an excerpt from "A Dialogue of Self and Soul" from COLLECTED POEMS of William Butler Yeats. Copyright © by the Macmillan Company, renewed 1961 by Bertha Georgie Yeats.

To New Directions Publishing Corporation, for excerpts from Denise Levertov, O TASTE AND SEE. Copyright © 1964 by Denise Levertov Goodman. Reprinted by permission of New Directions Publishing Corporation.
For excerpts from Denise Levertov, THE JACOB'S LADDER. Copyright © 1961 by Denise Levertov Goodman. Reprinted by permission of New Directions Publishing Corporation.
For an excerpt from Robert Duncan, THE OPENING OF THE FIELD. Copyright © 1960 by Robert Duncan. Reprinted by permission of New Directions Publishing Corporation.

To Juliet Rago McNamara, for an excerpt from A SKY OF LATE SUMMER by Henry Rago.

To Random House, Inc., and Alfred A. Knopf, Inc., for an excerpt from "Sunday Morning" in COLLECTED POEMS OF WALLACE STEVENS, copyright © 1954 by Wallace Stevens. Reprinted with permission of Random House, Inc., and Alfred A. Knopf, Inc.

To Gary Snyder, for "Above Pate Valley" from RIPRAP & COLD MOUNTAIN POEMS by Gary Snyder, Four Seasons Foundation, 1966.

To Wesleyan University Press, for excerpts from NOT THIS PIG by Philip Levine, copyright © 1968 by Philip Levine. Reprinted with permission of Wesleyan University Press.

To Helen, for the years—

"Like a choice
Returned to and returned to, like
A luminous choice"
Henry Rago

—and to my children, Natalie, Julian, and Brett, with love.

Acknowledgments

"Creation's Very Self" was originally delivered as the Cecil Williams Memorial Lecture in American Literature at Texas Christian University on May 7, 1969, and was issued as a small book by the University Press, with a foreword by William Burford. I am most grateful to Texas Christian University, its Press and editors, including Professor Betsy Colquitt, for permission to reprint this lecture in revised form.

The essay on Theodore Roethke first appeared in *Theodore Roethke: Essays on the Poetry*, edited by Arnold Stein. Thanks are due the editor and the University of Washington Press for permission to reprint it.

The studies of Galway Kinnell and Donald Hall were first published in *The Iowa Review*. I extend my warmest gratitude to that journal and its editor, Merle Brown, for his kindness and his receptivity to such lengthy essays, and for permission to reprint them.

"Earth Hard: The Poetry of David Ignatow" was initially published in slightly different form in *Boundary 2*. My thanks to the editors, particularly William V. Spanos, for allowing me to include it here.

The essay on Philip Levine was originally printed in *The American Poetry Review*. My gratitude to its editors, especially Stephen Berg, for permission to reprint it. Thanks are also due Philip Levine for providing me with copies of his work not easily obtainable.

Finally, I should like to indicate a considerable indebtedness to my friend and colleague, Michael Anania, who has read these essays at various times and in various stages and has offered his shrewd judgment and his strong encouragement when these were most needed.

Foreword

What I like about Ralph Mills is that he is not a didactic critic. He is not authoritarian. He is not dogmatic. He does not weave through the waters like a hammerhead shark. He is not out to kill you if you do not believe him.

He is an aesthetic critic, a man of sensibility who loves his subject and leads the reader with gentleness, justice, and enthusiasm, with sympathies and penetrations to let him see what he sees, feel what he feels, so that this kind of humane and nontoxic criticism can be a joy to read. If you know the poets, you may return to them refreshed by his insights. If you do not know them, or partially know them, his earnestness, sensitivity, and charm of relating are so genuine that you may wish to make your own total discoveries of the poets from his persuasions, his devotion to telling his truth.

Another way to say it is that some criticism is so severe that it is hard to read, so high-handed that as reader you lose the fundamental sense of poetry as giving pleasure in welters of intellection giving instead a kind of pain.

Mills's criticism is easy to read and is thus refreshing, and at the same time it is instructive, clarifying, and energizing. He shows the way but does not tell his reader how to feel. This new kind of criticism is better than the old so-called New Criticism which laid down the laws about a poem and if you did not take its teaching you were considered unworthy as a reader. If you did not conform, it paid a disrespect to your own true critical responses.

Why do I like what I call aesthetic criticism, or impressionistic criticism, or call it appreciative criticism better than dogmatic, didactic, hierarchical criticism? I feel that it must be due to the nature of the times. Our times are chaotic, kaleidoscopic. We have lived through depression, war, more war. I think of Spain, World War II, Korea, Vietnam, the cold war, atomic weapons, loss of religion, overpopulation, drugs, divorce, crime, dishonesty in government leading to Watergate; all these realities plus others militate against any one standard in criticism, any absolute value or value system.

Johnson in the eighteenth century had it easier than any of our critics today. He had a more or less stable society, indeed, an Age of Enlightenment, and he could deduce rules of writing from established rules of conduct. He could be reasonable, extol reason, and take a commonsense point of view.

In some ways we are better off because our times are so wild. But to be dogmatic now is to be absurd. And to uphold the absurd as a final value is more absurd. It is too late for Arnold. His brave idea that poetry will save us is true only in a delicate intellectual balancing act wherein supposedly we become better because more sensitive. But poetry did not alter the wars and other forces mentioned above.

Because of our present situation, and the splendid vigor of our diverse poetry, it seems to me that a personal, democratic criticism like that of Ralph Mills is much to the point of these times—a sharing of sensibility and enthusiasms with readers, a wish to show and to explain, in no way a wish to compel, or to beleaguer, but to exemplify relative attitudes as against absolute attitudes or dogmatic claims. These are relevant, too, and may appear again in the future, but I enjoy Ralph Mills's critical presentations of the poets he has chosen because of his love of poetry, which he expresses sincerely and convincingly.

The build of the book is refreshing. In an introductory chapter Mr. Mills looks over the field. The field of poetry is wide and great in America. He writes a chapter on Roethke which is informative, revealing, and gives a clear indication of his scope, interests, concerns, and progress. The bulk of the work is in three full chapters on Ignatow, Hall, and Kinnell. He could have chosen other poets from the wide contemporary field, and this book is so engaging that I hope he will engage other new poets in the future. His last chapter is a less full but rewarding chapter on Levine.

What I like about Ignatow is that you do not have to think about Marvell. He has no reference to Benlowes. He does not care about Beddoes. What I like about Ignatow is that he knows about Ignatow. I like the totality of his humanity. He is a people and I like the people.

What is the use of negative criticism? Fortunately, Mills is positive, yet not with a sledge hammer. Should I give Ignatow bad marks for not suggesting Marvell, or Benlowes, or Beddoes? He may know them, for all I know, but he does not show them. He shows himself, streets, people, the common sufferings of mankind, his, mine, yours. He tends to be prosaic, but what of that? Others tend to be poetic; read them.

Roethke had a sense of Elizabethan form and forms, and Berryman wrote a complicated imitation in the manner of Dante. Hall began in a convention of elders and in an early period wrote a moving poem about ancestors, nature, and New Hampshire, but then he suffered a sea change into the something rich and strange that Mills takes many pages to explain. Hall's change of style and interests shows the depths of his psychic penetration into arcane reaches of the spirit in a wide variety of poems in new makes of his own.

Kinnell knows that much of poetry comes from below the head. He could have learned this from Lawrence but he learned it from life, from himself. His personalism and passion, his unrelenting look at the truth preserve his deep knowledge in poems about the porcupine and the bear, the latter one of the best animal poems, surrogate for the animal man, of these times. To sophisticate dark places, bring a complex order to sprawling conditions, is a feat of Levine. "Everything we/say comes to nothing," but the rich nature of Levine alights on words to make poems anything but nothing, nothing if not anything but brilliant.

RICHARD EBERHART

Preface

The essays gathered in this book with one exception—a study of Theodore Roethke's last poems, written for an earlier occasion—represent my chief critical interests and efforts since the late 1960's. As such, I suppose they can be fairly viewed as a continuation along the lines indicated in a previous volume, *Contemporary American Poetry* (1965); indeed, the essay on Roethke included here picks up where the chapter on him in that collection left off. But the present book, unlike its predecessor, is not designed to offer a spectrum of poetic endeavor in this country in recent years, except insofar as the opening paper surveys an aspect of American poetry which gained prominence during the preceding decade or so. Nor are the other essays intended to support any sort of programmatic purpose. All the same, they follow naturally from the considerations and predilections evident in "Creation's Very Self," and the reader will perhaps discern even more correspondences and connections than the author can.

It remains, then, to say a few words on the essays treating the work of David Ignatow, Galway Kinnell, Donald Hall, and Philip Levine. My critical preference has always been for poets of substantial achievement whose writings either have been neglected or have received only minimal discussion, thus enabling me to approach their poems with a sense of freshness and discovery. That sense was very strong with the above-mentioned poets and led, in three of the instances, to considerably longer essays than I had at first anticipated, for the emergent patterns, themes, and imagery of their poems required increasing elaboration as the process of writing about them went on.

While the decision to write about these poets was personal, based

on my own deep attraction to their work, no apologies are necessary for the choices. Initially, each essay was composed with separate
publication in mind; later, at a friend's prompting, I saw that com-
bined with the Roethke study and "Creation's Very Self" they
formed a coherent but not binding whole. Ignatow, Kinnell, Hall,
and Levine demonstrate through powerful vision and originality
of style how the American poetic imagination has grappled fiercely
and inventively with the challenges set by the character of life since
the mid-century. The openness to experience and the search for
new, authentic modes of expression which are commented upon
within the somewhat generalized framework of "Creation's Very
Self" find exemplary figures for more detailed examination in
these accomplished and highly individual poets.

No doubt a number of other poets of similar forcefulness and
talent could be added to or substituted for those who are here.
Critics and readers will easily supply the important names of Bly,
Creeley, Olson, O'Hara, Ashbery, Simpson, Merwin, and so forth,
for themselves. But the overall conception of this book, as I see it,
belongs to the realm of the suggestive rather than the comprehensive, if it belongs to anything. It reflects my own feelings and taste,
too, and may, of course, imply my restrictions and blind spots. In
any event, it tries to sidestep theory and strict thesis, to refuse par-
tisanship and to maintain independence. A poet-critic friend, Al
Poulin, once observed that my criticism was romantic and per-
sonalist. I accept the definition. The ensuing essays result from a
basic sympathy for and imaginative commitment to the poetry and
poets that are their reason for being.

Contents

There can be for many writers no return to the traditional conception of God as the highest existence, creator of all other existences, transcending his creation as well as dwelling within it. If there is to be a God in the new world it must be a presence within things and not beyond them. The new poets have at the farthest limit of their experience caught a glimpse of a fugitive presence, something shared by all things in the fact that they are. This presence flows everywhere, like the light which makes things visible, and yet can never be seen as a thing in itself. It is the presence of things present. . . .

—J. Hillis Miller, *Poets of Reality*

And what I am proposing is that, toward the end of a new baptism for the modern imagination, a radically secular literature may have a profoundly fruitful religious function to perform. For, by the very resoluteness with which it may plunge us into the Dark, it may precipitate us out of our forgetfulness, so that, in a way, our deprivation of the Transcendent may itself bring us into fresh proximity to its Mystery.

—Nathan A. Scott, Jr., *Negative Capability*

1   Creation's Very Self: On the Personal Element in Recent American Poetry

Behind the poem is the human being . . .
  —Richard Lewis

Categories and classifications are among the dehumanizing evils of our time. Almost anywhere we turn in these bleak, disordered days of recent history there lies in wait one kind of mechanism or other which has as its end the obscuration or destruction of what is unique and particular, unmistakably itself: the very identity of a person, an experience, an object. Since nothing keeps alive our awareness of the concrete and specific more than poetry, it is the worst sort of folly to force it into convenient patterns or to make it demonstrate some invented principle. Such efforts are nets to catch the wind, a wind which has sacred sources because it is the Muse's or the spirit's motion, or, following Charles Olson's definition of the poetic line, because it is "the breathing of the man who writes, at the moment that he writes."[1] In spite of every attempt to do something with or to it, as W. H. Auden says in his elegy for Yeats, poetry "survives,/A way of happening, a mouth." And so it should be. The few distinctions and delineations that I make in the following pages are loose, not rigid, and are designed for the exigencies of the occasion. My purpose here will be neither that of the scholar nor the theorist, but, if you will, that of the enthusiast-commentator who wishes to bring to attention some contemporary poets and their poems, to remark on certain qualities that seem

1. Charles Olson, "Projective Verse," in *Human Universe and Other Essays*, ed. Donald M. Allen (New York, 1967), p. 54.

prominent and characteristic, and to disappear, leaving the reader, I hope, with a desire to know recent poetry better.

One distinction I do think necessary to draw before we can discuss current writing separates *modernist* poetry from *contemporary* poetry. I shall presume that the modernist poets are those whose names spring first to mind when we think of poetry in English in this century, the great pioneer figures such as Yeats, Eliot, Pound, Stevens, W. C. Williams, and Marianne Moore, most of them born a decade or more before the turn of the century and all but a few now dead. These modernists have in common the fact that each of them, in his or her own way, participated in the poetic revolution which cast aside the vestiges of Victorianism and outworn literary conventions, infused new vigor into diction and rhythm, disclosed new possibilities of form, and brought poetry into meaningful relationship with the actualities of modern life—a relationship which is being renewed by poets today. Having accomplished all this, the modernist poets proceeded into the years of their maturity and produced some of their finest work long after that revolutionary movement of what Randall Jarrell once aptly called "irregularly cooperative experimentalism"[2] was over. So, in a period ostensibly belonging to their successors, those poets who are the first of the ones I shall call contemporaries, we find extraordinary achievements such as Eliot's *Four Quartets*, Pound's later *Cantos*, Williams's *Paterson*, and Stevens's *The Auroras of Autumn* looming intimidatingly over the poetic landscape.

What separates the contemporaries from the modernists, to begin with, is the simple fact of being born too late to join in that radical movement which, beginning around 1910, overthrew reigning literary modes and aesthetic tastes, and, with increasing help from literary critics, itself solidified into an establishment. Not only did these younger poets emerge in the wake of a full-scale artistic revolution, whose chief participants were still alive and still quite productive, but they were also confronted with fresh versions of the

2. Randall Jarrell, "The End of the Line," in *Literary Opinion in America*, ed. M. D. Zabel (New York, 1951), p. 747.

literary past and a variety of prospects for using it which Eliot's notion of tradition, the practice of his poetry, and an expanding body of literary criticism made available. The liberating influence of William Carlos Williams was yet to be felt.

So it was that Stanley Kunitz, Richard Eberhart, Theodore Roethke, John Berryman, Robert Lowell, Karl Shapiro, Randall Jarrell, and others who began to write in the 1930's had to seek their own voices, searching them out through the arduous process of trying on and discarding models, guides, and influences from the poetic tradition and from modernist writers alike, without the benefit of any shared aesthetic principle or revolutionary artistic purpose. They did have in common a dogged attentiveness to the inner necessities of imaginative vision and to the difficult struggle for style. In this situation there were both burdens and blessings. If these poets, and many others who followed them in the late 1940's and the 1950's, felt overshadowed by most of their elders and confined by what Donald Hall terms a critical "orthodoxy" which required "a poetry of symmetry, intellect, irony, and wit,"[3] they were freed as individuals from the demands created by literary movements to an energetic and single-minded concentration on the making of poems, a concentration that brought, in due time, Roethke in *The Lost Son*, Lowell in *Life Studies*, Berryman in *Homage to Mistress Bradstreet* and *The Dream Songs*, and Shapiro in *The Bourgeois Poet*, for example, to the kind of poetic breakthrough James Dickey calls "The Second Birth"—an intense imaginative liberation, achieved at great personal cost, in which the poet, like a snake shedding his dead skin, frees himself of the weight of imposed styles and current critical criteria to come into the place of his own authentic speech. The secret of this renewal, Dickey observes, "does not, of course, reside in a complete originality, which does not and could not exist. It dwells, rather, in the development of the personality, with its unique weight of experience and memory, as a writing instrument, and in the ability to give literary influence a new dimension which has the quality of this

3. *Contemporary American Poetry*, ed. Donald Hall (Baltimore, 1962), p. 17.

personality as informing principle. The Second Birth is largely a matter of self-criticism and endless experiment, presided over by an unwavering effort to ascertain what is most satisfying to the poet's self as it develops, or as it remains more clearly what it has always been."[4]

It is precisely here, with Dickey's notion of the poet's personality "as informing principle," that I want to note an important difference between the critical views derived from the modernist movement and the practice of many contemporaries—a difference which has been heightened in the last decade and a half by the appearance of the Beat poets, the Projectivists, the confessional poets, the so-called New York School, and what is often called a new Surrealism or poetry of the unconscious. I have used in my chapter title the term "personal element," which is purposely more general than Dickey's "personality," so it might apply equally to the work of a number of poets who have differing aims and emphases. But both terms oppose the view handed down from Eliot and the New Criticism that poetry and the emotions it conveys are, or should be, impersonal, and that an author's personality and life ought to be excluded from his writings. In many of their poems Eliot, Pound, Stevens, and others stress the poet's anonymity by employing fictional masks, invented speakers or *personae*, thus enforcing a division between writer and work. The original motive for such objectivity seems genuine enough: to rid poetry of biographical excesses and the residue of the Romantics' preoccupation with personality which had seduced attention from the true object of interest, the poem itself. In his famous 1917 essay, "Tradition and the Individual Talent," Eliot declares, "The more perfect the artist, the more completely separate in him will be the man who suffers and the mind which creates"; and again he says, "The progress of the artist is a continual self-sacrifice, a continual extinction of personality."[5] While it cannot be gone into here, much of what Eliot says has great value and will continue to speak to later generations.

4. James Dickey, *The Suspect in Poetry* (Madison, Minn., 1964), pp. 55–56.
5. T. S. Eliot, *Selected Essays 1917–1932* (New York, 1932), pp. 8, 7.

But the emphasis on the poet as an impersonal or anonymous "medium" (actually, as various commentators have shown, to permit deeper, unconscious sources to aid in shaping poetic imagery and speech) passed out of Eliot's essay to become an important factor of the modern critical atmosphere. Subsequently, the poem came to be considered a neutral object, a vessel filled with the feelings of nobody, what Louis Simpson names "the so-called 'well-made' poem that lends itself to the little knives and formaldehyde of a graduate school."[6]

Among the pioneer modernists, William Carlos Williams, with his anti-academicism, interest in the immediacies of experience and the American spoken language, and sense of the singularity of form in the poem, and William Butler Yeats, with his insistence on the poet's creation of his personality, his anti-self, stand out in marked contrast to Eliot. The decidedly personal character of Yeats' voice, growing bolder and more idiosyncratic as his career lengthened out, could serve as a masterly example for Roethke, Kunitz, Lowell, Berryman, Nemerov, and other contemporary poets in quest of a personal idiom, a speech vibrating with their lives— something which Eliot's poetry does equally, though in perhaps subtler fashion, and in spite of his views. Writing in his autobiographies of what he saw in Dante and Villon, the Irish poet might have been describing the figure he makes in his own poems. "Such masters," he observes, "would not, when they speak through their art, change their luck; yet they are mirrored in all the suffering of desire. The two halves of their nature are so completely joined that they seem to labour for their objects, and yet to desire whatever happens, being at the same time predestinate and free, creation's very self. We gaze at such men in awe, because we gaze not at a work of art, but at the recreation of the man through that art. . . ."[7]

Contemporary poets, then, with a few forerunners providing guidance, begin to cultivate their own inwardness as material for

---

6. Louis Simpson, "Dead Horses and Live Issues," *The Nation* (April 24, 1967), p. 520.

7. *The Autobiography of William Butler Yeats* (New York, 1958), p. 183.

poetry or to look to the immediacies of their own situation for valid experience. In reaction to impersonality and rationalism, critical prescription and dissection, they seek a personal mode of utterance to embody perceivings and intuitions very much their own. As Robert Creeley comments, "Confronting such *rule* [i.e., a critical rule of rationality and taste], men were driven back upon the particulars of their own experience, the literal *things* of an immediate environment, wherewith to acknowledge the possibilities of their own lives."[8] With rare exceptions like Robert Duncan, poets no longer translate subjective experience into the kind of larger symbolic or metaphysical frameworks sustained by some of the modernists. Contemporary poets frequently give the impression of beginning their poems nearer the brink of private intuition and feeling, and of trying, for the sake of authentic testimony, to remain as close to it as they are able. Nor do these poets hesitate to speak in their poems as themselves, for the individual voice is likewise to be understood as a sign of authenticity. In general, there is a distrust among contemporaries of systematizing; those who have known some sort of visionary or mystical experience—Roethke or Eberhart, say—refuse to account for it by intellectual means or to locate it within some comprehensive explanation of things. Instead, these experiences are enclosed in the heart of the poems which sprang from them; as a result, they are not divisible from the selves to whom they occurred.

Contemporary poets might take one of their chief mottoes from Wordsworth. In the preface to the *Lyrical Ballads* of 1800, after asking himself "What is a Poet?" and "To whom does he address himself?" he answers unequivocally, "He is a man speaking to men." And we can add to this statement—thinking not only of Lowell, Eberhart, or Roethke, but also of more recent poets, of Anne Sexton or John Logan, Gary Snyder or Frank O'Hara, Denise Levertov or William Stafford—that each poet wishes to speak to us, without impediment, from the deep center of a personal engage-

8. Introduction to *The New Writing in the U.S.A.*, ed. Donald M. Allen and Robert Creeley (Harmondsworth, Middlesex, 1967), p. 18.

ment with existence. For the contemporary poet enters into himself and the particulars of his experience in order to bring into being in his work that true poetic "self which [he] is waiting to be," to borrow a phrase from Ortega y Gassett[9] that confirms Yeats' remarks. The activity in which he engages is not just the construction of objects but the fashioning of a language that will ultimately awaken and transform the inner world of his readers. We approach here Martin Buber's description of "the primary word *I—Thou*" which "can be spoken only with the full being." The artist who creates, in Buber's thought, "may withhold nothing of himself."[10] So, for our contemporary poets, we can perhaps say that poetic creation moves toward an intimacy, a communion of selves made available to the reader, if he will assume his part in it, through the agency of the unique poetic self we encounter speaking to us there. The contemporary poem requires dialogue to fulfill itself; once received, it inhabits us, unfolds a space within where we meet another presence, the poet's, through the order and resonance of words and images he has formed. "So," Kenneth Rexroth can rightly observe, "speech approaches in poetry not only the directness and the impact but the unlimited potential of act."[11]

Recent American poetry, with its chosen precursors in Whitman, Williams, Pound, Hart Crane, and the writing of European and Latin American poets influenced by Surrealism and Expressionism, as well as Chinese and Japanese verse, discards artificial barriers that put distance between poet, poem, and reader; searches out new kinds of informality in the attempt to be more congruent with the shapes of experience. The contemporary poet re-creates himself as a personality, an identifiable self within his poetry, that is, of course, a self who has been selected and heightened in the process, captured in essence, and so is not perhaps a full likeness of the author as a physical, workaday person outside the poem yet could not be mis-

9. Ortega y Gassett, *The Dehumanization of Art and Other Essays* (New York, 1956), p. 175.
10. Martin Buber, *I and Thou*, trans. R. G. Smith (New York, 1958), pp. 11, 10.
11. Kenneth Rexroth, *Bird in the Bush: Obvious Essays* (New York, 1959), p. 12.

taken for someone else. As we read the poems of our contemporaries, we recognize a certain magnanimous gesture in their acts of creation, a profoundly touching and human gesture through which the poet voluntarily stands exposed as "creation's very self" before us. In an age in which inner disorientation occurs because the individual's acts and thoughts appear to have no issue bearing his stamp, instead being swallowed by the vast technical apparatus of social, economic, and political forces that comprise our monolithic city-states, the poet invites us to share in his pursuit of identity; to witness the dramatization of the daily events of his experience—so closely resembling our own; to be haunted by the imagery of his dreams or the flowing stream of his consciousness; to eavesdrop on relationships with friends and lovers; to absorb the shock of his deep-seated fears and neuroses, even mental instability and madness, and through them to realize the torments of our time; and finally to reach with him that redeeming state of what Denise Levertov calls "Attention," which is no less than "the *exercise* of Reverence for the 'other forms of life that want to live.' "[12]

For the rest, let us see, in the abbreviated manner imposed by our limitations, some specific instances of the personal element in several poets and kinds of poetry of the last three decades. My first choice is Theodore Roethke, who died prematurely at the height of his powers in 1963. He produced work of such high quality that I feel sure he must be ranked as one of the finest American lyric poets. Appropriately enough for our subject, too, the pattern of his writing demonstrates in advance of many of his contemporaries the trying process of a "Second Birth," after an earlier period which merely hints at the penetrating experience he has yet to realize. The poems of his first collection, *Open House* (1941), show fundamental gifts: a fine ear, close acquaintance with the natural world, a good sense of language. But in spite of worthy pieces, one feels that all sorts of resources and energies remain still to be tapped. The declarations of the title poem support this feeling:

12. Denise Levertov, "Origins of a Poem," *Michigan Quarterly Review*, VII, 4 (Fall 1968), p. 238.

> My truths are all foreknown,
> This anguish self-revealed.
> I'm naked to the bone,
> With nakedness my shield.
> Myself is what I wear:
> I keep the spirit spare.

"Myself is what I wear"—the announcement might have been made somewhere in *Leaves of Grass*; however, Roethke has not quite earned the right to this declaration yet. In the next half-dozen years he broke through, in the so-called greenhouse poems, to those deeper layers of himself that would draw him on to the radical experimentation of "The Lost Son" and the subsequent poems of his childhood sequence. Commenting on the above-quoted passage three decades later, and only a few months before his death, Roethke remarked:

> This poem is a clumsy, innocent, desperate asseveration. I am not speaking of the empirical self, the flesh-bound ego; it's a single word: *myself*, the aggregate of the several selves, if you will. The spirit or soul—should we say the self, once perceived, *becomes* the soul?—this I was keeping "spare" in my desire for the essential. But the spirit need not be spare: it can grow gracefully and beautifully like a tendril, like a flower.[13]

With the 1940's Roethke started shattering the restraints upon his previous work, pressing beyond the surfaces of experience toward the hidden sources. What he was to discover was, of course, himself, or those "several selves" he mentions, through a return in memory and imagination to his childhood, his family's floral establishment with its huge greenhouses and the acreage of woods and fields beyond, his uncle's suicide and his father's death from cancer when the poet was only fifteen.[14] This return to the past, which was

---

13. "On Identity," in *On the Poet and His Craft: Selected Prose of Theodore Roethke*, ed. Ralph J. Mills, Jr. (Seattle, 1965), p. 21.

14. An illuminating account of these years is to be found in Allan Seager, *The Glass House: The Life of Theodore Roethke* (New York, 1968).

simultaneously a descent into himself, his psyche, could prove agonizing, if poetically rewarding, as he says in "The Return":

> A cold key let me in
> That self-infected lair;
> And I lay down with my life,
> With the rags and rotting clothes,
> With a stump of scraggy fang
> Bared for a hunter's boot.

But past experience which came alive then in his imagination
finds a language that carries it to the page with the urgency and
sensuous immediacy of life itself. At first, Roethke scrutinizes the
lives of flowers and plants, even the tiny insects inhabiting their
leaves. Yet he does not render this "vegetable realm" completely by
itself; everywhere the presence of the poet, both as child-observer
(since the poems draw upon vivid memories) and imaginative par-
ticipant, can be felt, however obliquely. In "Cuttings (*Later*)" he
claims his affinity with this world: the struggling into life visible
there parallels his efforts to renew and complete himself:

> I can hear, underground, that sucking and sobbing,
> In my veins, in my bones, I feel it,—
> The small waters seeping upward,
> The tight grains parting at last.
> When sprouts break out,
> Slippery as fish,
> I quail, lean to beginnings, sheath-wet.

The childhood sequence opening with "The Lost Son," which
takes a poetic leap beyond the greenhouse pieces, dramatizes what
is now Roethke's imaginative preoccupation—the evolution and
identity of the self. Through daring formal combinations, these
poems convey a direct apprehension of inner and outer experience,
the progressions and reversals of psychic life as the self seeks identity and spiritual reality. Beginning with early years, they proceed
through adolescence, the pains of sexuality, the loss of the father,
and on toward phases of illumination in which the self attains an

ecstatic, mystical communion with the surrounding animate and inanimate cosmos. Though Roethke indicates that the anonymous protagonist of these poems is meant to serve as a universal figure or everyman, both biographical detail and the intensity of the poetic experience reveal the poet's personal involvement with the speaker, whose consciousness and preconsciousness are realized in all their complexity through an impressive array of poetic devices. He lists their "ancestors" as "German and English folk literature, particularly Mother Goose; Elizabethan and Jacobean drama, especially the songs and rants; the Bible; Blake and Traherne; Dürer."[15] In these poems Roethke avoids at all costs the intervention of explanation, interpretation, or judgment. As readers, we are compelled to live through the experiences of the self, its sufferings and joys, presented directly, until we recognize that they are poet's and our own. Roethke also brings us to what technological man has forgotten—the inmost being of things, the essential existence we share with creation:

> Arch of air, my heart's original knock,
> I'm awake all over:
> I've crawled from the mire, alert as a saint or a dog;
> I know the back-stream's joy, and the stone's eternal
>   pulseless longing.
> Felicity I cannot hoard.
> My friend, the rat in the wall, brings me the clearest
>   messages;
> I bask in the bower of change;
> The plants wave me in, and the summer apples;
> My palm-sweat flashes gold;
> Many astounds before, I lost my identity to a pebble;
> The minnows love me, and the humped and spitting creatures.
>   —from *Praise to the End!*

In his love poems and later meditative pieces and metaphysical lyrics Roethke continues his relentless pursuit of personal unity of being through the relationship of self to the beloved, to the cos-

15. "Open Letter," in Mills, ed., *On the Poet and His Craft*, p. 41.

mos, and finally to God. Some of the last poems, written with an
instinctive awareness of approaching death, disclose a solitary confrontation with the Divine which becomes an excruciating course
of self-annihilation before it turns into a mystical union achieved
at the very boundaries of human life. My example here is "In a Dark
Time," the initial poem of *Sequence, Sometimes Metaphysical*:

> In a dark time, the eye begins to see,
> I meet my shadow in the deepening shade;
> I hear my echo in the echoing wood—
> A lord of nature weeping to a tree.
> I live between the heron and the wren,
> Beasts of the hill and serpents of the den.
>
> What's madness but nobility of soul
> At odds with circumstance? The day's on fire!
> I know the purity of pure despair,
> My shadow pinned against a sweating wall.
> That place among the rocks—is it a cave,
> Or winding path? The edge is what I have.
>
> A steady storm of correspondences!
> A night flowing with birds, a ragged moon,
> And in broad day the midnight come again!
> A man goes far to find out what he is—
> Death of the self in a long, tearless night,
> All natural shapes blazing unnatural light.
>
> Dark, dark my light, and darker my desire.
> My soul, like some heat-maddened summer fly,
> Keeps buzzing at the sill. Which I is *I*?
> A fallen man, I climb out of my fear.
> The mind enters itself, and God the mind,
> And one is One, free in the tearing wind.

While our limitations do not permit detailed comment at this
point,[16] let us anyway recognize in the poem an archetypal pattern

16. For discussions, see the next essay in the present volume, as well as *The
Contemporary Poet as Artist and Critic*, ed. Anthony Ostroff (Boston, 1964); Karl

of death and rebirth, of descent by the poet into his own nature, there to face its confusions, complexities, and impurities personified in the figure of his "shadow" or double, and to learn the agony of being parted from that in himself which must be abandoned— through a type of ritual or symbolic dying to oneself—if he is to find renewal in the form of communion with God, a communion that is likewise a moment of self-integration or unity of being. The poem gathers strength from the oppositions and perils of spiritual quest, but these qualities would not impress us so much were it not for the feeling of the poet's individual involvement with them. To be sure, the imagery and thematic design of the poem evoke abundant associations from various traditions of religious thought. Yet it is when we grasp these meanings as essential portions of a lived experience which is the poet's that they speak with undeniable conviction, the conviction born of personal witness. Roethke, in a symposium, says of the poem that it was "dictated . . . something given, scarcely mine at all. For about three days before its writing I felt disembodied, out of time; then the poem virtually wrote itself, on a day in summer, 1958."[17] The phrase "scarcely mine at all" does not, once we reflect on it in the context of this specific poem, contradict what I have been saying by separating the poet from his work. Rather, it points to an unusually heightened subjectivity, articulated in its totality from those regions of inwardness where the poem was prepared in secret. Roethke might also have commented on this poem, as on all of his poetry, with Whitman's words from "Song of Myself": "I am the man, I suffer'd, I was there. . . ."

Glancing around the current literary scene, we observe a number of younger poets who in certain ways stand in a line of descent from Roethke, though I should say at once that I am not speaking of direct imitation or obvious stylistic influence. Instead, I have in mind some of those poets who, however different from one another (and these differences are frequently considerable), create a poetry

---

Malkoff, *Theodore Roethke* (New York, 1966); *Theodore Roethke: Essays on the Poetry*, ed. Arnold Stein (Seattle, 1965).

17. Ostroff, ed., *The Contemporary Poet as Artist and Critic*, p. 49.

which depends heavily upon intuitive association, dreams, the preconscious and the unconscious, discontinuous or elliptical imagery;
a poetry highly responsive to the techniques of modern French,
German, Spanish, and Latin American poets; a poetry which proceeds by a "logic of the imagination" rather than a "logic of con-
cepts," to borrow Eliot's distinction with respect to St.-John Perse's
work.[18] Whether treating in some form or other the fusion of outer
and inner life, as, say, in various poems by Frank O'Hara, A. R.
Ammons, David Ignatow, William Stafford, Galway Kinnell,
Donald Justice, and John Logan; exploring avenues opened up by
the possibilities of Surrealism, as in the work of John Ashbery and
the recent poetry of Donald Hall; entering into the being of other
creatures or men by an imaginative extension, as in James Dickey's
writing; giving voice to the hidden dream life of America, as some
of the poems by Robert Bly, Louis Simpson, and James Wright do;
or fashioning a rich but hermetic language of association, evocation,
and prophecy, like W. S. Merwin's, this poetry continues to disclose
its highly personal character. In each instance the poet, tired of the
betrayal of his deepest feelings and most significant experiences by
attempting to force them into conventional forms, tired of the in-
trusion of intellect and reason (Roethke called the latter "That
dreary shed, that hutch for grubby schoolboys!" and countered,
"The hedgewren's song says something else.")[19] upon the free exercise of imagination, tired of the arid critical formulations of the
academies, has moved in the direction of the purely intuitive, the
illogical and irrational, the private and the intimate. Louis Simpson
calls this tendency Surrealist, though he clearly disavows any identification with the rigid theories and formulations proposed by
André Breton. In a recent anthology Simpson writes: "The next
step—it is already occurring—is to reveal the movements of the
subconscious. The Surrealist poet—rejecting on the one hand the

18. Preface to St.-John Perse, *Anabasis*, trans. T. S. Eliot (New York, 1949),
p. 10.
19. From "I Cry, Love! Love!" in *Collected Poems of Theodore Roethke* (New
York, 1966), p. 92.

clichés of the rational mind, and on the other, a mere projection of irrational images—will reveal the drama and narrative of the subconscious. The images move, with the logic of dreams." [20]

We know at once from this statement that Simpson does not wish merely to revive the Surrealist practice of automatic writing. In a later article he insists that "poetry represents not unreason but the total mind, including both reason and unreason," [21] by which he perhaps means the shaping powers of the conscious mind at work upon the materials provided by the subconscious. The French Surrealist poet Paul Eluard, who *is* convinced of the value of automatic writing, has a passage which is helpful in clarifying differences between dream and poem, the images issuing from below consciousness and the sensations which still come from without. In spite of certain discrepancies between Simpson's and Eluard's statements, both aim at a new fusion of interior and exterior experience which will result in radically altered poetic imagery. Eluard says:

> You don't take the story of a dream for a poem. Both are living reality, but the first is a memory, immediately altered and transformed, an adventure, and of the second nothing is lost, nothing is changed. The poet desensitizes the universe to the advantage of human faculties, permits man to see differently other things. His former vision is dead, or false. He discovers a new world, he becomes a new man.
>
> People have thought that automatic writing makes poems useless. On the contrary! It increases or develops the domain of examination of poetic awareness, by enriching it. If awareness is perfect, the elements which automatic writing draws from the inner world and the elements of the outer world are balanced. Thus made equal, they mingle and merge in order to form poetic unity. [22]

By whatever methods they proceed, the poets I am grouping very loosely here, as well as a great number not named (think of Michael Benedikt, Stephen Berg, Charles Simic, or Mark Strand,

---

20. *The Distinctive Voice*, ed. William J. Martz (Glenview, Ill., 1966), p. 247.
21. *The Nation* (April 24, 1967), p. 521.
22. *Mid-Century French Poets*, ed. Wallace Fowlie (New York, 1955), p. 175.

for example, as members of a still younger generation), tend to create work that develops with "the logic of dreams," to repeat Louis Simpson's phrase, or to achieve a transformation of outer reality through its assimilation by the inward self. Unlike Roethke, who had no talent for languages, most of them have been engaged in a considerable amount of translating, as well as reading, of foreign poets. In this respect they follow the lead not only of Pound and Eliot, but also of such extraordinarily accomplished poet/translators as Ben Belitt and Kenneth Rexroth. While it is not, as a rule, easy to indicate with assurance the influence of one poet upon another, familiarity with important modern poets from other countries, among them Neruda, Lorca, Vallejo, Char, Bonnefoy, Michaux, Trakl, Rilke, Benn, Mayakovsky, Pasternak, and Voznesensky, has helped to liberate American poetry from the confinements of logic and wit, "epithets and opinions."[23]

At this point, let me offer a brief anthology of poetic effects deriving from these tendencies. I offer it with some (but not too much) comment, since such poetry, coming as it does from the "total mind" of the poet, needs first to be taken in by the reader's or listener's "total mind."

In the poems of the late Frank O'Hara, whose accidental death at the age of forty cut off a great talent, there is considerable variety but also, in the end, a unity of impression. Like his friends Kenneth Koch, John Ashbery, and James Schuyler (each of whom writes a very different kind of poem), he gives the reader a sense of being talked to, rather than simply overheard. In fact, O'Hara thought of his writing in terms of just such direct address, a communication from one individual to another. In his work a voice speaks to us, or to someone of the poet's acquaintance whose person we share while reading the poem. This voice may be gay, breezy, and whimsical; it may be elegiac or remorseful, tender and erotic; or it may pour forth in a rich, bizarre stream the contents of the poet's consciousness in its ceaseless flow. As is often noted, O'Hara has close affinities with contemporary painters, especially those named Abstract

23. Louis Simpson in Martz, ed., *The Distinctive Voice*, p. 247.

Expressionists or the New York action painters: Jackson Pollock, Franz Kline, Willem de Kooning, Philip Guston, and others. Pollock, in a written statement, tells why he prefers his canvases laid out on the floor rather than on easel or wall: "I feel nearer, more a part of the painting, since this way I can walk around it, work from the four sides, and literally be *in* the painting."[24] These remarks apply equally to O'Hara, I think, in whose poems the poet's self is very evident, moving about freely, uninhibited by rules, concerned only with the realization of personal experience in language. "What is happening to me, allowing for lies and exaggerations which I try to avoid, goes into my poems," he explains in a statement on his poetics. "I don't think my experiences are clarified or made beautiful for myself or anyone else, they are just there in whatever form I can find them."[25] That form is the unpredictable, unliterary but highly poetic form of life itself. The poem "The Day Lady Died" begins with the rather trivial events surrounding O'Hara's preparations for a weekend out of New York visiting friends. Almost at the poem's conclusion he buys a newspaper, along with two cartons of cigarettes, and reads of the death of the great jazz singer Billie Holliday (nicknamed Lady Day, which adds to the implications of the title). In the closing lines a memory of her singing overwhelms the poet, as did the original occasion, though now her death leaves him with only that recollection of an extraordinary moment:

> It is 12:20 in New York a Friday
> three days after Bastille day, yes
> it is 1959 and I go get a shoeshine
> because I will get off the 4:19 in Easthampton
> at 7:15 and then go straight to dinner
> and I don't know the people who will feed me
>
> I walk up the muggy street beginning to sun
> and have a hamburger and a malted and buy

24. *The New American Painting* (New York, 1959), p. 64.

25. *The New American Poetry 1945–1960*, ed. Donald M. Allen (New York, 1960), p. 419. Readers may also want to consider O'Hara's remarks in "Personism: A Manifesto," included in *An Anthology of New York Poets*, ed. Ron Padgett and David Shapiro (New York, 1970), pp. xxxi–xxxiv.

an ugly NEW WORLD WRITING to see what the poets
in Ghana are doing these days
                                    I go on to the bank
and Miss Stillwagon (first name Linda I once heard)
doesn't even look up my balance for once in her life
and in the GOLDEN GRIFFIN I get a little Verlaine
for Patsy with drawings by Bonnard although I do
think of Hesiod, trans. Richmond Lattimore or
Brendan Behan's new play or *Le Balcon* or *Les Nègres*
of Genet, but I don't, I stick with Verlaine
after practically going to sleep with quandariness

and for Mike I just stroll into the PARK LANE
Liquor Store and ask for a bottle of Strega and
then I go back where I came from to 6th Avenue
and the tobacconist in the Ziegfeld Theatre and
casually ask for a carton of Gauloises and a carton
of Picayunes, and a NEW YORK POST with her face on it

and I am sweating a lot by now and thinking of
leaning on the john door in the 5 SPOT
while she whispered a song along the keyboard
to Mal Waldron and everyone and I stopped breathing

By way of contrast with the disarming openness of O'Hara's approach, a few stanzas from W. S. Merwin's "A Scale in May" suggest the poet's embarkation on a trying interior journey, frightening
in its solitude and challenge, for the goal is some kind of honest
understanding of existence, which is always threatened by death
and nothingness. Traveling light, Merwin takes with him only the
possibility of poetry and a resolute integrity. The subjective nature
of the poem's statements, their division into separate sections of
three lines, each having the quality of a gnomic utterance, lead us
to believe we have chanced upon the poet in profound conversation
with himself and are trespassers of his inner world. But that is not
really the case. Once we begin to listen to what he is saying, its
strange obliquity becomes at once evocative; its indefiniteness belongs to the elusive nature of spiritual quests. Then we cross over

into the world which Merwin has so beautifully realized through what he calls "the great language itself, the vernacular of the imagination":[26]

> Now all my teachers are dead except silence
> I am trying to read what the five poplars are writing
> On the void
>
> ---
>
> Of all the beasts to man alone death brings justice
> But I desire
> To kneel in a doorway empty except for the song
>
> ---
>
> Who made time provided also its fools
> Strapped in watches and with ballots for their choices
> Crossing the frontiers of invisible kingdoms
>
> ---
>
> To succeed consider what is as though it were past
> Deem yourself inevitable and take credit for it
> If you find you no longer believe enlarge the temple
>
> ---
>
> Through the day the nameless stars keep passing the door
> That have come all that way out of death
> Without questions

In a note written for the dust jacket of his collection *Drowning with Others* (1962) James Dickey declares, "My subject matter is inevitably my own life, my own obsessions, possessions and renunciations." He later adds, "In these poems I have tried to come into that place in myself which is mine." One of the most compelling features of Dickey's poetry is a power of imagination which enables him to feel or enter into the being of others as if it were his own, to be haunted by the living and the dead, and to perceive the universe as animistic, charged with forces and presences. Ordinary objects, situations, or patterns of nature in his poems suddenly assume the conformations of myth or participate in rituals of initiation and transformation, interchanging identities, and progressing toward

26. Martz, ed., *The Distinctive Voice*, pp. 269–270.

transcendent revelations. Here, to be specific, are the opening lines of "The Dream Flood," where the imaginative reenactment of archetypal details in a fluid, magical cosmos provides the aspect of personally experienced myth:

> I ask and receive
> The secret of falling unharmed
> Forty nights from the darkness of Heaven,
> Coming down in sheets and in atoms
> Until I descend to the moon
>
> Where it lies on the ground
> And finds in my surface the shining
> It knew it must have in the end.
> No longer increasing, I stand
> Taking sunlight transmitted by stone,
>
> And then begin over fields
> To expand like a mind seeking truth. . . .

Less cosmic in its proportions, Louis Simpson's brief poem "The Morning Light" projects, through a few suggestive images, those private associations by means of which the imagination quickens a sense of our individual lives or destinies:

> In the morning light a line
> Stretches forever. There my unlived life
> Rises, and I resist,
> Clinging to the steps of the throne.
>
> Day lifts the darkness from the hills,
> A bright blade cuts the reeds,
> And my life, pitilessly demanding,
> Rises forever in the morning light.

In a poem of this sort, as Jacques Maritain would say, "the conceptual utterances have either disappeared or they are reduced to a minimum or are merely allusive . . . there is no longer any *explicit* intelligible sense, even carried by the images. The intelligible sense drawing in the images is . . . *implicit*."[27] That is to say, if we try to translate into logical prose sense the substance of what we might call the poetic thought (as distinct from straightforward rational thought) in this poem, we will come up with very little, for it is inherent in an imagery completely implicated with inward feeling. We can only understand these images by immersing ourselves in their reality. If we do so, allowing imagination and intuition to lead us, Louis Simpson's poem takes on new aspects, and we experience them with an intimacy close to bodily sensation. There occurs to us a sense of something like pictorial space in the poem, but it is an interior space we see, an arena of desires, fears, frustrations, and possibilities glimpsed as a barely sketched landscape suffused with "morning light." In keeping with his own conviction that "the deepest image, if it does not move, is only an object,"[28] Simpson sets the poem in motion. The tension between his life's possibilities and demands, associated with the light of day and the indefinite horizon, and the resistance to them, the wish to remain motionless, "clinging to the steps of the throne," increases with the awareness of "rising light." Indeed, the general movement within the space disclosed by the poem is upward—until the gesture of the "bright blade," stroking horizontally across this vertical tendency, severs the poet's "life" like a balloon from its mooring, and "pitilessly demanding," it ascends eternally into the brightened heavens, presumably drawing him after or at least compelling his undistracted gaze. Having said these things about the poem, we have still hardly touched the suggestiveness of the images and their movements. Their sense is "implicit," to repeat Maritain's term, and will be apparent to us only when we place ourselves within the poem's precincts.

A new sort of political poem has emerged from the new poetry of dream, surrealist inclination, or pure imagination which we

27. Jacques Maritain, *Creative Intuition in Art and Poetry* (New York, 1955), p. 197.
28. Martz, ed., *The Distinctive Voice*, p. 247.

have been discussing. It likewise relies upon an imagery of the subconscious or of affective association; but now this imagery must
reflect something of the buried collective life of the nation, even as
Louis Simpson's or W. S. Merwin's poems grow from submerged
areas of their individual lives. Kenneth Patchen's explosive poetry
of political and social horror, with its juxtapositions of brutality,
irrationalism, outraged innocence, and savage satire, together with
Weldon Kees' ominous, unrelenting poems of decay and destruction are chief among the forerunners of more recent work by others.
Standing alone, independent and fierce, as an exemplary precursor
in this respect is the figure of Stanley Kunitz, whose work is a
dramatic embodiment of his own personal life, with its torments
and anxieties, and the character of the age in which he exists. Subjective existence and apocalyptic vision accumulate terrible force,
as in these first lines from "Open the Gates":

> Within the city of the burning cloud,
> Dragging my life behind me in a sack,
> Naked I prowl, scourged by the black
> Temptation of the blood grown proud.

Among the chief acknowledged influences for this poetry of political and historical interest are such poets as Whitman, Pasternak,
Neruda, and Vallejo. Robert Bly, an eloquent proponent and a
practitioner of this sort of writing, makes some useful remarks in
an essay, "On Political Poetry," where he stresses the need for poets
to "penetrate the husk around their own personalities" and probe
the lower regions of the psyche. "Once inside the psyche," Bly maintains, "[they] can speak of inward and political things with the
same assurance. . . . Paradoxically, what is needed to write true
poems about the outward world is inwardness."[29] He wants to
divorce such poems from "personal" poems or poems of political
"opinions"; however, his very definition of the requirements of inwardness implies that political poems of the kind he favors are at

29. Robert Bly, "On Political Poetry," *The Nation* (April 24, 1967), p. 522.

the same time personal as well, for the psyche of the poet is inseparable from its intuitions of the nation's psyche.

> The life of the country can be imagined as a psyche larger than the psyche of anyone living, a larger sphere, floating above everyone. In order for the poet to write a true political poem, he has to be able to have such a grasp of his own concerns that he can leave them for a while, and then leap up, like a grasshopper, into this other psyche. In that sphere he finds strange plants and curious many-eyed creatures which he brings back with him. This half-visible psychic life he entangles in his language.[30]

With the reservations I have expressed, let me abandon theoretical disagreement and permit these statements by Bly to stand by themselves without further comment, then place next to them James Wright's "Confession to J. Edgar Hoover," which reveals this poet's almost unbearably intense human concerns, his undeniably personal involvement with the substance of the poem, coupled with an imaginative capacity for raising into view levels of existence invisible to the naked eye and unavailable to the reasoning mind. Wright by-passes headlines, news reports, speeches, and platitudes to sound those mysterious depths of the self where the guilt, terror, alienation, and anxiety that make themselves felt in the external affairs of society in other forms have their dark, tentacular roots:

> Hiding in the church of an abandoned stone,
> A Negro soldier
> Is flipping the pages of the Articles of War,
> That he can't read.

> Our father,
> Last evening I devoured the wing
> Of a cloud.
> And, in the city, I sneaked down
> To pray with a sick tree.

30. Ibid., p. 522.

> I labor to die, father,
> I ride the great stones,
> I hide under stars and maples,
> And yet I cannot find my own face.
> In the mountains of blast furnaces,
> The trees turned their backs on me.
>
> Father, the dark moths
> Crouch at the sills of the earth, waiting.
>
> And I am afraid of my own prayers.
> Father, forgive me.
> I did not know what I was doing.

Departing these twilight regions of the psyche—without, it must be said, trying here to specify other forms of commitment to social themes in such poets as David Ignatow, Philip Levine, Charles Reznikoff, or Carl Rakosi, to mention but a few names—for different areas of consciousness equally tense with disturbance, we are faced with a large, impressive body of writing which has earned in the past decade the title of "confessional" poetry or, as it has been called by the British critic A. Alvarez, "Extremist art."[31] While the term "confessional" is now widely applied, its origin with respect to contemporary poetry lies in the startling transition which occurred in Robert Lowell's career with the publication of *Life Studies* in 1959. Since that book first appeared, Lowell's work has continued to change and to be exploratory, but it has taken on a new surge of power, as a result both of an unsparing scrutiny of his own life, family, and background, and of an open confrontation with our perilous moment in history. The reader must imagine for himself at what cost Lowell effected this alteration in his poetry (though the recent work has obvious connections and continuities with the earlier books), an alteration which recalls exactly Yeats's previously quoted notion of "the recreation of the man through [his] art."

In his early poetry Lowell displays considerable rhythmic and

31. See A. Alvarez, *Beyond All This Fiddle* (London, 1968); also on confessional poetry, M. L. Rosenthal, *The New Poets* (New York, 1967).

imagistic strength, which operates in the service of a somber, apocalyptic vision of life, growing out of the conflict between his New
England heritage and his conversion to Roman Catholicism. That
vision is conveyed with great rhetorical force in the poems of *Lord
Weary's Castle* (1946). This style becomes, I think, overworked and
rather heavy-handed in his third book, *The Mills of the Kavanaughs* (1951), and it is a sign of Lowell's poetic intelligence,
imagination, and inner resourcefulness that he could remake himself and his art together in the years immediately following. *Life
Studies* gives us a poetry which seems the living tissue of the man
who has written it, for he is never completely out of sight. As he
says in a later poem, "one life, one writing."

Not only are the new poems of this volume freer, prosier in style;
many of them are also unashamedly autobiographical. They are
composed of intimate details, close sketches and glimpses of the
poet's parents and grandparents, his friends, several other writers
he has known or admired, his wife, and himself. But their most
radical and unsettling aspect remains the candid, often frightening
revelations of the poet's mental illness and hospitalization in such
poems as "Waking in the Blue" and "Skunk Hour." Lowell's admitted interest in the possibilities of prose narrative (which he explores in the memoir "91 Revere Street," included in *Life Studies*);
his liking for the masters of Russian realism, Tolstoy and Chekov,
for example; his acquaintance with the poems of his student W. D.
Snodgrass (whose first collection, *Heart's Needle*, also was published in 1959) which treat the details and crises of private life[32]—
all these factors point the way toward a transformation of his writing into a manner closer to existence itself and less literary or
artificial.

Lowell is extremely frank about himself and his family, though
he is perhaps outdone in this respect by Anne Sexton, the late Sylvia
Plath, and John Berryman in books such as his *Love & Fame*
(1970). What he says may or may not be true in every detail to the

32. See Frederick Seidel's interview with Lowell, in *Robert Lowell: A Collection
of Critical Essays*, ed. Thomas Parkinson (Englewood Cliffs, N.J., 1968).

actual lives and personalities he portrays, but we cannot be judges of that. What we know are the poems alone. We may object to the use of such private material in poetry, but I believe we must prove our objections on the grounds of the poem—that is, whether the use of the material is justified by what is made of it.

To my mind, the poems do justify themselves, for wry and critical or disturbingly self-revealing as some may be, they are conceived in clarity of vision and tempered with compassion and love. If we think of the poems as sketches or studies, in the way of the visual artist, not as finished portraits, final and irrevocable, we will observe in them the benefits of freedom and informality Lowell is seeking which will permit him to achieve, in his words, "some breakthrough back into life."[33] And these poems vibrate with life, its changing moods and order, the pain and pleasure of close relationship, the humor and bittersweetness of remembrance and loss; and through all of these elements of existence, the sweep of time, the knowledge of death.

The poem "Grandparents," for instance, begins humorously, even flippantly, though that is hardly its main line of feeling. As it proceeds, a few images taken from memories of his adolescence help to evoke the poet's grandmother and grandfather, and to give their world an impression of remoteness from our own. The first stanza ends by echoing the opening of an elegiac poem by the seventeenth-century English poet Henry Vaughan which starts, "They are all gone into the world of light!/And I alone sit ling'ring here. . . ." Then we learn that the poet has inherited his grandparents' farm and now visits it by himself, only to be haunted by recollections of the past. The poetic echo from Vaughan actually sounds an alteration in mood as returning memories continue to build up emotional pressure in the poet, until he recognizes what we all know intellectually but don't really understand without experiencing its forceful blows upon our deepest affections, our hidden but vital loves: he perceives the irreversible nature of time and events. This realization creates the sudden emotional climax of the

---

33. *Robert Lowell: A Collection of Critical Essays*, p. 19.

poem, which is Lowell's momentary anguished cry of love and
need hurled against the inevitable deprivations that our lives accumulate. His emotion released, however, he becomes once more
the whimsical, slightly irreverent self we encountered at the outset
of the poem. His idle doodling with a pencil at the poem's close
indicates, in spite of persistent affections, the sharp division prevailing between the poet's attitudes and his grandparents' luxurious
but trivial mode of living, shut off from the harsher realities of the
world and secure in a religiousness that ignored them. The poem
compels us to acknowledge the complex ties between past and
present in an individual, as well as the wide range of feelings those
ties can generate.

> They're altogether otherworldly now,
> those adults champing for their ritual Friday spin
> to pharmacist and five-and-ten in Brockton.
> Back in my throwaway and shaggy span
> of adolescence, Grandpa still waves his stick
> like a policeman;
> Grandmother, like a Mohammedan, still wears her thick
> lavendar mourning and touring veil;
> the Pierce Arrow clears its throat in a horse-stall.
> Then the dry road dust rises to whiten
> the fatigued elm leaves—
> the nineteenth century, tired of children, is gone.
> They're all gone into a world of light; the farm's my own.
>
> The farm's my own!
> Back there alone,
> I keep indoors, and spoil another season.
> I hear the rattley little country gramophone
> racking its five foot horn:
> "O Summer Time!"
> Even at noon here the formidable
> *Ancien Régime* still keeps nature at a distance. Five
> green shaded light bulbs spider the billiards-table;
> no field is greener than its cloth,
> where Grandpa, dipping sugar for us both,

once spilled his demitasse.
His favorite ball, the number three,
still hides the coffee stain.

Never again
to walk there, chalk our cues,
insist on shooting for us both.
Grandpa! Have me, hold me, cherish me!
Tears smut my fingers. There
half my life-lease later,
I hold an *Illustrated London News*—;
disloyal still,
I doodle handlebar
mustaches on the last Russian Czar.

Of course, the poems from *Life Studies* which are most unsettling
and caused the greatest stir are those treating mental breakdown
and hospitalization. The title of the poem "Waking in the Blue"
refers to the thoughts and sensations that occur to the poet as he
wakes early in the morning in a Massachusetts mental hospital. The
"azure day" he can see through his window, with its suggestions of
freedom and promise, is in biting contrast to his own confined state.
Lowell's poem records, among other things, that first waking when
we still have a moment before full consciousness returns and we
must face our daily reality, whatever it may be. But the instant of
total recollection with which the first stanza concludes is a mur-
derous thrust:

The night attendant, a B.U. sophomore,
rouses from the mare's-nest of his drowsy head
propped on *The Meaning of Meaning*.
He catwalks down our corridor.
Azure day
makes my agonized blue window bleaker.
Crows maunder on the petrified fairway.
Absence! My heart grows tense
as though a harpoon were sparring for the kill.
(This is the house for the "mentally ill.")

Lowell proceeds to describe the wasted lives of various patients, whose figures merely intensify his own feeling of restriction, near-hopelessness; a fear for the future lurks beneath every word. The last stanza combines, in its image of the poet before the mirror, a momentary but ironical sense of jauntiness and contentment with the recurrence of quiet desperation over what is yet to be:

> After a hearty New England breakfast,
> I weigh two hundred pounds
> this morning. Cock of the walk,
> I strut in my turtle-necked French sailor's jersey
> before the metal shaving mirrors,
> and see the shaky future grow familiar
> in the pinched, indigenous faces
> of these thoroughbred mental cases,
> twice my age and half my weight.
> We are all old-timers,
> each of us holds a locked razor.

This poem, and "Skunk Hour," which focuses on an agonized moment of mental disorder yet ends on a note of stubborn persistence in living, are terrible disclosures. In them Lowell takes a more candid, searching look at himself and his situation than most of us would care to, even under reasonably normal conditions. But such poems spring from a passion born of sheer necessity, and they strike the reader with the full force of the poet's individual being. Entering into areas usually marked "Private" in Lowell's work, we do not escape our own existence; rather, we find it and the larger life of our time reflected there, and in an aspect anything but comforting. More recently, Lowell has turned to the public world in a considerable number of poems, though here again he places himself as sensitive, tormented witness to the brutality, ugliness, frightened coldness, and power-craving of America today. "Agonies are one of my changes of garments," Whitman says in *Leaves of Grass*, and Lowell knows only too well the truth of that statement. Four stanzas from another poem of waking, a much later one called "Waking Sunday Morning," included in *Near the Ocean* (1967), give us the dilemmas of Lowell the man, conscientious, honest, spiritually bereft, in the midst of a society which has bred them. In a small New England town where Sunday church bells ring, the poet, now churchless but not irreligious, ponders the fate of belief in an America "top-heavy" with military might and envisages the country's collapse along the lines of an Old Testament precedent:

> O Bible chopped and crucified
> in hymns we hear but do not read,
> none of the milder subtleties
> of grace or art will sweeten these
> stiff quatrains shovelled out four-square—
> they sing of peace, and preach despair;
> yet they gave darkness some control,
> and left a loophole for the soul.
>
> No, put old clothes on, and explore
> the corners of the woodshed for
> its dregs and dreck: tools with no handle,
> ten candle-ends not worth a candle,
> old lumber banished from the Temple,
> damned by Paul's precept and example,
> cast from the kingdom, banned in Israel,
> the wordless sign, the tinkling cymbal.
>
> When will we see Him face to face?
> Each day, He shines through darker glass.
> In this small town where everything
> is known, I see His vanishing
> emblems, His white spire and flag-
> pole sticking out above the fog,
> like old white china doorknobs, sad,
> slight, useless things to calm the mad.
>
> Hammering military splendor,
> top-heavy Goliath in full armor—
> little redemption in the mass
> liquidations of their brass,
> elephant and phalanx moving
> with the times and still improving,

> when that kingdom hit the crash:
> a million foreskins stacked like trash ...

While resorting to formal poetic devices to maintain a certain control and emphasis, as in these stanzas, Lowell becomes simultaneously elliptic, allusive, and fast-moving. He manages to create the semblance of his mind's activity as it responds to the experience of contemporary life. Unlike Wright or Bly, who seek to articulate the voices lingering in a dark substratum of collective dreams as the means for comprehending our common condition, or Allen Ginsberg, who fashions a socio-political idiom in certain poems from a speech which incorporates elements of his private vision with others derived from Blake, the Old Testament, and Eastern mysticism, Lowell projects himself as a type of representative consciousness, absorbing and suffering the jolts and jars administered from without, and answering them with honesty, directness, and the strength of a very gifted, perceptive poet who no longer finds it possible to appeal to an order higher than the human. The spiritual order with which he had substantial familiarity in the period of his Catholic poems has not vanished entirely; rather, it has become clouded, indefinite, its signs as cryptic for him as for the protagonists of Kafka's tales. In Lowell's poetry since *Life Studies*, there is the man himself, as A. Alvarez says, "a man of great contradictions, tenderness and violence, a man obsessed equally by his own crack-ups and by the symptoms of crack-up in the society around him."[34]

Similar qualities and obsessions govern a rather extensive body of contemporary poetry which, for all the skill, inventiveness, and imagination that go into its composition, still communicates a naked revelation of tormented selfhood seemingly devoid of aesthetic intention. Prufrock's lines, with their implicit pain and frustration, characterize this poetry very well:

> It is impossible to say just what I mean!
> But as if a magic lantern threw the nerves in
> patterns on a screen....

34. Alvarez, *Beyond All This Fiddle*, p. 14.

The most elaborate work in this canon of confessional or extremist writing is the lengthy sequence of John Berryman's *Dream Songs*, which began with the *77 Dream Songs* published in 1964 and concluded with the bulky *His Toy, His Dream, His Rest: 308 Dream Songs*, which appeared in 1968. Surely the impulse for these poems reaches from the early "Nervous Songs" and some other pieces through the startling transformation of Berryman's art initiated by his *Homage to Mistress Bradstreet*, a poem in which the author's voice alternates at times with the imagined voice of the early American poet, and where the tight, elliptic style with inverted, idiosyncratic syntax which we encounter in the *Dream Songs* makes its debut. The speaker in all of these frequently untitled poems is Henry Pussycat, middle-aged, white, and, as the sequence progresses, more and more obviously a thinly disguised *version* of Berryman himself—or, to play upon Yeats, a self which is distinctly *his* creation. Since the poems constitute a stylization of the dreaming mind, there is a constant shifting back and forth between the first, second, and third persons to correspond with altering moods and changes in the climate of consciousness, and to heighten dramatic tensions. In addition, a part of Henry occasionally adopts minstrel's black face, talks in a stagey Negro dialect, and then addresses the primary self of Henry as Mr. Bones —a traditional title which carries both social and personal overtones in terms of the whole poetic sequence. Curiously, in the second volume of *Dream Songs*, where the materials of Henry's experience seem to match so closely those of Berryman's, and where internal references to the poems themselves occur, the poet has supplied a prefatory note indicating that he is not to be mistaken for the speaker. Doubtless, as Lowell notes with respect to *Life Studies*, liberty is taken with fact, for the purposes of art. It is Berryman's consciousness remade by poetry which we inhabit, an image of his personal experience which we perceive through the sharp, difficult figure of Henry, with his tormented spirit of a lapsed Catholic (though there is an unexpected return to religious conviction, due to some visionary awareness, in the last poems of the recent book,

Love & Fame) confronted with the spectacle of "a sickening century" of war, mass extermination, racial hatred, and power politics. Perhaps the best way to describe the complicated relationship between poet and speaker is to adopt a line from *Dream Song #370* to the purpose: "Naked the man came forth in his mask, to be."

These poems take for themes, as a rule, the details of an individual life: loves, marriages, friendship and enmity, poetry, and death. They move outward from such preoccupations into politics, the sufferings of others, various manifestations of evil in the present age, celebrations and lamentations for several figures, usually (though not exclusively) poets whom Berryman admires and whose loss is keenly felt: Frost, Roethke, Delmore Schwartz, Louis Mac-Neice, R. P. Blackmur, and Randall Jarrell among them. Intermixed with the toughness, harshness, irrationality, and pain in the poems are recurrent strains of comedy and tender lyricism. Underlying the sequence is a gnawing anxiety and guilt, as well as what Berryman calls "an irreversible loss" which Henry has suffered. The latter assumes many forms: the death of friends, failures of love, the suicide of the poet's father, his collapsed religious faith, or the terrible nameless dread that can seize him, as in *Dream Song #29*:

> There sat down, once, a thing on Henry's heart
> só heavy, if he had a hundred years
> & more, & weeping, sleepless, in all them time
> Henry could not make good.
> Starts again always in Henry's ears
> the little cough somewhere, an odour, a chime.
>
> And there is another thing he has in mind
> like a grave Sienese face a thousand years
> would fail to blur the still profiled reproach of. Ghastly,
> with open eyes, he attends, blind.
> All the bells say: too late. This is not for tears;
> thinking.
>
> But never did Henry, as he thought he did,
> end anyone and hacks her body up

and hide the pieces where they may be found.
He knows: he went over everyone, & nobody's missing.
Often he reckons, in the dawn, them up.
Nobody is ever missing.

Though this sequence explores private associations and the details of personal life, rendering the most lucid and the most illogical states of mind, nothing about it is more remarkable than Berryman's combination of formal exactness—the poems are composed around three six-line stanzas, freely rhymed—with bold experiment —he coins words, uses slang, dialect, inverted syntax, and so forth. As a result, no matter how irrational the dream elements may be at times, they are presented with a precision and tautness of language which is enviable. Paul Valéry says, "It is the very one who wants to write down his dream who is obliged to be extremely wide awake."[35] In the eighth *Dream Song* Berryman dramatizes the nightmare of the self's destruction by a vicious, anonymous company referred to only as "they." These grim processes are conveyed (as also in Stanley Kunitz's "My Surgeons," built upon a similar theme) in a language that embodies the full nature of what is happening without itself succumbing to emotional chaos:

> The weather was fine. They took away his teeth,
> white & helpful; bothered his backhand;
> halved his green hair.
> They blew out his loves, his interests. 'Underneath,'
> (they called in iron voices) 'understand,
> is nothing. So there.'
>
> The weather was very fine. They lifted off
> his covers till he showed, and cringed & pled
> to see himself less.
> They installed mirrors till he flowed. 'Enough'
> (murmured they) 'if you will watch Us instead,
> yet you may saved be. Yes.'

35. Paul Valéry, *The Art of Poetry*, trans. Denise Folliot (New York, 1958), p. 11.

The weather fleured. They weakened all his eyes,
and burning thumbs into his ears, and shook
his hand like a notch.
They flung long silent speeches. (Off the hook!)
They sandpapered his plumpest hope. (So capsize.)
They took away his crotch.

"The way is to the destructive element submit yourself," Stein advises Marlowe in a famous passage in Conrad's *Lord Jim*. Many of our contemporary poets seem bent on following this course, pursuing it though the attendant hazards of madness and death loom perilously near for anyone who, through an exposed, vulnerable psyche and nervous system, tries to cross thresholds where the self is strained beyond endurance and shatters. For them, "the destructive element" alone, rather than Stein's survival techniques, matters —unless the act of poetry itself can become a mode of release and self-protection. Anne Sexton and Sylvia Plath, two richly endowed poets, walk such a narrow, dizzying boundary line in their work, sometimes overstepping it. The price is high—life itself—and neither of them returns. The poetry of both these women rises from the turbulence of private emotions, mental breakdown, spiritual quandaries, and strong attractions to death. To have produced the poems they have given us, charged with beauty and terror, and to have remade themselves as distinctive poetic personalities within those poems by transmuting inner crises and a compulsion toward self-destruction is a moral and artistic triumph for both of them— in spite of their tragic suicides.

In "For the Year of the Insane," subtitled "a prayer," Anne Sexton, a confessed "unbeliever," still holds in her hand a "black rosary with its silver Christ" and addresses the Virgin Mary. The theme of her reflective speech is the passage of time, the steady encroachment of age and death, her fear, loneliness, spiritual desolation, and mental instability. No poetry could be more personal.

Closer and closer
comes the hour of my death
as I rearrange my face, grow back,

grow undeveloped and straight-haired.
All this is death.
In the mind there is a thin alley called death
and I move through it as
through water.
My body is useless.
It lies, curled like a dog on the carpet.
It has given up.
There are no words here except the half-learned,
the *Hail Mary* and the *full of grace*.
Now I have entered the year without words.
I note the queer entrance and the exact voltage.
Without words they exist.
Without words one may touch bread
and be handed bread
and make no sound.

O Mary, tender physician,
come with powders and herbs
for I am in the center.
It is very small and the air is gray
as in a steam house.
I am handed wine as a child is handed milk.
It is presented in a delicate glass
with a round bowl and a thin lip.
The wine itself is pitch-colored, musty and secret.
The glass rises on its own toward my mouth
and I notice this and understand this
only because it has happened.
I have this fear of coughing
but I do not speak,
a fear of rain, a fear of the horseman
who comes riding into my mouth.
The glass tilts on its own
and I am on fire.
I see two thin streaks burn down my chin.
I see myself as one would see another.
I have been cut in two.

O Mary, open your eyelids.
I am in the domain of silence,
the kingdom of the crazy and the sleeper.
There is blood here
and I have eaten it.
O mother of the womb,
did I come for blood alone?
O little mother,
I am in my own mind.
I am locked in the wrong house.

This experience which Anne Sexton so vividly depicts, with its intense, visionary qualities, its feeling of being divided in two, may remind us of the drama of Roethke's "In a Dark Time." Though the poem strikes into the most intimate domains of consciousness and alternates between self-examination, supplication, and a hallucination that appears to approach madness yet is also strangely ritual and sacramental (the glass changes into a chalice; the wine, as in communion, into Christ's blood or presence, which in turn brings the "fear of the horseman," or death), the mind of the poet reflects the spiritual unrest and tension in which many of us may share and the terrible frustration we feel at being trapped by the limited perspective of our own egos.

The same may be said for Sylvia Plath, particularly with respect to the poems of her posthumous collection *Ariel* (1966), where her own "controlled hallucination," as Robert Lowell calls it in his foreword to the book, and the poetic powers freed by her neuropathic state permit her entry into the most extreme conditions of awareness and emotion. These poems are filled with inexorable motion, relentless energy, abrupt, shifting imagery, and the expanding, altering identity of the poet herself. In "Getting There," for instance, conceiving herself involved in "some war or other," she is moving in a train across Russia through a veritable hell of death, destruction, and brutality. The images follow one another in rapid succession, with the poet both witnessing and participating in what occurs. At the conclusion of the poem she has survived all the desolation and carnage, as if miraculously, and is reborn. If the experience seems confused, disordered, that is Plath's imaginative intention and not the failures of the neurotic; no matter what perceptions and hallucinatory visions her mental states provoke, these are worked with consummate, determined skill and craft into her poems. As she remarked in an interview not long before her death:

> ... I must say I cannot sympathize with these cries from the heart that are informed by nothing except a needle or a knife, or whatever it is. I believe that one should be able to control and manipulate experiences, even the most terrifying, like madness, being tortured, this sort of experience, and one should be able to manipulate these experiences with an informed and an intelligent mind. I think that personal experience is very important, but certainly it shouldn't be a kind of shut-box and mirror-looking, narcissistic experience. I believe it should be *relevant*, and relevant to the larger things, the bigger things such as Hiroshima and Dachau and so on.[36]

So the nervous and emotional illness which assails her inner life becomes for Plath a means whereby she can gain access to experience not outwardly hers; the imagination thus liberated takes on the existence of others. An identification of this sort is evident in "Getting There." The last half of the poem follows:

> How far is it?
> It is so small
> The place I am getting to, why are there these obstacles—
> The body of this woman,
> Charred skirts and deathmask
> Mourned by religious figures, by garlanded children.
> And now detonations—
> Thunder and guns.
> The fire's between us.
> Is there no still place
> Turning and turning in the middle air,
> Untouched and untouchable.
> The train is dragging itself, it is screaming—

36. *The Poet Speaks*, ed. Peter Orr (London, 1966), pp. 169–170.

An animal
Insane for the destination,
The bloodspot,
The face at the end of the flare.
I shall bury the wounded like pupas,
I shall count and bury the dead.
Let their souls writhe in a dew,
Incense in my track.
The carriages rock, they are cradles.
And I, stepping from this skin
Of old bandages, boredoms, old faces

Step to you from the black car of Lethe,
Pure as a baby.

In the last turning that this limited survey of various manifestations of the personal element among contemporary poets will take, I want to cite the work of a few poets who have, each in his or her singular fashion, followed the leads suggested both in theory and in practice by William Carlos Williams and Ezra Pound—and to a certain extent by H. D., Louis Zukofsky, and Kenneth Rexroth as well. A number of these poets are frequently called the Black Mountain group, named after the experimental Black Mountain College, where many of them first met to study or to teach and began to formulate their notions of poetry; or they are called Projectivists, after the late Charles Olson's influential and descriptive essay on "Projective Verse." What links them together, beyond a recognition of Olson as a seminal force and leader, beyond friendships and apparently a great amount of literary correspondence, is less a close or confining similarity of poetic practice than the acceptance of Williams and the other poets mentioned as their guides and mentors. As Denise Levertov writes in "September 1961," a profound tribute to Pound, Williams, and H. D.:

They have told us
the road leads to the sea,
and given
the language into our hands.

In his essays Williams urges the abandonment of iambic pentameter, the sonnet form, and other English poetic conventions which he strongly believes prevent America from producing its own unique poetry, a poetry deriving from our native speech and its rhythms, and from developing a new and relative kind of "measure," to use his favorite term, in opposition to the fixed poetic foot. But, more than that, in his poems and prose there is a concentrated attention to particulars, to immediate environment, to objects in all their detailed concreteness and specificity which simultaneously helps to define the self perceiving them. Williams notes in the introduction to a book of his poems, *The Wedge*:

> When a man makes a poem, makes it, mind you, he takes words as he finds them interrelated about him and composes them—without distortion which would mar their exact significances—into an intense expression of his perceptions and ardors that they may constitute a revelation in the speech that he uses. It isn't what he *says* that counts as a work of art, it's what he makes, with such intensity of perception that it lives with an intrinsic movement of its own to verify its authenticity.[37]

In the work of Denise Levertov, Robert Creeley, Charles Olson, Robert Duncan, Gary Snyder, Edward Dorn, Larry Eigner, and Paul Blackburn, among others, we discover the poetic realization in several forms of the process Williams describes. The poet's focus is frequently on his life as a person: his daily encounter with *things*, with others; the character of his relationships, even the most intimate ones; the movements of his thought and sensation; the nature of his interior being as it emerges in dream or vision, or is interwoven with traditional and occult symbols, as in Robert Duncan's poetry, into the shape of a mythology both personal and cosmic. Finally, there is, for certain of these writers, a poetry of place. The most notable and ambitious example is Charles Olson's long sequence, *The Maximus Poems*, combining the history, geography, and topography of his native town, Gloucester, Massachusetts (the

---

37. *Selected Essays of William Carlos Williams* (New York, 1954), p. 257.

"Dogtown" of the poems), with personal perceptions, biography, and, intermingled with these, elements of various mythologies. He writes in the fourth poem: "An American/is a complex of occasions,/themselves a geometry/of spatial nature," a view which grew out of his visit, years earlier, to the Yucatan Peninsula, where he studied closely the ancient Mayan culture and set down his thoughts and discoveries in a correspondence with Robert Creeley, now included in the volume of Olson's *Selected Writings* (1966).

However personal some of the work of the Projectivists and Black Mountain poets may be, it can never be mistaken for the writing of the confessional poets. While it does not avoid the harsh actualities of present-day existence or disguise painful areas of private experience, it also does not display much interest in psychic disturbance, emotional and spiritual torment, the sense of victimization, and nervous pressures which threaten to explode into madness. For these poets the act of poetry—and all of them, I believe, are fascinated with the process of composition itself—is a matter of the most profound significance to the individual, because it is through that act that he fashions his own single identity. Becoming a proper human being and making a poem properly are two sides of the same endeavor. In Charles Olson's words:

> . . . a man, carved
> out of himself, so wrought he
> fills his given space, makes
> traceries sufficient to
> others' needs. . . .[38]

Denise Levertov, who quotes in a lecture this statement by Olson, has a remark of her own which, together with Olson's, brings out the double emphasis of their poetics: the stress on the fulfillment of the poet's self and on the poem as directed to readers. She says: "The act of realizing inner experience in material substance is in itself an action *towards others*, even when the conscious intention has not gone beyond the desire for self-expression."[39]

38. Quoted by Denise Levertov, *Michigan Quarterly Review* (Fall 1968), p. 236.
39. Ibid., p. 235.

In Denise Levertov's poems, or Robert Creeley's, or Robert Duncan's, the reader receives an impression of having stepped into a new kind of space, an invisible but nonetheless real zone bounded by an interlocking form of words yet acquiring its substance from the felt presence of the poet. The first poem in Robert Duncan's important collection *The Opening of the Field* (1960) introduces a location which is at once an amalgam of memory and dream in the author's mind and the actual space or "field" of language the poem creates:

> ...a scene made-up by the mind,
> that is not mine, but is a made place,
>
> that is mine, it is so near to the heart,
> an eternal pasture folded in all thought
> so that there is a hall therein
>
> that is a made place, created by light
> wherefrom the shadows that are forms fall.

This space is, in correspondence with Charles Olson's attitudes, an essential aspect of the poet's being, a part of his life. Admittedly, what I am saying may seem difficult to understand clearly, but it can be grasped readily through the experience of the poetry. Or we might think of how our bodies create what we could call their own individual space around themselves as we perform all the gestures and activities of living. It is that sense of presence, involving the total self of the writer, physical and spiritual, which reaches us in the work of these poets.

Again I shall offer only a couple of examples out of many possible ones, rather than to aim at comprehensiveness here. The last section of Levertov's "The Coming Fall" blends description of an external setting with the gradual effects of this situation as it is felt inwardly by the poet herself, coming initially through bodily sensations:

> Down by the fallen fruit in the old orchard
> the air grows cold. The hill
> hides the sun.

> A sense of the present
> rises out of earth and grass,
> enters the feet, ascends
>
> into the genitals, constricting
> the breast, lightening
> the head—a wisdom,
>
> a shiver, a delight
> that what is passing
>
> is here, as if
> a snake went by, green in the
> gray leaves.

Here the "sense of the present," an evanescent trace of feeling and physical sensation which would normally elude words, is beautifully caught; it remains true to its origins, for there is no attempt to put intellectual constructions upon it. Levertov tries to return us, through the poem, to the moment of the experience itself. In another poem, "A Common Ground," she tells us how, ideally, poetry should so transform reality that in perceiving the elements which comprise our world, in carrying out the tasks and necessities of daily life, we would be absorbing poetry:

> Poems stirred
> into paper coffee-cups, eaten
> with petals on rye in the
> sun—the cold shadows in back,
> and the traffic grinding the
> borders of spring—entering
> human lives forever,
> unobserved, a spring element....

Levertov's search, as she says in "Matins," is for "the authentic," which appears both in dreams, the inward life, and in waking actualities; it is "the known/appearing fully itself, and/more itself than one knew." In discovering the true abundance and nature of knowable reality, the poet fashions her—and our—solidarity, human community, with it.

Gary Snyder's poetry, surely some of the finest of recent years, often draws on his experiences of camping and mountain-climbing, working in logging camps in the forests of the Pacific Northwest, laboring as a tanker hand, studying the life and lore of American Indians, and, finally, spending years in Japan studying under a Zen master in Kyoto. He has remarked in a dust-jacket comment for one of his books: "As a poet I hold the most archaic values on earth. They go back to the late Paleolithic; the fertility of the soil, the magic of animals, the power-vision in solitude, the terrifying initiation and rebirth; the love and ecstasy of the dance, the common work of the tribe. I try to hold both history and wilderness in mind, that my poems may approach the true measure of things and stand against the unbalance and ignorance of our times." In certain poems from his *Riprap* (1959), for example, Snyder provides a feeling of the immensity of the wilderness, of nonhuman nature, of its seemingly eternal, mute history, against which human activity, culture, and consciousness appear insignificant. By his control of rhythm and language, his accuracy and precision of detail, he resists being overwhelmed; the poem, in turn, while re-creating the man and his experience, humanizes it, if you will. The recognition is not less disturbing but has at least been assimilated to consciousness, made part of our awareness of reality. To repeat Denise Levertov's words: "the known/appearing fully itself, and/more itself than one knew." One such poem of Snyder's is "Above Pate Valley":

> We finished clearing the last
> Section of trail by noon,
> High on the ridge-side
> Two thousand feet above the creek
> Reached the pass, went on
> Beyond the white pine groves,
> Granite shoulders, to a small
> Green meadow watered by the snow,
> Edged with Aspen—sun
> Straight high and blazing

But the air was cool.
Ate a cold fried trout in the
Trembling shadows. I spied
A glitter, and found a flake
Black volcanic glass—obsidian—
By a flower. Hands and knees
Pushing the Bear grass, thousands
Of arrowhead leavings over a
Hundred yards. Not one good
Head, just razor flakes
On a hill snowed all but summer,
A land of fat summer deer,
They came to camp. On their
Own trails. I followed my own
Trail here. Picked up the cold-drill,
Pick, singlejack, and sack
Of dynamite.
Ten thousand years.

Something of the enormous range and vitality of American poetry today has, I hope, impressed itself in the course of these remarks, which I intended both to distinguish certain of the pronounced personal qualities evident among contemporary poets of the last three decades or so, and to provide a partial—but only partial—survey of the very different kinds of writers and writings involved. I have avoided, as I said I would, any attempt at close definition; that should come later, as the job of the sympathetic, imaginative literary historian. Instead, I have tried to be both suggestive and illustrative, and to focus on examples of the poetry itself, since it, after all, is more important than anything I might have to say about it. There are other poets too numerous to name whom I should have liked to introduce here, but such an effort is impracticable, the matter for a large book. I have confined myself, more or less, to three prominent tendencies for the purposes at hand. Within the landscape of contemporary poetry, as I believe my choices demonstrated, there are many talented writers, and their styles, their notions of what a poem ought to be or do, diverge widely. Yet it is not too much to say that they have in common a concern for the experience which lies nearest them, within the radius of their actual lives: the space—to return to that metaphor— outside themselves, through which they move and possess the legacies of history, in which they act and meet others; or the space within, the interior world of dream, vision, and meditation. This concern enables them, whether consciously or not, to combat those abstracting, tabulating, depersonalizing forces which our society produces by asserting through poems the value of their unique human nature and experience. Again Denise Levertov helps us; she writes of the stages of awareness leading up to poetic activity: "The progression seems clear to me: from Reverence for Life to Attention to Life, from Attention to Life to a highly developed Seeing and Hearing, from Seeing and Hearing (faculties almost indistinguishable for the poet) to the Discovery and Revelation of Form, from Form to Song."[40] A similar process, however aware of it the poet may be, however it might differ in certain particulars, appears to me to govern the work of those poets we have discussed, and many others as well. I can say little more now except that the burden of proof is in the reading of our contemporaries, and that careful attention will be repaid by an encounter with poems bold and various in form, attitude, and insight; poems which, like the poets we discover within them, are unimpeachable in their integrity, intense in their vision. In Yeats' pregnant phrase, "creation's very self" is what we look for, and find. In the third of her "Three Meditations," Levertov offers us an image of the poet's activity in our time with which I should like to finish:

> We breathe an ill wind,
> nevertheless our kind
> in mushroom multitudes
> jostles for elbow-room
> moonwards
>
> an equalization of
> hazards

40. Ibid., p. 238.

bringing the poet
back to song
as before

to sing of death
as before
and life, while he
has it, energy

beinging in him a singing,
a beating of gongs, efficacious
to drive away devils,
response to

the wonder that
as before
shows a double face,

to be
what he is
being his virtue

filling his whole space
so no devil
may enter.

2 In the Way of Becoming: Theodore Roethke's Last Poems

We end in joy
—T.R., "The Moment"

The primary thematic concern in Theodore Roethke's poetry is with the evolution and identity of the self, its beginnings with an individual's birth, its organic growth which resembles the growth of things in nature, and its attainment of a maturity and independence that bring it into a new, harmonious relationship with creation.[1] I want to call attention here to the different phases of the self's evolution as we find them treated in the last poems of *The Far Field*, especially in those two parts of the book called "North American Sequence" and "Sequence, Sometimes Metaphysical" in which the poet exceeds the limits of previous development and sets forth on an arduous but successful quest for mystical illumination.

This undertaking, as we shall see more concretely in the poems themselves, requires a moral or spiritual trimming, a divesting of self which cannot be accomplished in one gesture and which, though it might at first appear so, is not a reversal of the process of growth in the self that occupies so much of Roethke's earlier work. It is, rather, evidence of the genuine fulfillment of that process, and it brings the body of his art to a strong and moving com-

1. That relationship is extended and deepened in the love lyrics, where cosmic resonances are sounded by the sensual and spiritual exchange between poet and beloved. These matters I have discussed in more detail in *Theodore Roethke* (Minneapolis, 1963).

pletion. Such poems of supernatural consciousness are anyway not without precedent in Roethke's writing; indeed, they are prepared for by many poems in the second half of *Words for the Wind*, and by a consistent use of certain metaphors and types of imagery to designate the operations of the inner life. Then, too, in manner the poems of "North American Sequence" derive from techniques put to work in previous poems of psychic growth in *The Lost Son* and *Praise to the End!,* as well as from those of the later "Meditations of an Old Woman," while the closing "Sequence, Sometimes Metaphysical" recalls Roethke's predilection for a taut, economical lyricism which he continued to practice throughout his career. Thus the two sequences emphasize the main tendencies of his poetic manner—the one freer, Whitmanesque at times, answering his demands for "the breath unit, the language that is natural to the immediate thing," "the catalogue," and "the eye close on the object"[2] —the other constructed along more traditional lines, capable of containing and concentrating immense pressures of feeling. These manners are most appropriate to the use Roethke makes of them in *The Far Field*: the long, free, variable lines of "North American Sequence" carry the burden of natural and geographical detail, the experience of the outer world of nature, of creatures and things that is intimately related to the poet's states of consciousness, their rising and falling, their stillness and motion. The spare, and more formal, character of the lyrics in "Sequence, Sometimes Metaphysical" parallels the further stage of visionary experience they embody, for at this point the focus of activity is almost entirely inward or spiritual, and considerations of external reality are, at best, secondary.

Within the evolutionary scheme of Roethke's poetry, the scheme which traces the course of the emergent self, there is a simultaneous development of what is variously called soul or spirit, which we might say is the inner or ruling principle of the self. The term

2. "Some Remarks on Rhythm," *Poetry*, XCVII (October, 1960), p. 45. Reprinted in *On the Poet and His Craft: Selected Prose of Theodore Roethke*, ed. Ralph J. Mills, Jr. (Seattle, 1965).

"self" appears to embrace and unite both the physical and spiritual components of the individual into a whole of particular identity. The spirit is perhaps the bloom, the last and highest glory of the self, and so becomes the guiding and motivating principle in its experience, its ascent on the scale of being. Roethke portrays it similarly in "A Light Breather," indicating connections between his title and traditional associations of breath and wind with spirit:

> The spirit moves,
> Yet stays:
> Stirs as a blossom stirs,
> Still wet from its bud-sheath,
> Slowly unfolding,
> Turning in the light with its tendrils;
> Plays as a minnow plays,
> Tethered to a limp weed, swinging,
> Tail around, nosing in and out of the current,
> Its shadows loose, a watery finger;
> Moves, like the snail,
> Still inward,
> Taking and embracing its surroundings,
> Never wishing itself away,
> Unafraid of what it is,
> A music in a hood,
> A small thing,
> Singing.

This brief poem holds the implications for the spiritual journey out of the self which begins in an organized way with "North American Sequence." The spirit as essence of the organic self seeks finally to go beyond that self's circumference. What Roethke tells us in the first two lines above is revealed many times over in his later work: the spirit retains its central position and yet seems to step outside itself, to merge with things other than itself. Thus the spirit is fluid, can expand indefinitely, a potentiality that is fundamental to mystical experience. But this expansion is not new to Roethke's poetry; here are two examples from *Words for the Wind*:

> I know the motion of the deepest stone.
> Each one's himself, yet each one's everyone.
> > —"The Sententious Man"

> Dry bones! Dry bones! I find my loving heart,
> Illumination brought to such a pitch
> I see the rubblestones begin to stretch
> As if reality had split apart
> And the whole motion of the soul lay bare:
> I find that love, and I am everywhere.
> > —"The Renewal"

These extreme moments vividly demonstrate the kind of experience implicit in "A Light Breather" and also qualify as illustrations of the earlier stages of mystical awakening. But such positive instances, leading the way to greater visionary knowledge, do not continue unimpeded; there are occasions of spiritual setback constantly to be faced, with their nearly overwhelming atmosphere of negation, nothingness, and terrible human desolation. In "'The Shimmer of Evil'" the poet, and all creatures and things, remain imprisoned in their selfhood. Everything loses its depth and luminosity and shows only hard, impenetrable surfaces which forbid communion and force the poet back into himself; the spirit, to borrow Roethkean metaphors, back into its sheath or shell: ". . . and I was only I./ There was no light, there was no light at all. . . ."

One could multiply examples of this sort; even poems like "The Lost Son" display the delays and retreats of the self as well as its forward movements. But in the last poems, where the intention to achieve mystical illumination is more sustained, this negative experience becomes more terrifying and, if possible, more purposive. Among the pieces from *Words for the Wind* depicting negative spiritual states of lassitude, guilt, and deprivation, I think not only of "'The Shimmer of Evil'" but also of "Elegy," "The Beast," "The Song," and particularly of "The Exorcism," in which the poet undergoes a frightening purgation. Self-questioning and interior stagnation haunt the reflective consciousness of the speaker in

"Meditations of an Old Woman"; she fluctuates between ecstasy (a sense of harmony with creation) and periods of dryness (failures of vision), such as provide the ground rhythm of "North American Sequence." "By dying daily, I have come to be," writes Roethke in the fourth poem of "The Dying Man." This alternation between contrary states is the basic pattern of experience on the path to intensifying mystical perception. Evelyn Underhill says:

> We are to expect, then, as part of the condition under which human consciousness appears to work, that for every affirmation of the mystic life there will be a negation waiting for the unstable self. Progress in contemplation, for instance, is marked by just such an alternation between light and shade: at first between "consolation" and aridity; then between "dark contemplation" and sharp intuitions of Reality . . . each joyous ecstasy entails a painful or negative ecstasy. The states of darkness and illumination coexist over a long period, alternating sharply and rapidly.[3]

True to his personal experience and to his insight, Roethke carries these "states of darkness and illumination" into the midst of his poetic work, where they fall quite readily into its course of development. In *The Far Field* he begins to purify and purge himself as he aims toward a union with or experience of the Divine. That process reaches its zenith in the lyrics of "Sequence, Sometimes Metaphysical."

Appropriately enough, "North American Sequence" begins in a condition of spiritual emptiness and torpor. The poet is at the nadir, sunk in a world of the senses, tormented by a hypersensitive awareness of physical and moral decay:[4]

> On things asleep, no balm:
> A kingdom of stinks and sighs,
> Fetor of cockroaches, dead fish, petroleum,

3. *Mysticism* (New York, 1955), p. 383.
4. Some of my remarks parallel those of Hugh Staples, whose "The Rose in the Sea-Wind: A Reading of Theodore Roethke's 'North American Sequence,'" *American Literature*, XXXVI (May, 1964), pp. 189–203, I had not read at the time of this writing.

> Worse than castoreum of mink or weasels,
> Saliva dripping from warm microphones,
> Agony of crucifixion on barstools.
> —"The Longing"

These lines do more than convey the living death of modern existence; they reveal the poet's feeling of disaffection from his true or spiritual nature. The soul withers in this climate, sickens on its fare; the effects are manifested outwardly in speech, gestures, looks. This "agony of crucifixion" calls for resurrection, and the poet asks "How to transcend this sensual emptiness?" Dreams will not suffice. Actuality surrounds him everywhere in images of industrial urban landscape, dead and locked in itself; as a result, "the spirit fails to move forward,/. . . shrinks into a half-life, less than itself. . . ." Yet, in Part Two, the value of this "wretchedness" appears perhaps as cleansing preparatory to another dream, large "enough to breathe in," which we see in the striking images of the next lines shifting from dark to a light whose strange flare beckons the poet. Both the image of the rose (with all its traditional symbolic weight) and the light (a source of grace and revelation in many recorded mystical experiences) announce a transcendent reality. The stanza's concluding lines imply an accompanying spiritual renewal and potency ("bud" and "worm"). Another short stanza ending this section shows the pattern of death and rebirth which is the spirit's destiny if it chooses the route to mystical communion. This pattern is further predicted in the image of the waning moon, the close of the lunar cycle which, we know, merely precedes the beginning of a new moon that will wax to the full:[5]

> What dream's enough to breathe in? A dark dream.
> The rose exceeds, the rose exceeds us all.
> Who'd think the moon could pare itself so thin?
> A great flame rises from the sunless sea;
> The light cries out, and I am there to hear—

5. For a discussion of lunar cycles, see Mircea Eliade, *The Sacred and the Profane*, trans. Willard Trask (New York, 1959), pp. 155–159.

> I'd be beyond; I'd be beyond the moon,
> Bare as a bud, and naked as a worm.
>
> To this extent I'm a stalk.
> —How free; how all alone.
> Out of these nothings
> —All beginnings come.

The absolute character of Roethke's quest is demonstrated by his desire to "be beyond the moon," that is, beyond the recurrence of spiritual death and rebirth. This wish is intensified as the poems proceed and may put us in mind of Plotinus' memorable expression of the search for Divine union, "the flight of the alone to the Alone." But while the call to that union seems clearly uttered above, the realization is not so simple. We will not be surprised, then, to find that the third part of the poem returns to a middle ground of recollection and meditation. The poet is no longer vexed by the horrors of the poem's start, but neither is he being swept up on waves of holy rapture to a beatific vision; the journey has only begun. The long variable lines of this section move with the currents of the poet's mind as he awaits the impulse to spiritual movement which usually arrives without activity of the will, its origins located in that

> agency outside me.
> Unprayed-for,
> And final.
> —"What Can I Tell My Bones?"

(Very often, as we might expect, the impulse is symbolized naturalistically, normally by two of the four elements, air and water, in the forms of wind and flowing waters or rivers.) Without this impulse, the spirit remains resident at the center of the self, though not necessarily in a state of depression or emptiness. Sometimes it engages in a period of collecting itself, setting out its aims, calmly and beautifully affirming the deep ties between human life and the natural world that are such a remarkable feature of Roethke's poetry.

"Meditation at Oyster River" gets under way, as the title suggests, in a specific place and sustains a familiar mood of passive observation. The poet watches carefully "the first tide ripples, moving." His activity is minimal, his attention directed at the spirit within to catch the first signs of an awakening. The second section is a brief meditation provoked by the spiritual inactivity of the first:

> The self persists like a dying star,
> In sleep, afraid. Death's face rises afresh,
> Among the shy beasts, the deer at the salt-lick,
> The doe with its sloped shoulders loping across
>   the highway,
> The young snake, poised in green leaves, waiting
>   for its fly,
> The hummingbird, whirring from quince-blossom to
>   morning-glory—
> With these I would be.

A wish to discard the self, or at least to purify it to essentials, seems obvious here. In the first image Roethke exhibits the difficulty, for the self stays on as a residue in the same way that stars many light years away are still visible on earth long after they have actually been extinguished. The fear of losing oneself also clings; human nature and living creatures are further reminders of mortality, but this remembrance is changed into something more positive by identification of the poet with these creatures and, in the next stanza, with "the waves" and "the tongues of water" presaging spiritual movement. The longed-for dispersal of self into the beloved realms of nature is also integral to the course of mystical experience.

Memory takes command in the poem's third section, calls up river scenes from childhood that correspond with the present condition of the poet's inner life. The exploding of the ice-blocked Tittebawasee River, so that "the whole river begins to move forward," is analogous to his own spiritual advance. In the dusky evening he sees the light of a new day breaking, feels at one with creation, and gives himself up to the "will" and direction of the water on whose surface the spirit will skim. In the last lines the moon reappears, inaugurating a new cycle.

"Journey to the Interior" acknowledges in its opening "the long journey out of the self" and, like "The Far Field," supplies examples of it which end in frustration. Roethke uses automobile trips through a variety of landscapes as outward counterparts of the expedition to the center of the self, that is, to the spirit. Much of the poem is devoted to rich geographical detail; in this it is very near to "The Long Waters" and "The Far Field" as well as to preceding pieces in the sequence. Things are viewed from the window of a passing car: small towns, bridges, animals, and birds; elsewhere they are the things contemplated at the water's edge by river or lake, or those others seen "at the field's end, in the corner missed by the mower." Roethke keeps us conscious during the entire sequence that his travels are basically interior, and so the by now familiar pattern of spiritual elation and depression, motion and relaxation, is never obscured: "I rise and fall, and time folds/Into a long moment. . . ." The self is now in what Miss Underhill would call the "Way of Becoming" and receives from time to time in the sequence the vision which accompanies a state of heightened meditation. The last section of "Journey to the Interior" presents the images visible to the poet in this elevated condition. The experience comes again, somewhat less sharply, at the finish of "The Long Waters"; assuming a more reflective cast, it closes "The Far Field" with thoughts of the plan of human existence; "The Rose" folds such experiences into the comprehensive image of that flower, causing us to think of some of its other appearances, in Dante, Eliot, and Yeats.

Each of the poems in the "North American Sequence" is occupied not only with the spiritual journey but also with details of place, through or from which moments of vision occur. There is in every poem a substantial portion of magnificent descriptive writing, important in its links with the inner life but delightful and evocative in itself. All this is evident in "The Rose," toward which the other poems have been leading. Place is insisted upon in the poet's position "where sea and fresh water meet." When the busy life of birds slackens and silence falls, he proceeds out of himself "Into the darkening currents. . . ." Section Two enlarges this exodus by a kind of epic simile of sea voyage and the continuous "motion" of spiritual quest, but then turns to the stable, unmoving yet surpassing image of the rose, rooted in our world though extending beyond it. Stillness and movement, the journey and its goal, are contained in these lines:

> But this rose, this rose in the sea-wind,
> Stays,
> Stays in its true place,
> Flowering out of the dark,
> Widening at high noon, face upward,
> A single wild rose, struggling out of the white
>   embrace of the morning-glory. . . .

But again memory draws him back to childhood, to the familiar greenhouse of Roethke's early work, filled with roses: ". . . how those flowerheads seemed to flow toward me, to beckon me, only a child, out of myself." Just so, the mystical rose of his mature experience attracts him.

A long passage in Section Three catalogues a multitude of things in the American landscape, specifically elements of "sound and silence," but also whatever arrests the eye. The rose image returns at the end and is pictured as a source of nourishment to the thirsting spirit (see the kindred "flower of all water, above and below me, the never receding,/Moving, unmoving in a parched land" of "Journey to the Interior") that will bring about the birth of a new self from the old in the poet. Roethke introduces bird and flower images to suggest the freedom and transcendence of this change, which may permit him to taste eternity and yet not leave the world as we commonly know it. A balance between earthly and superior reality is implied in the ultimate stanza in the alternation of stone and light, sound and silence, self and sea-wind (the latter a vehicle

of spiritual impulse). Roethke nears "the Unitive Life," to borrow
from Evelyn Underhill again, a life symbolically represented by the
unchanging rose, whose shape and petals might also remind us in
a more Jungian fashion of individuation and self-fulfillment in the
mandala figure:

> Near this rose, in this grove of sun-parched, wind-
>   warped madronas,
> Among the half-dead trees, I came upon the true ease
>   of myself,
> As if another man appeared out of the depths of my
>   being,
> And I stood outside myself,
> Beyond becoming and perishing,
> A something wholly other,
> As if I swayed out on the wildest wave alive,
> And yet was still.
> And I rejoiced in being what I was:
> In the lilac change, the white reptilian calm,
> In the bird beyond the bough, the single one
> With all the air to greet him as he flies,
> The dolphin rising from the darkening waves;
>
> And in this rose, this rose in the sea-wind,
> Rooted in stone, keeping the whole of light,
> Gathering to itself sound and silence—
> Mine and the sea-wind's.

Among the other lyrics and love poems of *The Far Field* which
come between "North American Sequence" and "Sequence, Sometimes Metaphysical," there is a slightly longer piece called "The
Abyss," composed in the manner of "Meditations of an Old Woman" and much more tense and vertiginous than the poems we have
just discussed. It opens on a nervous interior colloquy:

> Is the stair here?
> Where's the stair?
> "The stair's right there,
> But it goes nowhere."

> And the abyss? the abyss?
> "The abyss you can't miss:
> It's right where you are—
> A step down the stair."

We are close to the "edge" here, that precarious border in Roethke's poems between ecstasy and the void. In spite of the calm and reconciliation at the end of "The Rose," he has merely "been spoken to variously/But heard little" and now lapses into a state not unlike the one which began "The Longing." As in the second poem of "The Dying Man" cycle, death approaches, "a sly surly attendant," but finally departs, leaving the poet possessed of unpleasant images of himself as a crawling caterpillar, a mole "winding through earth,/A night-fishing otter." This part of the poem discloses a reverse-motion of the spiritual life, a fall away from vision; this experience of the abyss is that of a subjective hell, or, as it is spoken of a few lines later, "A flash into the burning heart of the abominable."

In Section Four of "The Abyss" Roethke's statements become even more explicitly religious. His beginning rhetorical questions again press him toward a supernatural goal:

> How can I dream except beyond this life?
> Can I outleap the sea—
> The edge of all the land, the final sea?

We find, too, the flowing waters of the Way of Becoming, and then two stanzas about the poet's "knowing" and "not-knowing" with regard to this spiritual process in which he is so completely absorbed. "Not-knowing" is related to the unbidden spiritual impulse bringing him to visionary knowledge. Reason gives no answers about this generating force: "We come to something without knowing why," Roethke says in "The Manifestation." But an attitude of religious reverence unmistakably marks the last stanza:

> The shade speaks slowly:
> "Adore and draw near.
> Who knows this—
> Knows all."

This attitude is carried into the final section, where the poet reveals his pleasure at communion with the Divine and at his release from the "heaviness" of spirit which tormented him before.

"North American Sequence" concludes under the symbol of the rose, but the lyrics of "Sequence, Sometimes Metaphysical" finish with the possibly more comprehensive, and certainly more energetic, image of a cosmic dance. The poems of this second sequence are, because of their formal manner, condensed in the presentation of experience; they bring their material to sudden, lively focus and seem to increase the range and depth of Roethke's mystical perceptions by striking inward steadily with little recourse to external affairs. Unrelieved by descriptive writing, the atmosphere is highly charged and passionate. Roethke goes past the achievements of the previous sequence in approximating the instant of naked revelation.

"In a Dark Time" was the subject of a brilliant symposium by John Crowe Ransom, Babette Deutsch, Stanley Kunitz, and Roethke himself,[6] but I must venture to discuss the poem because of its primary importance in the sequence. The poem is clearly about a moment of mystical illumination, but it also deals with the peripheral experiences, including spiritual unrest and agony, which precede and surround such a moment. Roethke plays on the word "dark" throughout the poem: the world of appearances darkens to physical sight, permitting a second or inner sight to take over; there is the dark of spiritual ignorance and of purgation to be endured; then we know, too, that there is a long tradition of mystical imagery in which the blazing light of God appears to our limited, impure human vision as an enveloping darkness. In the "echoing wood," recalling Dante, the poet meets, as he has said, "my double, my Other, usually tied to me, my reminder that I am going to die,"[7] and advances into a personal darkness, which he characterizes as a "Hades." There he loses dignity and control in the midst of

6. "The Poet and His Critics," ed. Anthony Ostroff, *New World Writing* XIX (1961), pp. 189–219. Reprinted in *The Contemporary Poet as Artist and Critic*, ed. Anthony Ostroff (Boston, 1964).

7. Ibid., p. 215.

familiar nature: "A lord of nature weeping to a tree." The humiliation and self-abasement of weeping are replaced by suggestions of madness as an exalted defiance of "circumstance" and of despair while the self descends into the inferno of its undoing. A "place among the rocks" at which the poet next arrives is a decisive threshold in the journey, since it must be either a dead end, and thus a real place of death, or a point where movement alters direction and goes upward out of these depths: "That place among the rocks— is it a cave,/Or winding path? The edge is what I have." Fortunately, it is the "winding path," reminiscent of the path spirits traverse between the natural and supernatural worlds in Yeats's "Byzantium." These two worlds seem to mix in Roethke's vision as well: things are seen as transparent and symbolic, unveiling their higher significances. The last lines of stanza three indicate that a "death of the self" or self-purgation is necessary in order to see "All natural shapes blazing unnatural light" (by "unnatural" Roethke surely means "supernatural").

The final stanza powerfully sets forth the urgency of the soul's desire for a Divine union:

> Dark, dark my light, and darker my desire.
> My soul, like some heat-maddened summer fly,
> Keeps buzzing at the sill. Which I is *I*?
> A fallen man, I climb out of my fear.
> The mind enters itself, and God the mind,
> And one is One, free in the tearing wind.

Again Roethke emphasizes the darkness of his vision. The greater darkness of his "desire," I suppose, connotes his aim to win an even more intimate meeting with God. The soul, freed momentarily of the attachments of self, seeks a total release from earthly reality but is restrained, in part at least, by the poet's double nature which emerges once more in the question, "Which I is *I*?" These dilemmas are temporarily healed in the Divine embrace of the closing lines, where the mind regains unity, is seized and assimilated by God, and so learns a kind of absolute freedom. The "tearing wind" is obviously the breath of spiritual force we have often noticed; at this instant it is, understandably, at its strongest.

Roethke said of this poem that it was "the first of a sequence, part of a hunt, a drive toward God. . . ."[8] We can expect, therefore, that the other pieces will be involved with such mystical experience or with interpretations of it. These concerns hold the sequence together, as do recurrent words and images. "In Evening Air" offers a respite from the intense strain of Divine vision, allowing the poet to ruminate on that vision, its demands upon the self, and to reassert his artistic vocation: "I'll make a broken music, or I'll die." Most important, he can still utter his love for creation and his prayerful request for transcendence at the same time. The rose image is used again to blend natural and supernatural spheres of being:

> Ye littles, lie more close!
> Make me, O Lord, a last, a simple thing
> Time cannot overwhelm.
> Once I transcended time:
> A bud broke to a rose,
> And I rose from a last diminishing.

Roethke begins "The Sequel" as a poem of self-questioning, querying his motives and the character of his experience. But soon he sees "a body dancing in the wind" which distracts his attention. This is a figure of more than one meaning: first, his guide, his Beatrice, who appears frequently in love poems and other earlier lyrics; second, the *anima* or soul, which is a female principle in the male (see "The Restored" in this sequence, where it has a poem to itself). The figure heralds another spiritual awakening and engages the poet in a dance of universal celebration that continues into "The Restored" and reaches a climax in "Once More, the Round." Corresponding rather closely to the dance and the female figure is the image of "An old wind-tattered butterfly" that "pulsed its wings upon the dusty ground" in "stretchings of the spirit" at

8. Ibid., p. 214.

the start of "The Motion." The conclusion of this poem is another realization of possibility which aids the poet on his trying way: "O, motion O, our chance is still to be!"

Located near the middle, "Infirmity" summarizes various themes worked through the entire sequence, much as "The Lost Son" does in the "Praise to the End" sequence. "Infirmity" explores at first Roethke's wish to retain his individual identity and yet "to be something else." Pride, fear, and self-love prevent him from abandoning himself wholly to the spirit: this is one aspect of infirmity in the poem. The second stanza, concerned with his physical nature, describes another sort of infirmity: the slow death of the body which will force the poet out of himself, into the realm of the spirit, by killing him. A little wryly, he thinks Christ must be pleased with this inevitability:

> Sweet Christ, rejoice in my infirmity;
> There's little left I care to call my own.
> Today they drained the fluid from a knee
> And pumped a shoulder full of cortisone;
> Thus I conform to my divinity
> By dying inward, like an aging tree.

Here the tree refers explicitly to the poet's life, and the description of that life's gradual collapse extends through the next stanza, where "a pure extreme of light/Breaks" on the poet as his "meager flesh breaks down" and he becomes "son and father of [his] only death." The increase of spiritual life seems exactly proportionate to the decrease of physical powers, and "The soul delights in that extremity." Roethke muses on this terrible and frightening transformation of himself in stanza four; there "the deep eye" of second sight "sees the shimmer on the stone," an altered version of the dance we have noted, and also the play of Divine light. "The eternal seeks, and finds, the temporal," he writes; we feel something of the enormous pressure of that spiritual impulse which leads the poet where it will. He is brought one more time, through the symbolism of the lunar cycle, to a death of the self and a rebirth "beyond the reach of wind and fire." In the subsequent stanza he again states his abiding love for the creatures of the natural world and recognizes that he has not lost everything he valued as his own, for, as he says, "My soul is still my soul, and still the Son,/ And knowing this, I am not yet undone." The soul is, in other words, born of the body's decrepitude and, at last, its death, but it keeps a personal quality, the signs of the individual's life and loves:

> Things without hands take hands: there is no choice,—
> Eternity's not easily come by.
> When opposites come suddenly in place,
> I teach my eyes to hear, my ears to see
> How body from spirit slowly does unwind
> Until we are pure spirit at the end.

Roethke gives voice in these final lines to the transforming process he knows himself to be undergoing. His means of apprehending experience change to conform with the radically different zones of reality into which he is being thrust, and so the ordinary sensory perception is replaced by synesthesia (reputedly common in mystical experience). Indeed, we might say that the moment of mystical union in "In a Dark Time" is a conditioning for this last journey in death of which Roethke speaks in the concluding line above. Such a journey, of course, lies beyond the province of poetry, except as it is glimpsed in vision.

"The Decision," "The Marrow," "I Waited," and "The Tree, the Bird" all concentrate in strong fashion on episodes in the Way of Becoming: periods of waiting, discontent; the agony involved in choosing to pursue this Way; the acts of sacrifice and self-annihilation required to progress toward God ("I bleed my bones, their marrow to bestow/Upon that God who knows what I would know"); the tension of inner division; and those hard-won but rewarding visions that pierce through time:

> The present falls, the present falls away;
> How pure the motion of the rising day,
> The white sea widening on a farther shore.

> The bird, the beating bird, extending wings—.
> Thus I endure this last pure stretch of joy,
> The dire dimension of a final thing.
> —"The Tree, the Bird"

Roethke intends, I believe, by "dire" not something evil or fatal, in a pejorative sense, but rather something overpowering that puts aside whatever has preceded it.

Even though the spiritual journey Roethke has embarked upon and carried through, in spite of considerable pain and uncertainty, to a peak of mystical knowledge may appear to us as anything but a pleasurable venture, he can still persuade us in "The Right Thing" that he is "the happy man."[9] This poem is primarily about that spiritual impulse, often seen in the form of wind and water, to which the poet submits himself throughout these late poems. Determinacy of a spiritual nature, or perhaps we should call it Divine necessity, brings Roethke to a transcending joy. He "takes to himself what mystery he can,"

> And, praising change as the slow night comes on,
> Wills what he would, surrendering his will
> Till mystery is no more: No more he can.
> The right thing happens to the happy man.

The final poem of the sequence maintains the same elated feelings. It begins with a question—"What's greater, Pebble or Pond?"— about the worth of the isolated spirit as it is drawn into the heart of Absolute Reality, and repeats the desire for knowledge of "The Unknown." In this initial stanza we discover also the image of the "true self" running toward "a Hill" (which recalls Dante's "purgatorial hill" to which Roethke refers in "Four for Sir John Davies") or, ultimately, toward God. That self is the real "I" of the two confusing the poet in "In a Dark Time," and it is a new self born of the spirit, purged of dross and yet keeping its attachment to cre-

---

9. "I count myself among the happy poets," Roethke wrote earlier in "Open Letter," in *Mid-Century American Poets*, ed. John Ciardi (New York, 1950), p. 70. Reprinted in Mills, ed., *On the Poet and His Craft*.

ation. The poet celebrates this spiritual birth by joining in a dance of cosmic proportions with all creatures and things, and with Blake, whose vision ("the Eye altering all"), like Roethke's, can find God living in everything and everything living in God. All are in One and One is in all:

> Now I adore my life
> With the Bird, the abiding Leaf,
> With the Fish, the questing Snail,
> And the Eye altering all;
> And I dance with William Blake
> For love, for Love's sake;
>
> And everything comes to One,
> As we dance on, dance on, dance on.

Roethke's search for God ends poetically in that inclusive and joyous representation of a Divine unity. Theodore Roethke, it seems to me, is one of our great American poets; in "North American Sequence" and "Sequence, Sometimes Metaphysical" he has left us not only some of his finest work, but also a number of the most astonishing mystical poems in the language.

3   Earth Hard: David Ignatow's Poetry

Earth hard to my heels
bear me up like a child . . .
                    —Davd Ignatow

Multitude, solitude: identical
terms and interchangeable by the
active and fertile poet.
                    —Baudelaire

David Ignatow is a latecomer, a dark horse in contemporary American poetry, chiefly because he was never recognized—
nor did he think of himself—as a member of the poetic generation
to which he properly belongs by age—that is, the generation which
includes, among others, Lowell, Berryman, Nims, Schwartz, and
Shapiro. He has written steadily in isolation and independence for
several decades. His earliest books, *Poems* (1948) and *The Gentle
Weight Lifter* (1955), were published by small presses, one of them
a New York art gallery. Only with the appearance of three succes-
sive volumes in the Wesleyan Poetry series, beginning with *Say
Pardon* (1961) and culminating recently in a fourth, comprehensive collection of *Poems 1934–1969* (1970), has Ignatow's work become generally known for its remarkable imaginative and stylistic
accomplishment, and then among a younger generation of poets
and readers. A look at the developing course of his art over thirty-
five years discovers no abrupt changes in manner but rather an extraordinary firmness of purpose and direction, the cultivation of a
language and approach to experience that could derive only from
the most severe demands upon himself.
     The reader can merely guess at the private cost of these demands,

but he can discern their sources in Ignatow's work and his comments about it. First, there is his will to face himself squarely, to bear witness to every failure, weakness, destructive impulse, and to a nearly overwhelming feeling of guilt ("Guilt is my one attachment to reality," he writes in a much-quoted line). Ignatow constantly explores his inner life, carrying what he finds into the light, bearing whatever pain it may cause him. But such self-examination is just one side of the coin in his poetry; the second side involves him in the lives of others, for his aim, beyond the earliest poems, is to become a poet of the city—specifically, of New York—to make himself, as he says, "the metaphor of his community."[1] Awareness of identity and of self-integrity depend not simply upon the ability to scrutinize with honesty and care one's inward being, but also on the capacity for extending the self outward into immediately surrounding existence. "My kind of writing forces me to go out among people," Ignatow remarks. "I'm not a social poet. I'm a poet of individuality and I only know my individuality by interacting with others. I can't do less than respond as I'm made to respond by environment. Yet I'm conscious, as a poet, of exactly what's happened to me."[2] Precisely here, at the margin of daily existence, where the self encounters others or turns away to look within, the elements of his experience take the shape of a unique poetic articulation. The word "poetic" does not in this instance awaken any of the usual lyric connotations; the speech of Ignatow's poems, mined from the spoken language, earns its victory the hard way, by educating the reader's ear to realize and appreciate its marvelous flexibility and strength, its subtle beauty.

The creation of that poetic speech or voice which lends Ignatow's writing so much forceful singularity can be traced in part to influences avowedly decisive for him. These include, he tells us, Baudelaire, Whitman, William Carlos Williams, and the Bible.[3]

1. Scott Chisholm, "An Interview with David Ignatow," *Tennessee Poetry Journal* III, 2 (Winter 1970), p. 27.
2. Ibid., p. 27.
3. See "On Writing," *Tennessee Poetry Journal* III, 2 (Winter 1970), pp. 14–15.

For Ignatow the ideals and values of Whitman are questioned and counterbalanced by the sombre, pessimistic vision of urban life to be found in Baudelaire's poetry and prose poems. The former's optimistic view of America—to which the French poet might well reply, "Dreams! Always dreams! And the more ambitious and delicate the soul, all the more impossible the dreams" (translated by Louise Varèse)—are vigorously challenged, inverted, by the harsh realities of the twentieth-century America which Ignatow's poetry so stunningly captures. In "Communion" Ignatow begins each of the poem's three stanzas with the same declaration of Whitman's desire for brotherhood, and proceeds to demolish it through the bitterly ironic disclosure of the fate of such hopes for America. Enmity and death pervade the poem's atmosphere, and a desolate prophecy of annihilation brings it to conclusion, thus simultaneously effacing Whitman's vision—though not, of course, his imaginative or poetic greatness which Ignatow surely admires. The delicate, unobtrusive way in which he uses the word "contended" in the first stanza, allowing it to accumulate a terrible suggestive power in terms of the spirit of free enterprise as the poem progresses inexorably toward its suicidal climax, is indicative of Ignatow's characteristic skill:

> Let us be friends, said Walt,
> and buildings sprang up
> quick as corn and people
> were born into them, stock
> brokers, admen, lawyers and doctors
> and they contended
>   among themselves
> that they might know
>   each other.
>
> Let us be friends, said Walt.
> We are one and occasionally two
> of which the one is made
> and cemeteries were laid out
> miles in all directions

to fill the plots with the old
and young, dead of murder, disease,
rape, hatred, heartbreak and insanity
to make way for the new
and the cemeteries spread over the land
their white scab monuments.

Let us be friends, said Walt, and the graves
were opened and coffins laid on top
of one another for lack of space.
It was then the gravediggers slit
their throats, being alone in the world,
not a friend to bury.

When national and historical ideals are perverted, employed as tools for self-promotion or as weapons against others, Ignatow finds himself in the difficult situation of so many contemporary poets who also lack any kind of religious commitment, namely, that of possessing no ideological or metaphysical frame of reference from which to comprehend experience, derive values, and order imaginative vision. This condition assumes primary importance in Ignatow's case, for he turns this deprivation to positive account and develops from it his own notably anti-poetic "flat style," which likewise owes its inception to a close study of the abstract techniques of pioneer modern painters, as well as his wish to fashion a poetry utilizing the idiom of urban American speech. He comments:

> The *flat* style is precisely the style of Picasso when he is working with urban images. The *flat* style is the style of Matisse for which he was condemned at the beginning. It is the cubist and abstract style divorcing itself from perspective. In fact, there no longer is perspective. There is the thing itself—that which we must concentrate on. We can no longer put anything or any idea in a context of references to other or more distant goals or larger perspectives in life. We must work with what we have, and what we have lived through —our sensibilities, and nothing else.
>
> This is especially true in the arts where the authenticity or originality of the work derives from the uniqueness of the artist's expres-

sion. The fact of the matter is that I studied the flat style of Picasso and Matisse and Mondrian and saw its usefulness—let me say, significance—for poetry, and I began to use it. At that point, I abandoned the romantic rhetoric I was enjoying in myself so immensely, finding it inadequate to my experience. The work of William Carlos Williams confirmed the direction I began to take.[4]

It becomes evident from these remarks on the loss of perspective that the enterprise of religious and/or cultural allusion which *does* lend perspective to the work of Eliot and Pound—and, later, in varying degrees, to that of David Jones, Robert Duncan, Charles Olson, and Nathaniel Tarn, let us say—is for Ignatow, as man and poet, quite impossible to sustain without fabrication. Alternatively, he returns to the immediacies of existence, the particulars of here and now, "the thing itself," and concentrates singlemindedly upon them. Two brief poems, printed next to each other in *Figures of the Human* (1964), reflect this preoccupation. In "The Sky Is Blue," a recollection from childhood of his mother's angry command and his own view at that moment of the blank sky outside the window in which the sole thing visible is the contingent one of a neighboring roof, he obliquely challenges, through his boyish (but now pointed) query, her presumed belief in some kind of fixed order comprehending everything, with even a niche for his toy soldier:

> Put things in their place,
> my mother shouts. I am looking
> out the window, my plastic soldier
> at my feet. The sky is blue
> and empty. In it floats
> the roof across the street.
> What place, I ask her.

"The Song," which follows, emphasizes more directly and definitely the absence of transcendental meanings for existence. The "emptiness" to which the song is surrendered in the opening line

4. Ibid., p. 14.

Ignatow refers to elsewhere as "the emptiness of consolation"; he continues: "How do we console ourselves in a world that can no longer be motivated by the ideals of the nineteenth century? We haven't any ideals to speak of now and the spirituality is the sense of defeat. For us it's a defeat that forces us into a kind of humbleness."[5] As the poem implies, in the appearance and disappearance of creatures and things in the universe, in the activities of men, whether recreations, hobbies, or the writing of poetry, there is no further significance. For Ignatow, nothing will be rescued from oblivion by the benevolence of a Divine eye: living beings, the acts and gestures that occur within time and space, are simply and finally themselves and are subject to the fate imposed by the temporal order, which is to vanish, in the longer reaches of history, without a trace:

> The song is to emptiness.
> One may come and go
> without a ripple. You see it
> among fish in the sea,
> in the woods among the silent
> running animals, in a plane
> overhead, gone; man
> bowling or collecting coins,
> writing about it.

Having taken these poems as representative of a fundamental attitude underlying Ignatow's work, a conviction of the severely reduced scope of possible beliefs or ideals for himself and contemporary man, one must still account for certain poems in the third section of *Say Pardon* in which the figure of God appears, for they will help us to discern what values he struggles for through his writing. Altogether, these poems at first create an effect of ambiguity and uncertainty. In "A Semblance" the poet, standing at his mother's graveside, hears the rabbi's prayer for the dead with bewilderment and can only "follow unsteadily/its meaning"; in conclusion he asserts: "You pray/to the air." He wonders, in "Without

5. Chisholm, "An Interview with David Ignatow," p. 25.

Fear," if the "self-pity,/terror and love" which comprise the constant ingredients of human feeling aren't in themselves sufficient "to preserve us" so we might affirm, in a phrase echoing Eliot's in "Little Gidding" (in turn borrowed from the fourteenth-century mystic Juliana of Norwich), that "all will be well," since it is through the rhythm of these contrasting, recurrent states that the Divine becomes manifest: "Without fear of contradiction," he ends, "I give you God in my life."

Two other poems, "I Felt" and "The Rightful One," come closest to establishing the kind of basic principle we grow conscious of as we read through Ignatow's poetry. Here the Divine and the human belong to the same dimension of reality, which is earthly, mortal, and also profoundly Christian in a certain sense, one might add, though completely devoid of ecclesiastical, transcendental, or supernatural implications, thus once more confirming a belief in the closed perspective and the resulting necessary confrontation with existence as it is at each moment. An obligation is placed upon the poet in "I Felt" to authenticate his life, to make it his own by loving and caring for another. The poem plainly indicates that the poet must deliver his life from the Lord—which I understand as meaning to take it away from the realm of potential or idealized virtue and into the world of specific activity, turn it into the realized gesture of himself toward another person; in this manner alone can he win the attribute of selfless love ordinarily relegated to the Divine, and so enter also his own existence through the fulfillment of its inherent possibilities:

> I felt I had met the Lord.
> He calmed me, calling me
> to look into my child's room.
> He said, I am love,
> and you will win your life
> out of my hands
> by taking up your child.

"The Rightful One," a longer, more dramatic poem, begins with the poet's son announcing excitedly the presence of God in his room, arrived there because the boy, unlike his father, "had searched for Him." The appearance of the Divine figure is all too human: He is scarred by experience, worn with fatigue and the burden of too much knowledge, and comes to disclose the inevitability of weakness, the necessity of suffering, and, in spite of that, the need to bless, to bestow love and "forgiveness":

> He had come. I saw Him standing,
> his hair long, face exhausted, eyes sad
> and knowing, and I bent my knee,
> terrified at the reality,
> but he restrained me with a hand
> and said, I am a sufferer like yourself.
> I have come to let you know.
> And I arose, my heart swelling, and said,
> I have failed and bitterness is in me.
> And he replied, And forgiveness too.
> Bless your son. And I blessed him
> and his face brightened. And the Rightful One
> was gone and left a power to feel free.

Such freedom as is available here depends, I believe, on the acceptance of one's own life, which, as in "I Felt," achieves completeness only when it includes responsibility and love for others. (This freedom stands in absolute opposition to the negative or selfish state of being free from obligation to anyone but oneself which Ignatow countenances in the later "Ritual" poems and "Rescue the Dead.") In both poems blessedness, freedom, and integrity must be earned in terms of present existence; what value they might have elsewhere Ignatow does not know, for, as we have seen, he has no faith in the transcendent, in perspective, and admonishes us to recognize the "emptiness" beyond which we have already encountered. Value, when it does emerge, as in the poems just discussed, has been labored for and discovered within the context of the work, or rather in the difficult, complex process of transforming daily experience and perception into the language of poems. Ignatow repeatedly uses walking—frequently in the sense of a dogged persistence against the odds and of bearing the onus of pain and guilt—as a highly evocative metaphor for the slow, hard progression through a lifetime and, by implication, for the strenuous activity of writing poems along the way:

> I've got to have the things that hurt me.
> People want to deprive me of them in pity.
> It is they who are made miserable
> by my painful life, and I am sorry
> for them without weights upon their feet,
> walking.
>
> —"Walking"

With the realms of idealism sealed off for him in both the religious and socio-political sense, Ignatow abandons himself to the world of the actual, the day-to-day, and to the environment he inhabits. Ignatow grew up in Brooklyn, which, after he began to know New York as a city in his teens, he came to think of as suburban, "as that great part of America that lived under the trees and among the grasses";[6] subsequently, at the age of eighteen, he moved to the city. The earliest pieces in *Poems 1934–1969* do not reflect the deep impression resulting from his exposure to the city but are instead love poems; if they are not as yet revelatory of the dramatic interaction between the poet's self and his urban surroundings, certain of them, such as "Pardon Keeps the Sun," are notable for their candid self-scrutiny and careful delineation of the relationship of lover and beloved, both of which are important and enduring themes in Ignatow's writing. Other poems of the 1930's —"For a Friend," "Forks with Points Up," and "My Neighbor" are among the best—show an increasing preoccupation with rendering the complicated mode of life into which he had thrust himself, in other words, with "writing a poetry of New York." That attempt, to be successful, required the creation of a style, a form of language and rhythmic movement avoiding the "poetical," through which his urban experience could be incarnated:

6. Ibid., p. 22.

I had to meet the city on its own terms if I was going to get it into my work. And that meant being overwhelmed by the city's life in order to emerge with all the facts. This is how language becomes transformed from one historical period to the next, through history or the individual. I was not going to write in the iambic pentameter when the very tone and pace of the city denied such a regular, predictable and comfortable style—comfortable, of course, from long use and its acceptance, as *style*. I wanted the spirit of the city in my poems while I, as a city man, knew how to manipulate the spirit in terms of its language. I was the city's artist and as its artist I could feel both in and out of the city at the same time.[7]

In these observations and aesthetic convictions Ignatow demonstrates his affinity with William Carlos Williams, whose poetic career was dedicated to developing a new metric, a "measure" evolved from American speech and liberated from the bond with traditional English rhythms and forms. Williams immersed himself in his New Jersey environment of Rutherford and Paterson and in the details of his life as a man and a practicing physician. In "The Wanderer," the opening piece in his *Collected Earlier Poems*, he symbolizes his artistic ties with the immediacies of existence and its location by his leap into "the filthy Passaic" river, where he receives, as in an initiation rite, new knowledge within himself, including even the "rottenness" and "degradation" of the place and the lives closely surrounding his. This poetry of location or environment, which may incorporate geography, topography, and history as well, and puts the poet in the personal context created by direct contacts and relationships with the past or the present or both—that is, the milieu of his life—is visible in different ways in the writings of Charles Olson (its chief theoretician), Louis Zukofsky, Edward Dorn, Gary Snyder, and Denise Levertov, to name the most prominent. For Ignatow, who can be linked with them, though only in his own independent fashion, the poetry which he sets out to write must be capable of embodying the joy, terror, evil, shame, and tragedy discovered each day in himself and in the lives of other

7. Ibid., p. 23.

city inhabitants, but it also demands a plain, unvarnished language that can, in the interests of accuracy and truth to experience, present those qualities in all of their intensity, drawing out their basic human implications while resolutely avoiding any kind of adornment. The reader, abruptly greeted by these bare essentials, gradually realizes how much poetry is in them. A strong, if partial, statement of the aesthetics of Ignatow's type of poem can be found in the poetry itself, and in a variety of different pieces. One of them, "Singers of Provence" from *The Gentle Weight Lifter*, contains an unmistakable refusal to hide, beautify, or dissemble in writing. Unlike the Provençal poets who, fearing for their safety, disguised the significance of their songs, the contemporary poet needs to bear testimony, to make known what he has seen:

> You made music
> to cover your guilt, you were all scared;
> and you sang to bring on the ecstasy of lies;
> while we with the door wide open
> on the scene of the crime face the day
> clearly with these words: We were here
> and we witnessed the deaths and drownings,
> the deeds too dark for words;
> they would rumble in the belly meaninglessly,
> but we speak our minds and the song sticks.
> The people sing it, the singer believes it,
> the air springs with a new song.

Evidence of this receptivity and honesty is inscribed on every page of Ignatow's poetry and stems directly from his dedication to the hard, often frightening and dangerous task of exposing himself to, even assimilating, the experiences and torments of others ("My life has been a seeking/to identify with pain and suffering . . ."), frequently reaching out to adopt their voices and identities so as to recognize them in himself, himself in them. Penetration of the existence of another person becomes simultaneously a means of self-knowledge. In "Day My Dream" Ignatow comprehends those unpleasant or destructive aspects of life which the majority of people like to ignore, content with themselves and their own well-being, or to protect themselves from, armored with conventions which proscribe sensibility and empathy. Startlingly, the poet acknowledges that he feels contradictory behavior is "normal" because he has intimate acquaintance with all sides of himself, the secret impulses toward pleasure or negation at work in the depths of the psyche when sleep loosens the control of reason and conscience. The dying fish, unnoticed by passersby, the "terror" of the stalked deer to which the hunters are insensitive, the slovenly, decrepit old woman who embarrasses the bus passengers by her reminder of the frailty of human dignity and poise Ignatow can fully understand, for he has uncovered the same fears, weaknesses, and incongruities in his own psyche:

> Fish tossed on sand,
> flopping for air; overhead
> two-legged people stride about.
> Such a scene is normal to me.
>
> Deer hunted through the woods,
> heads high in terror. Men train
> normal guns on them.
>   The explosive
> mouth that fragments the atmosphere;
> the old woman who drools on a bus
> crowded with intensely dressed salesmen.
> How they look away in disgust.
> All this is normal to me,
> as the face in my mirror each morning—
> lined by guilt of the night;
> lips relaxed from rightness, creases
> under the eyes enfolding pleasure
> in dark folds.
>   Since the tunnel
> in which I have acted out my dreams
> has been lit with these passions,
> revealing my form, I converse with all,
> as if night were day and my dream.

In another poem, "Nocturne," from the same period (the 1940's) the poet puts himself clearly on view, again rejecting subterfuge or masquerade. He shows us himself "Sitting at [his] window" at night, with lights on and the shade up; and just as he willingly reveals himself in the interests of truth, so he may expect to

> look into the windows of others,
> giving warning to those
> who like to hide.

His admitted intention here is to probe degradation, to perceive "that moment when human passes/into beast," obviously not for sensational purposes or out of prurient motives but essentially "to distinguish the difference" and thus locate some groundwork for what is properly human. Once more, as in "Day My Dream" and many another poem, Ignatow has involved himself with the scale of man's behavior, sounding those subconscious layers of the mind that dictate our actions but which we usually prefer to forget since cognizance of them breaks down pride and self-esteem, opens a window on our fears, guilt, and covert energies. But the poet does not flinch from these realities and asks us to observe exactly those elements present in ourselves. How else shall we begin to try to live as humans, brought together in a mutually shared world?

> Ugly is the word
> and do not be scared of mirrors.
> The sewer runs through the neatest block,
> the tide carrying crud and contraceptives,
> and I have thoughts to make the hair
> of strangers stand on end.
>   We are together
> by contact of our hands on furniture,
> books, plates and fruits of the corner peddler's
> busiest intersection.

So, as he writes in another poem, "To say what has to be said here,/one must literally take off one's clothes," and proceeds to do it, finding in his nakedness a relationship: "I am/of my own kind/

and my heart beats./I have brothers." Self-exposure and vulnera-
bility enable Ignatow to participate in the common life of humanity
and bring to his poems revelations of moods and emotions otherwise unspoken. A second poem with the title "Communion" contains as much irony as the one already discussed but of a different
sort:

> In the subway I had the impulse to kill
> and sat and stared straight ahead
> to avoid the eyes of strangers
> who might read my dread
> and when finally I had the courage
> to shift my gaze from the poster above
> I saw to my dismay the eyes of others
> turning away.

Ignatow's characteristically plain, conversational diction and his
quiet tone lend this little poem an almost placid surface which is
suddenly disturbed by words such as "kill" and "dread," as well as
the phrase "eyes of strangers" that creates for a moment a spasm of
paranoiac terror. The absence of any punctuation forces the reader
more completely into the poem to find for himself its rhythmic
flow, a movement which, because of its lack of ordinary guideposts,
comes to seem synonymous with the felt time of the experience
itself. The thematic implications remain purposely indefinite yet
highly suggestive. The poet senses in himself a terrible initiative to
destroy, not for a discernible reason but apparently from a con-
catenation of psychic causes whose motives are invisible. At the
same time, he has enough self-possession to realize that this eruption
of malevolent desire must be held in check, and here the poem
pivots about the word "dread." "Dread" catches up the various
ramifications of his condition: fear at what has announced itself
within him, anxiety over the problem of maintaining self-control
in a public place, and, of course, a kind of horror that what is going
on inwardly—the struggle of will, the tumult of emotions—might
be read on his face by the other passengers. With an effort, he fixes

his gaze on an advertising poster until the impulse passes, or is at least manageable. Only then is he struck with another disclosure, more far-reaching than the first. With "dismay" he discovers that he has been watched during his bout with his feelings and, in addition, that those feelings have been interpreted, a fact which draws him into a strange union (or "communion") with the passengers, since they must also, at times, have known the same inspiration to murder in order to perceive it and now look aside, abandoning to the poet a part of themselves they should best like to forget. Through this haunting brief episode, Ignatow again forges the links of fraternity.

Living in New York, working at a variety of jobs to maintain himself and his family, always under the threat of economic insecurity, the pressures of his superiors, Ignatow has realized comprehensively the nature of modern urban experience; it has formed the very substance of his existence for a period of more than thirty years. As a result, his poetry abounds in instances of closely rendered observation of individuals at their tasks, at lunch, in the streets, during the working day. It is impossible in an essay to cover all such poems, but "The Fisherwoman," as an example, with its extremely sensitive description of mundane labor, manages to simulate, through the skillful progression of its lines, the actual physical feeling and pattern of this woman's procedures, the movement of her body and the movement of her day:

> She took from her basket four fishes
> and carved each into four slices
> and scaled them with her long knife,
> this fisherwoman, and wrapped them;
> and took four more and worked
> in this rhythm through the day,
> each action ending on a package
> of old newspapers; and when it came
> to close, dark coming upon the streets,
> she had done one thing, she felt, well,
> making one complete day.

Occasionally, a poem of this kind may open a dimension beyond
itself, assume something of the quality of a parable, in which the
activities of the particular person depicted take on a more porten-
tous aspect than mere facts allow, as if, indeed, they signified in
their peculiar fashion the larger configurations of life. Two poems,
"The Errand Boy I" and its sequel, among others from *Say Pardon*,
are representative; I quote only the first:

> To get quicker through the day
> and to bring on night as a blessing,
> to lie down in a sleep that is a dream
> of completion, he takes up his package
> from the floor—he has been ordered
> to do so, heavy as it is, his knees weakening
> as he walks, one would never know
> by his long stride—and carries it
> to the other end of the room.

Readily enough, one can detect in these lines the sort of symbolic
implications I've referred to: the burdensome task is not simply
detailed for its own sake, as in "The Fisherwoman," but tends,
especially through the resonant, allusive diction of the opening half
of the poem, to suggest something of the character of man's lot.
The biblical overtones aroused here hardly need mentioning, particularly those in which God, expelling Adam and Eve from Eden,
places upon them the requirements of hard labor. What Ignatow
adds is the notion of reward and fulfillment man finds for himself
in doing the things imposed upon him by implacable necessity,
and doing them without exhibiting their arduousness. Yet this
"dream of completion" many also carry connotations of death, the
point at which rest occurs after a lifetime of such days as the poem
describes. If that is so, perhaps there is some irony in the fact that
a man tries "to get quicker through the day," that is, hurry through
the duration of his existence, in order to discover his only lasting
refuge and satisfaction in his demise.

If ordinary work brings on exhaustion, it further permits release of pressures and drives which otherwise might seek destruc-

tive outlets; that is the idea behind "Sales Talk," where at first Ignatow appears to be defending the frenzied pace of business life as a safety valve:

> Better than to kill each other off
> with our extra energy is to run after the bus,
> though another be right behind. To run
> and to explain to ourselves we have no time
> to waste, when it is time that hangs
> dangerously on our hands, so that the faster
> we run the quicker the breezes rushing by
> take time away.

But once more a thread of irony runs through the poem's fabric, and it is the irony of a momentarily detached, appraising eye which views things as they are, the demands of circumstance. Doubtless, this critical attitude tacitly implies that our modern human situation should not be what it is, for to avoid killing one another we are forced to kill ourselves, or at least to use up time, our precious commodity. Moreover, as the latter part of the poem indicates, the environment of the city breeds murderousness and enforces a conformity beyond the limits of which exist isolation and danger. The business "uniform" signifies membership in the ranks of regularity and normalcy, prohibits any close inspection of our nakedness, especially of the kind we have already seen Ignatow undertake for himself:

> For comfort we must work
> this way, because in the end we find
> fume-filled streets and murder headlines:
> one out of insanity breaks loose:
> he could not make that extra effort
> to keep connected with us. Loneliness
> like a wheeling condor was attracted
> to the particle that had strayed apart.
> The brief case we carry, the pressed trousers,
> the knotted tie under a white collar add up
> to unity and morale.

"The Business Life," in the poem of that title, offers a type of exposure to the hardness and antipathy of individuals at their jobs. In this instance it is the ethos of the office or white-collar job Ignatow attends to; thus the poem contrasts markedly with the sympathetic portraits of the much humbler positions on the economic ladder held by the errand boy and the fisherwoman or "The Gentle Weight Lifter," who achieves "love and honor by lifting barrels" and wins the poet's praise as opposed to those with "a soft job, pushing a pencil/or racketeering, the numbers game." The poem finally brings about a conditioning experience, a realization and acceptance of the brutal, intemperate terms for working fostered by a competitive system. The poet, if he will survive, must learn to "live" with the viciousness of others while retaining his own gentleness; gradually, the initial reaction of horror and dread will pass into a relatively stable feeling of illness—bearable illness—at this daily encounter with sheer malice:

> When someone hangs up, having said
> to you, "Don't come around again,"
> and you have never heard the phone
> banged down with such violence
> nor the voice vibrate with such venom,
> pick up your receiver gently and dial
> again, get the same reply; and dial
> again, until he threatens. You will
> then get used to it, be sick only
> instead of shocked. You will live,
> and have a pattern to go by, familiar
> to your ear, your senses and your dignity.

Ignatow has noted that "the one overriding experience we have had in this country and which we will probably continue to have [is] a sense of violence about ourselves."[8] This poem reveals such active animosity exercised routinely as part of making one's living. Yet the closing lines, if ironical, are not totally negative, bleak and desolate as they seem; for the poet remains sickened by this situation, a sign that he will not abandon his sensitivity to its evils. He

8. Ibid., p. 27.

finds, in the end, a means of surviving in extremely trying circumstances without being overwhelmed by them or relinquishing his own humanity and "dignity" to become himself a figure of violence and ruthlessness. In general, that is the moral history of Ignatow's art.

"Tenderness is our posture," he writes in another poem; and the cultivation of gentleness and love in the specific acts and practical affairs of daily living is Ignatow's mode of asserting value concretely in the midst of the dehumanizing "business life." But it is made unmistakable in this poem that love, when genuine, never wears the guise of some remote spiritual ideal, the "golden trophies or fair kisses" mentioned below; rather, it is a force working through the particulars of an individual's existence, a generative, driving energy that discriminates between the objects of experience and bestows worth as it goes. At last, love discards us, handing us over to death, but we are "racing" toward that conclusion in any event; "tenderness and waiting," with their air of attentiveness and gentle restraint, are, the poem insists, the true expression of love in a temporal, mortal world and provide the strength and integrity to stand "upright" in a valid, fulfilled selfhood:

> Be torn by lions of the day,
> love rends us. Or we must walk among our fellow men,
> at peace in our deaths, not knowing
> the difference between a flower and a spittoon,
> between sitting and walking, running and racing,
> and the panting breath at the far end
> of the field where nothing awaits us
> but a fence over which the ash heap lies:
> dumping grounds that someday shall become
> new racing fields. In our panted breath
> we shall expend ourselves, seeking no cause
> or climax: golden trophies or fair kisses,
> too tired, too happy in our weariness:
> loss of the heavy part of us, run
> to be rid of it: love forcing us, living us,
> wearing us. Finally, when we are useless

> to other needs, tearing us to pieces by lions
> before the crowd.
>   For love is when we are racing,
> expressed in tenderness and waiting.
> Wait always. Waiting we are racing.
> And tenderness is our posture, not crouched,
> not forward, nor leaning backwards but upright
> like a man in which love can recognize itself.

Again, in this passage, we encounter the type of spirituality noted previously in "I Felt," "The Rightful One," and other poems. Here, as specific allusions to the grim fate of early Christians in Rome vividly demonstrate, love is envisaged in terms of martyrdom. But obviously, for Ignatow, life is not sacrificed to love in the expectation of gaining an extra-terrestrial paradise; instead, it defines the right way to live out present existence. A paradox underlies this conception of the poet's, a religious paradox central to the teachings of the Gospels as well, namely, that selflessness opens the path to self-fulfillment. The "upright" figure at the poem's conclusion has won that "posture" or stance of the spirit through "tenderness and waiting," which certainly require nothing less than self-abnegation and a kind of humility, an intention of self toward others. In "The Dream," a beautiful small poem from *Say Pardon*, Ignatow dramatizes the same theme, using the simplest yet most evocative language and detail, creating something which seems endowed with the clarity and luminosity of a vision:

> Someone approaches to say his life is ruined
> and to fall down at your feet
> and pound his head upon the sidewalk.
> Blood spreads in a puddle.
> And you, in a weak voice, plead
> with those nearby for help;
> your life takes on his desperation.
> He keeps pounding his head.
> It is you who are fated;
> and you fall down beside him.
> It is then you are awakened,

the body gone, the blood washed from the ground,
the stores lit up with their goods.

With a marvelous stroke of intuition, Ignatow employs the pronoun "you" here so as to include both poet and reader, drawing the latter into the heart of the situation the poem presents. Assuming another person's agony and deprivation as he attempts to aid him, his life and the victim's merge until his action redeems them both. It is worth observing that while the poem shows some of the qualities of parable, Ignatow does not neglect to give it an urban setting, as if to remind us that the drama belongs to daily experience. The closing line puts the events and figures in touch with material reality, with city environment; at the same time, the details, particularly of light, contribute vitally to the aura of purification and renewal that characterizes the end.

The relation of self to others also demands acknowledgment of the individuality and integrity of each person, even under somewhat unlikely circumstances, as in the poem "Say Pardon," where Ignatow achieves a perfect mixture of humor and irony with the possibilities for humiliation to enforce the affirmation of identity and freedom in the final lines:

> Say pardon to a bum,
> brushing past him.
> He could lean back
> and spit
> and you would have to wipe it off.
> How would you explain
> that you have insulted
> this man's identity,
> of his own choosing;
> and others could only scratch
> their heads and advise you
> to move on
> and be quiet.
> Say pardon
> and follow your own will
> in the open spaces ahead.

The reference to space at the finish, and the suggestion of movement through it, put us in mind of Ignatow's recurrent metaphor of walking, mentioned before, which he introduces usually to designate some sort of progression of the self in the search for wholeness and completion. For the poet does not discover himself or the direction he needs to pursue solely through his exchanges with others; there are numerous poems in which he gazes inward or adopts a meditative attitude toward objects or elements of nature that become charged with significance for him. "And Step" is such a poem. In it Ignatow confronts reflectively his own physical nature and that of a stone. With this inanimate object he does share his material substance, but he wonders if he should think himself inferior because he lacks the hardness and durability of stone. On the other hand, he possesses a voice and a mind, the potentiality for thought, and he decides to stand on his merits, "proud/and fragile" as he is, and then respectfully move on. The "step" he proposes at the end is obviously kindred to the procedure indicated at the finish of "Say Pardon." In both poems an experience is concluded which enlightens and magnifies the poet's sense of identity, and his way lies clear to continue:

> I understand myself
> in relation to a stone,
> flesh and bone.
> Shall I bow down
> to stone? Mine
> is the voice
> I hear. I will
> stand up to stone.
> I will be proud
> and fragile, I will
> be personable
> and step over
> stone.

In an extremely short poem, "All Comes," Ignatow finds cause for celebration in the most ordinary combination of things, sunlight and the form of a bird in flight. If they appear to us common-place, he implies, that is because we fail to see them as he now does, reading them as signs available in nature which conceal a message of hope in the brightness of air, in the lifting of wings, a direction to pursue mapped by the flying bird:

> All comes to sunlight.
> A bird stirring its wings.
> In the air it has the shape of a dream.
> It too is perfect off the ground,
> I follow its flight.

Ignatow can also withdraw into a silence that seeks self-integra-tion and individual assurance which his life needs for its continu-ance. The wall, in "Blessing Myself," serves to symbolize both the isolation he has chosen and the blankness he faces in consequence. He speaks to it, wishing to obtain grace, but nothing miraculous occurs; he receives no answer from the wall, and the reader suspects that he never anticipated a reply. What this strange meeting with the wall effects is a dialogue within the poet which leads to a state of balance allowing him to bestow this desired grace or blessedness upon himself. Ignatow has been forced, then, into an examination of conscience, as it were, an inventory of his own being; only when he can approve himself in honest judgment with scrupulous stan-dards can he win the exaltation of the poem's direct, moving conclusion:

> I believe in stillness,
> I close a door
> and surrender myself
> to a wall and converse
> with it and ask it
> to bless me.
> The wall is silent.
> I speak for it,
> blessing myself.

Such poems represent a strong and important strain in Ignatow's work, that of the personal meditation in which, turned away from the external matters of urban life, he contemplates himself and his nature—both in a personal fashion and as *human* nature, concentrating on his intimate problems, awareness of guilt and failures, the inevitable slow approach of death. Closely related to these poems are the recent pieces, most of them included in *Rescue the Dead* (1968), treating his marriage (other love and marriage poems are, of course, scattered throughout his work), which similarly belongs to the sphere of his private emotions and intimate perceptions of himself. One can say without exaggeration that the distinguishing feature of Ignatow's poetry as his career lengthens out through the 1960's is an increasing intensity in his approach to experience, a tendency to probe even more boldly, thrusting himself forward so as to become as completely engaged as possible with aspects of pain and suffering, violence and death; as he comes more completely to grips with his condition, he does so with man's condition in mid-twentieth-century America as well. This intensity dominates the later poems of social and political affairs—"The Appointment Card," "A First on TV," "My Native Land," "1965," "Emergency Clinic," "Play Again," and the brilliant prose poems, "The Cookout," "America America," "Where There Is Life," and "A Political Cartoon"—to the same degree it does the personal or inward pieces. Any reader of Ignatow knows quite well the extent to which these elements pervade all of his writing, yet now he makes us feel that he must enter more fully into contact with the negative, terrifying forces which erupt everywhere in the modern world as a means of validating not only his own individual existence but even existence as such. He undertakes, as a result, what might be called a descent into the hell of contemporary experience which appears simultaneously as his private inferno; there, divested of traditional spiritual values and with every human impulse and emotion, measure of good and evil, under question, he must attempt to make his passage, literally, save his life.

Nowhere do we see these preoccupations more dramatically and powerfully articulated than in the poems of *Rescue the Dead* and a few others written afterward and now included in the closing section of *Poems 1934–1969*. Ignatow has supplied his own epigraph for *Rescue the Dead*, and its three lines again recall the metaphor of the journey or walking with its corresponding desire for a route away from confinement, toward freedom and harmony. The phrase "edges of life," which occurs in the epigraph, further suggests a tentative, often perilous testing of the perimeters and extremities of human experience that is so prominent a feature of much of the ensuing poetry:

> I feel along the edges of life
> for a way
> that will lead to open land.

In several poems from the book's opening section Ignatow frankly countenances personal feelings of guilt, self-estrangement, and failure which encourage in him states of terror or despondency and, frequently, a longing for death. "Nourish the Crops" begins with the poet standing in sunlight, "warmed on body, face and hands," yet nonetheless desperate within himself, searching for his "life's goodness" before this solar source of nature's fertility. In doubt of his own motives, accusing himself of an endeavor to escape his guiltiness through self-deception, he quickly reaches a condition of fear and trembling so severe that his very life seems momentarily threatened. But the seizure passes, permitting the poet to regain his mood of calm reflection, which is almost pantheistic in its implications of an individual's place in the natural order under the sun:

> True as I breathe, I tell myself.
> It is just as I say. Back to this understanding
> of myself, my breathing becomes normal.
> Guilty in the sun. My peace now is truthful,
> I am truthfully at peace. Oh sun,
> your kindness is a mystery to me.
> How dark I am to myself. How cold I am to myself.
> How close to death I bring myself.
> Because I see you shine on me, I am amazed
> at a loss about myself. I stop to reconsider

> my purpose. Whose death am I seeking?
> I feel myself inconsequential in your warmth
> as it descends on me and on birds, flowers
> and beasts. You give us life, no matter.
> I feel humiliated in my self-importance.
> My wish to die in retribution for my sins
> is laughable. I die in any case like a flower
> or bee or dog. Should I live then as you do
> in brightness and warmth, without question?
> Because I am a product of you to whom all life
> is equal. Do I not sin against you
> by staying dark to myself? You who have given
> the tiger and the snake life
> and nourish the crops?

The poem does not end here but its meditations do, leaving Ignatow with questions that may have answers, though he cannot be sure. His attack of guilt has abated, his thinking has traced a line of possibilities terminating in the notion of self-forgiveness as a virtue, which still remains only a query, a hypothesis brought forth from the situation of unbelief where the poet must try to read what truths he can from his surroundings. The closing stanza shows him persisting in his quest:

> Slowly I move over the field,
> one tired foot ahead of the other,
> feeling through my soles
> the rise and fall of the land.

This sensitive meeting of his feet with the earth as he proceeds, obviously reminiscent of the book's epigraph discussed above, indicates the poet's cautious, perhaps one should say empirical, approach to the events of life, at the same time implying, through the connotations of "rise and fall," the alternating highs and lows, periods of light and darkness, which characterize the climate of his inner being.

The very next poem in sequence, much briefer, confirms this pattern of ascent and decline as if by intentional design. Not surprisingly, since "Nourish the Crops" focuses upon the sun's life-giving rays which appear to the poet to demand the obliteration of darkness, anguish, and deathward inclinations, this poem is called "The Moon." In it Ignatow divides his perceivings between awareness of lunar (or cosmic) ignorance of and alienation from the concerns of men and a sharp cognizance of his own movements and frame of mind, which is bleak:

> I walk beneath it, seeing a stranger
> look down on my familiar state. I walk,
> and it does not know where or for what
> reason on the black surface of the earth.
> I hurry, it is late. I disappear
> into the dark shadow of a building,
> running, and ask of the moon
> what does it expect to discover,
> what does it do in the sky,
> staring down on the intimate
> despairing actions of a man?

The atmosphere of night, "the black surface of the earth," "the dark shadow" into which the poet hurries, as if in flight, combine to create an overall effect of both fear and desolation. The moon hangs over this scene like a blank, stone-faced god who continues to gaze at man's world in utter incomprehension of it and the activities of the poet, caught up in the flux of time ("I hurry, it is late"). One recalls other such "despairing," dead-end poems of the night as Elizabeth Bishop's "The Man-Moth" and Eliot's "Rhapsody on a Windy Night." Whatever considerable differences exist between these various pieces, they all share a common element in their use of fantasy and the irrational. Ignatow in his later work frequently establishes a surrealist or dreamlike situation through which he can expose hidden aspects of thought or behavior. In "The Moon" the darkness that was contained within himself and, so to speak, neutralized by the energy of the sun in "Nourish the Crops" achieves release; the shadowy realm of night becomes a vast projection of the poet's anxiety. Finally, the poem leaves us with a firm

impression of the mute indifference of the universe, quite opposite
to the indiscriminate benevolence of the sun entertained by the
poet in thought in "Nourish the Crops," as the backdrop against
which man makes the futile, frustrated gestures of living.

Subsequently, Ignatow examines some of these gestures in even
more personal fashion, moving relentlessly toward the book's terrible nadir of violence and suffering in the group of three "Rituals."
The title poem, "Rescue the Dead," starts the second section, and
its somewhat generalized statements prepare for the particular,
private pieces to come; it also raises fundamental questions of
value with regard to human relationships.[9] The development of the
poem depends upon an apparent alternating pair of choices: to live
or to love. The latter has the aura of sacrifice and is associated with
the incapacity for survival, while the former is clearly compounded
of sheer practicality, an attitude which, in sum, looks selfish and
predatory. The first stanza begins by relinquishing love without
regret, and the initial lines point a return to the state of nature, of
primitive man who accepts and respects the rules of rudimentary
living, puts no ideal constructions on them in the sense in which
religions do, but then the poem shifts suddenly to reveal this primitive type as modern urban man, the dweller in mass society who
must keep on his mettle in order to feed himself and stay alive in
the jungle of his cities:

> Finally, to forgo love is to kiss a leaf,
> is to let rain fall nakedly upon your head,
> is to respect fire,
> is to study man's eyes and his gestures
> as he talks,
> is to set bread upon the table
> and a knife discreetly by,
> is to pass through crowds
> like a crowd of oneself.
> Not to love is to live.

9. I am indebted in part here to Ignatow's discussion of the poem. Ibid., pp.
31–33.

Of the poem's three remaining quatrains the next introduces the theme of love with exotic and romantic imagery, allusions to death and the unfathomable enigmas of existence, which are neither denied nor avoided but are indissolubly bound to the pursuit of love. In this stanza love appears magical, hypnotic perhaps, and ultimately quite perilous for the individual who follows its seductive course. The contrast between this reckless quest for the ideal or the absolute in love's terms and the wary role of self-protective pragmatism previously advocated for survival in the world could not be more deliberately defined:

> To love is to be led away
> into a forest where the secret grave
> is dug, singing, praising darkness
> under the trees.

Enchanted, rapturous, the believer in love, like an ecstatic mystic or visionary, willingly embraces death as part of the whole to which he has dedicated himself and leaves behind the concerns of mortality and ordinary existence in favor of the hidden principle that animates them. But the next stanza balances the scales on the opposite side:

> To live is to sign your name,
> is to ignore the dead,
> is to carry a wallet
> and shake hands.

These lines return us to mundane affairs, the practical and commercial life in which a person of necessity carefully preserves his surface identity (the assumption here must be, I think, that he never looks far within), faces always the present moment and its expediencies. To carry a wallet is to pay one's way, to be self-reliant, and again to hold those cards with signatures that indisputably prove identification, while shaking hands, in this context, is less an expression of friendship than a conventional act placing both parties on an equal but separate footing, poised to do business. Thus Ignatow has set up in the poem two irreconcilable attitudes or modes of being; and at least on one level, a very important one, he is scrutinizing approaches to life in modern society which are widespread, especially in the instance of the hard-headed, pragmatic view. The poem's conclusion finally brings the poet himself into sight, along with the title's implications, which now, as he has noted, carry ironic overtones:[10]

> To love is to be a fish.
> My boat wallows in the sea.
> You who are free,
> rescue the dead.

The first line above, which might at a glance seem merely odd, has direct relevance to what has gone before in the poem. The fish can survive only in its own element, not in the earth-and-air environment of men; the sea is linked in this stanza with the remote setting of forest and trees in the earlier quatrain on love. Yet the crucial image here remains that of the poet who, speaking about himself, says he "wallows in the sea," not quite a fish then (that is, presumably, committed to the vision of love), yet closer to that than to the ruthlessly self-seeking conduct of those "who are free" of such illusions and dreams, dealing only in the brute facts of existence. Ignatow's "boat" tips dangerously, for his position is still precarious and uncertain. Yet his command in the last line really constitutes a challenge to the liberated "realists" to deliver those trusting in love from the death to the world's actualities their faith imposes and guide them to the authentic life—if they can. The suggestion is that, in any event, they cannot.

Subsequently, Ignatow plunges into areas of experience where love is negated, human sympathy and feeling denied, perverted, or corrupted into violence, whether that of war or individual criminal acts. "A Suite for Marriage," "Sediment," and "For Your Fear" probe with painful precision the dilemmas and agonies of the poet's relationship with his wife. In the first of these poems he envisages the abolition of his personality and identity, finally, his life itself,

---

10. Ibid., p. 32.

within the circumscribed world of domesticity in which husband
and wife, locked in their respective solitudes, struggle beneath the
surface, almost like characters in Nathalie Sarraute's novels, to endure, even to dominate the situation:

> You keep eating and raising a family
> in an orderly, calm fashion
> for the sake of the child,
> but behind you at your heels
> in a humble mass
> lies a figure.
>
> Do you own me?
> I sense it in your nervous
> irritated talk, as for someone
> who has become a burden—
> when what is possessed
> becomes equally demanding
> for being possessed.
>
> I am not sure that you wish me to live.
> I am not sure that I can.
> We circle each other
> with the taut courtesy
> of two respectful opponents.
> Difficult to say what next,
> this could be all,
> to confront each other
> in suspense.
>
> Your eyes are so cold-looking,
> rejecting me silently
> as I talk in low, cultured tones
> to convince you
> of my superiority.

With the next stanza the child, Ignatow's daughter, enters the
poem; in ignorance of her parents' conflict and misery "she stands
between them/like a light of many colors, turning/and dancing."
(One should read this poem together with "Steps for Three—A

Prose Poem" which dramatizes the same problems.) Her appearance mediates to a degree the marital combat and urges the poet—
he does not presume to speak for his wife, whose role with the girl
must anyway be different—to partial resolutions, the effort to elicit
benefits for his daughter's existence. We observe in this attempt
something of the selflessness recommended in earlier poems as the
means for achieving grace or spiritual welfare for another and so,
at last, for oneself:

> My daughter, I cry to you from my solitude.
> I play the yea-sayer, most bitter,
> to spare you with deeds I know can win
> good from evil, my despair
> a blessing for your life.

The poet's own suffering persists, however, without diminishing;
though he is able to wrest value from it for someone else, his relations with his wife stay unchanged, as the powerful and strange
concentration of imagery in "Sediment" proves. In the dream landscape of this poem Ignatow envisages himself as "a lake for you"—
addressing his wife—"not to see you shrivel up," for she looks, in
the opening lines, like "a well-rounded sponge/from head to foot."
As the poem progresses, he adds further detail to the setting—trees,
sky, a mountain—until it seems complete, a world in which their
relationship is at the center. Since the sky is cloudless, the season
dry, the sponge keeps absorbing the lake's unreplenished waters,
and such is the odd vision of their mutual fate the poet entertains
in the end. Apparently the bond between them precludes any other
possibilities, and besides, the poem's events bear the inexorability
of nightmare. The image of sediment in the closing line again indicates a sacrifice of self which is reductive for Ignatow, leaving him,
in this instance, quite literally emptied out:

> No rain comes while you and I float together,
> your reflection in me, and then slowly
> you settle down, filled.

> I think you are going to drown
> and I will go dry, utterly absorbed in you,
> my mud and rock showing. I worry about us,
> you swollen and out of shape
> and I tasting of sediment.

Plainly enough, this situation works hardships and performs distortions on both parties involved, though our main interest naturally focuses on the poet since it is he who struggles in these domestic poems through the primal levels of his experience, staring hard at his "mud and rock showing." In "For Your Fear" he tries to strike a temporary balance that will be true to his uncertainties as well as responsive and fair to his wife. His most promising effort here is "to think/and keep open between us lines/which might someday carry messages/when it's with you as with me"; and he finishes with a request: "Love me for my desperation/that I may love you for your fear."

Desperation is a word increasingly appropriate to the poems of *Rescue the Dead*, as the reader proceeds through the book, page after page. "The Room," which immediately precedes the trio of "Ritual" poems, prepares an entrance of a sombre kind into the tortuous labyrinth of these pieces. Like the lonely, deprived figures of Samuel Beckett's fiction and plays, the poet occupies a place of isolation, a room which is equivalent to the bare, reduced circumstances of his own existence. There he is left to confront the rudiments of his relationships and endeavors, the thinking and writing ("charts/and prescriptions and matches") with the aid of which he attempts to navigate the psyche's dark channels:

> There's a door to my name
> shutting me in, with a seat
> at a table behind the wall
> where I suck of the lemon seed.
> Farther in is the bed
> I have made of the fallen hairs
> of my love, naked, her head dry.

> I speak of the making of charts
> and prescriptions and matches
> that light tunnels
> under the sea.

Yet Ignatow can merely "speak of the making" of such guidelines and maps; when we reach the second stanza, we realize that the harsh conditions already described comprise only a beginning, which now gives way to frightening sensations of vertigo forcing the poet to cling to the form and density of ordinary objects to maintain his equilibrium:

> A chair, a table, a leg of a chair—
> I hold these with my eyes to keep from falling,
> my thoughts holding to these shapes,
> my breathing of them that make my body
> mine through the working of my eyes.
> All else is silence and falling.

In the extremity of this state only the most commonplace *things* suffice to keep the mind occupied and away from the storm of nerves and emotions, the eruptions of thought which send the self toppling into an abyss of disorder and madness. (Again one thinks of Beckett's characters, obsessed with object rituals like Molloy's pebble game and Malone's endless check on his meagre belongings, and of the young American novelist Rudolph Wurlitzer, who introduces similar figures that devote themselves to collecting and arranging cigarette packages, penknives, etc. —the debris of modern life.) The poem's last stanza finds visibility gone and the poet maneuvering in blackness. The void around him becomes alive with the movement of wings which he, in turn, emulates, circling about in the confines of his small space at the end:

> In the dark
> I hear wings beating
> and move my arms around
> and above
> to touch.

> My arms go up and down
> and around
> as I circle the room.

This conclusion leaves the poet intact, keeping himself going, but directionless and unsure of his bearings. The "dark" through which he flies seems purposefully to serve as a preliminary setting for "Ritual One." The latter begins in a theater, as if a curtain lifted in the darkness of "The Room" and the poet suddenly found himself on foot again, now at the threshold of his worst nightmares; for his "falling" has finished, but only in the sense that Ignatow has reached the depths and has no alternative to seeing through the imminent horrors to their completion. The play, already in performance when he arrives, appears composed of banal complaints and reports of mechanical breakdown uttered by a father and son. Yet, odd as this dialogue may be, our attention is suddenly caught by the poet's declaration of his own overwrought state and a startling announcement of the appalling drama that rapidly unfolds, not on the stage as might be expected, but in the audience, involving him completely:

> Tiptoeing down the aisle, I find my seat,
> edge my way in across a dozen kneecaps
> as I tremble for my sanity.
> I have heard doomed voices calling on god the
>   electrode.
> Sure enough, as I start to sit
> a scream rises from beneath me.
> It is one of the players.
> If I come down, I'll break his neck,
> caught between the seat and the backrest.
> Now the audience and the players on stage,
> their heads turned towards me, are waiting
> for the sound of the break. Must I?
> Those in the aisle nod slowly, reading my mind,
> their eyes fixed on me, and I understand
> that each has done the same.

> Must I kill this man as the price of my admission
> to this play? His screams continue loud and long.
> I am at a loss as to what to do,
> I panic, I freeze.

The stanza develops with the inescapable logic of a brutal dream, but one from which the poet is helpless to rouse himself. The demands upon him as the price of entrance to this play—a play which, incidentally, bears something of the negative aspects of everyday living with its pointless hagglings, its routine irritations—really take the form of an ordeal of initiation that severely tests his hardness, his willingness to look out for himself and secure his niche, and thus to have no qualms about taking another's life. At this point we should note how the present poem draws out to their conclusion the attitudes of those who "forgo love" in "Rescue the Dead." The appeal of the "doomed" like the player trapped in the poet's chair is made in vain; "god the electrode" certainly refers to a universe without a deity sensitive to man's dilemmas. Yet Ignatow himself is not lacking in human sympathy; to kill another person contradicts his basic impulses, though the entire audience has found it possible to do. Finally, we realize—there is no other way; he cannot turn back or simply depart; this theater *is* existence.

The second stanza starts with a mixture of memories which recount the growth of his feeling and affection for other humans through love for his father, but it likewise reveals his acquaintance with man's capacity for slaughtering animals. The first line indicates how the poet, whose heritage is Jewish, has been forced from the beginning to live according to the rules of a profane, even repugnant reality, to get used to it and to learn kindness and love in its midst. In spite of this backward glance, the actuality of the present reasserts itself, and the poet completes his initiation only under physical pressure:

> My training has been to eat the flesh of pig.
> I might even have been able to slit a throat.
> As a child I witnessed the dead chickens

over a barrel of sawdust absorbing their blood.
I then brought them in a bag to my father
who sold them across his counter. Liking him,
I learned to like people and enjoy their company
   too,
which of course brought me to this play.
But how angry I become.
Now everybody is shouting at me to sit down,
sit down or I'll be thrown out.
The father and son have stepped off stage
and come striding down the aisle side by side.
They reach me, grab me by the shoulder
and force me down. I scream, I scream,
as if to cover the sound of the neck breaking.

Desirous of a participation in existence, he is unwillingly compelled to become a murderer like the other members of the audience and the players. His hysteria continues into the closing stanza, where at first he is treated as something of a celebrity—presumably because he has now been initiated—but then his mood changes to one of rage and he attacks the players with particular violence, which merely creates amusement. Finally, however, his reasoning prevails, eliciting its stark conclusions from the paradoxical nature of this theater and the behavior required of the occupants. Ignatow sits down to watch a new performance, a crude and ugly act with children as participants, which leads directly into "Ritual Two":

All through the play I scream
and am invited on stage to take a bow.
I lose my senses and kick the actors in the teeth.
There is more laughter
and the actors acknowledge my performance with a bow.
How should I understand this?
Is it to say that if I machine-gun the theatre
from left to right they will respond with applause
that would only gradually diminish with each death?
I wonder then whether logically I should kill myself

> too out of admiration. A question indeed,
> as I return to my seat and observe a new act
> of children playfully aiming their kicks
> at each other's groins.

Clearly, the realm into which the poet has been introduced with so much reluctance on his part to pay the cost exists without benefit of any traditional convictions or creeds and apparently neither knows nor respects humanistic values; on the other hand, there is no indulgence in pretense here either. The picture Ignatow so shockingly sketches discloses a type of naked, primitivistic humanity whose primary concerns are the aggressive activities necessary to individual endurance. Violence and death constitute the ordinary practice rather than the exception, and variations on them provoke interest, even laughter (as in the poet's anger and physical assault upon the actors), for watching fights or other kinds of violent acts supplies the chief form of entertainment in this hellish auditorium.[11]

A poem from the same period which has affinities with these "Ritual" pieces and the atmosphere they generate is the equally excruciating "A First on TV," in which Ignatow openly announces his intention of portraying the unfeeling fascination and complicity with violence done to humans that characterizes our age:

> This is the twentieth century,
> you are there, preparing to skin
> a human being alive. Your part
> will be to remain calm
> and to participate with the flayer
> in his work as you follow his hand,
> the slow delicate way with the knife
> between the skin and flesh,
> and see the red meat emerge.

11. There are similarities in this treatment of and insight into violence between Ignatow and the extraordinary French poet Henri Michaux. See, for example, the latter's "Chez les hacs," in *Selected Writings of Henri Michaux*, ed. and trans. Richard Ellmann (New York, 1968).

> Tiny rivulets of blood will flow
> from the naked flesh and over the hands
> of the flayer. Your eyes will waver
> and turn away but turn back to witness
> the unprecedented, the incredible,
> for you are there
> and your part will be to remain calm.

A second stanza brings out the watcher's reaction of indignation and fury, approximating the poet's in the theater, but, as Ignatow insists through his repetitions of the phrases "to remain calm" and "you are there," a person's response is incapable of altering the entire complex of his society and his time. In the end he is hopelessly enmeshed in a frightening network of events which appear immediately before him, yet his blows struck against these evils are wild flailings that cannot touch their object. The calmness which finally arrives—or is perhaps predicted with assurance—suggests both a kind of resignation to brutal actuality and an accommodation to it, or the first gradually becoming the second:

> You will smash at the screen
> with your fist and try to reach
> this program on the phone, like a madman
> gripping it by the neck
> as it were the neck of the flayer
> and you will scream into the receiver,
> "Get me Station ZXY at once, at once,
> do you hear!" But your part
> will be to remain calm.

With "Ritual Two" the children kicking "at each other's groins" in the previous poem have regressed even further toward a savage state, lashing themselves into frenzied activity punctuated by their single nihilistic cry which echoes throughout:

> The kids yell and paint their bodies
> black and brown, their eyes bulging.
> As they brush, they dance, weaving

> contorted shapes. They drive each other
> to the wall, to the floor, to the bed,
> to the john, yelling, "Nothing!"

No reader can fail to recognize in this and the following stanzas a brilliant, though terrifying, dramatization of the purposeful reversion to the primitivistic by many young people in the midst of an increasingly streamlined technocratic society, a society which, to repeat, has taught them "to forgo love" or demanded false allegiances and now reaps the harvest of hypocrisy in frantic horror. As the poem continues, the kids tear up the stage "on which they stand" (literally, destroy the world in which they find themselves) with ferocious intentness until the poet himself arrives to stand among them, offering them with hand and mouth what would seem to be signs of his identity as a writer, then entering on a death dance which they surround him to watch with anticipation and pleasure. The progression of the dance involves Ignatow in the abandonment of the ordinary accoutrements of civilized Western man, his clothing and his bank account; all of these movements are accompanied by the kids' refrain of denial: " 'Nothing, Nothing!' " The last stanza, however, finds the poet enacting what might at first appear to be a different drama but is actually a continuation of his fatal dance onto another phase, climaxed by his death and a rebirth as his own child:

> I pretend to hold a child by the hand
> and walk as though strolling up a street
> with him and stoop to listen to this child
> and talk to him, when suddenly I act
> as if shot, slowly falling to the ground,
> kissing the child goodby with my fingertips,
> but I spring up and pretend to be the child,
> lost, abandoned, bewildered, wanting to die,
> crouching as the circle keeps chanting,
> "Nothing, Nothing!"
> I then rise slowly to my full height,
> having grown up through my agony.

> I throw my head back proudly
> and join hands with others as they dance,
> chanting their theme. We converge in the center,
> bang against each other, scream and scatter.

In losing his parent the imagined child loses love, security, direction; worse than this, the elder person dies by senseless or gratuitous violence, and this death must be assumed to tell us something of the character of the world the two inhabit. The poet, having died, now mimes the boy's role and knows in himself the isolation, confusion, and suffering to which the youth is subject. But he passes beyond these pains to achieve a stature and independence of his own. This resolution still contains its ambiguities, however, for the pride and maturity lead to a freely chosen participation in the kids' dance and its ending in chaos, probable belligerence and terror—though it is difficult to be certain of the full implications of the final line except for its unequivocal statement of disorder. The poem should be read, I think, like its predecessor, as an initiation ritual; growing up through "agony" here does not possess the same redemptive connotations as we have observed in other poems but signifies instead a decision to proceed from pain and abandonment and to live, though that entails an acceptance of existence as founded upon "Nothing."

Such an interpretation may be further justified by the substance of the two reflective sections comprising the whole of "Ritual Three," a poem which penetrates to the very center of "the heart of darkness" Ignatow pursues in spite of everything. The poem has for preface a single sentence designating the matter on which the poet subsequently meditates, acts of an insane cruelty that defies rational comprehension or explanation: "In England, the slow methodical torture of two children was recorded on tape by the murderers." Ignatow's mood at the beginning might be described as one of somber exhaustion, for it appears that he has lived through, at the deepest levels of himself, the evil and horror of those children's murders (though he refers only to one of them), probably after reading a detailed account of what occurred, and

has felt vicariously their agony and also the maiming of his own
spirit at the realization of the unspeakable crimes perpetrated by
these killers. The child's suffering is over, he admits at the outset,
simultaneously recalling his own mortality; but as his thoughts
turn to the offenders he veers dangerously toward a precipice, prepared for by the earlier initiations of the previous "Ritual" poems
and by such other pieces as "Rescue the Dead" and "A First on
TV." If at first he acknowledges the bond of humanity with the
murderers, while adding that he has never shared their perverse
and base impulses, yet, as he reflects, the savage creature latent in
himself (and in all of us), devoid of reason or sympathy, awakens
to action:

> Let me rest, let me rest from their mistakes.
> They were human like myself, somehow
> gone in a direction to a depth I've never known.
> I am not thinking,
> I am contemptuous of thought.
> I growl in my depths, I find blood flowing
> across my tongue and enjoy its taste.
> Call me man, I don't care.
> I am content with myself,
> I have a brain that gives me the pleasure.
> Come here and I will tear you to pieces,
> it'll be catch as catch can
> but I can throw you who are weakened with the horror
> of what I say, so surrender peacefully
> and let me take my first bite directly above your heart.
> I am a man, your life lost in feeling,
> I never knew what mercy meant,
> I am free.

We are witnesses in this disturbing passage to the poet in troubled
dialogue with himself. For once he relinquishes his tormented
thinking and emotional suffering over the killings and those involved, tries to find some respite from the state of mind he has
come to, then immediately the predatory voice, a constant element

in the human composition, dedicated only to the ends of self-gratification (in whatever form desire may dictate to the individual), rises up within him and, taking advantage of his spiritually exhausted condition, attempts to dominate. The last line of the stanza connects this poem directly with "Rescue the Dead," where at the conclusion Ignatow admonishes: "You who are free,/rescue the dead." The dead, we recall, are those who believe in love (in terms of the present poem, those with "life lost in feeling"), while the free "forgo love" in favor of self-seeking and survival, unencumbered by the moral baggage of feeling for others. The monstrous presence who announces his intentions above is merely a more completely defined—and thus more frightening—version of the "free" man of the earlier poem; as this voice echoes and elaborates in its speech the ending of "Rescue the Dead," we can see how cutting is the irony of the poet's final words there. The free will "rescue" no one: the act of rescuing implies a care for the welfare or the life of someone else, an idea totally alien to the free. The single thing they will do for persons of sensitivity, love, and mercy is destroy them, a literal fulfillment of the word by which the feeling are identified—"the dead."

The closing section of the poem, addressed to the murdered child, finishes the series of initiation rituals by confirming the poet in the attitudes of the free and unfeeling. Wishing for the guise of a crocodile, he commits himself, not to the nightmare of hideous criminal activities ("I will not run a knife across the skin/or cut off a nose or tear off the genitals,/as screams fade in exhaustion") but to the requisites of self-preservation:

> Child gone to a calm grave,
> I want to be a crocodile,
> opening the two blades of my mouth.
> I'll slide through swamp, taking in small fish and flies.

So he becomes convinced that while perverse extremities must be avoided and rejected as forms of behavior, given the circumstances of life as we find it men must accommodate themselves to living

with the jaws and scaly armor of reptiles rather than aiming toward ideals or kinds of goodness beyond their capacities and the
harsh rules of the world:

> ... I dream I am sane, purposeful
> and on my course, dreaming that we no longer
>   should trouble
> to live as human beings, that we should discuss this,
> putting aside our wives and children,
> for to live is to act in terms of death.

The group of "Ritual" poems comes full circle here, leading us back
to the killing imposed upon the poet as the entrance fee to the
theater of existence. If a man can win his life only at the expense
of taking another's, then he surely cannot with honesty pretend
to exist in accord with the ideals of humanism or Christianity, the
spiritual legacy of the Western tradition. Struggling for survival
within his own species, he paradoxically regresses on the evolutionary scale (at the same time he has been developing tremendous
technical skills and powers), turned at last into a grim creature
fending for himself in a swamp in the midst of an earth which is
nothing but jungle. Ignatow's unflinching need for truthfulness
brings him to the poem's sobering finish, where the vestments of
aspiration and finer feeling have been discarded and the rude facts
laid bare.

The anguish of this exposure for Ignatow—and it is obvious from
the poems how he has proceeded personally step by step into these
fearful depths of thought and vision—manifests itself in the three
pieces following the "Rituals": "The Open Boat," "A Dialogue,"
and "From a Dream." The first returns again to "Rescue the Dead"
to pick up the image of the poet at sea in a boat; in this instance his
isolation and distraught emotions derive from the enervating course
of experience in the "Ritual" poems—or so its placement suggests.
But more is to be discovered here than the inevitable sense of anguish, fatigue, and solitude which results from traveling perilously
far in pursuit of valid grounds for human existence. The poem ends

with a shocking confirmation of all the poet has realized, rendered the more frightful because it occurs through the gesture of a supposedly lesser creature than man and symbolizes the rejection of him by the remainder of living beings:

> With no place to lay my head
> beside a friend
> who could give peace,
> none to guard my door
> nor still my house,
> I am five miles out: the sea
> flexes its muscles
> and I have gulls for companions
> overhead—veering off,
> afraid, afraid
> of a human.

"A Dialogue" leaves no alternative to its speaker, who chooses suicide as a way to "express sorrow in its pure form" but is prevented, declared "insane" and carried off to the hospital to "die there/in sorrow." Death provides the single resolution to the unspecified suffering in this poem, which is another expression of Ignatow's despairing state or a momentary exorcism of it. And in "From a Dream" he vividly relates his feelings of frustration and terror during a dreamlike descent that takes him uncontrollably further and further away from the ordinary amenities and habits of daily life. Once more we see him walking, but now in a direction he cannot determine for himself, which elicits his nervous speculation at the close:

> I'm on a stair going down.
> I must get to a landing
> where I can order food
> and relax with a newspaper.
> I should retrace my steps to be sure,
> but the stairs above disappear into clouds.
> But down is where I want to go,

> these stairs were built to lead somewhere
> and I would find out.
> As I keep walking,
> ever more slowly,
> I leave notes such as this on the steps.
> There must be an end to them
> and I will get to it,
> just as did the builders,
> if only I were sure now
> that these stairs were built
> by human hands.

The concluding phrase, with "human" as the modifier, creates an extremely disturbing ambiguity in terms of the poems which have gone before. A first response, perhaps, is to experience a quick, conventional flash of hope, reassurance, and familiarity at the sight of this word. But once we recollect its fundamental implications, the uses to which it has been put, in Ignatow's dark imaginative vision through the poems leading up to this one, we are struck suddenly with the knowledge that the human may be something to arouse apprehension, that its designs possibly offer no more assurance than those of nonhuman hands.

The present section of the book, which began with "Ritual One," comes to an end with two poems of public violence. "East Bronx" discloses "two children" who "sharpen/knives against the curb," while parents and elders "leaning from the window" above this scene of mounting antagonism and viciousness not only make no effort to prevent it but even turn away as from a wearying commonplace, retreating into their bathrooms to read of exotic and nonhuman affairs: "of the happiness of two tortoises/on an island in the Pacific—/always alone and always/the sun shining." In "I See a Truck" a similar but more widespread spectacle of violence as an acceptable or routine part of everyday life assumes large, grotesque proportions. A truck goes wild in the city streets, running over citizens who are participants in some sort of parade; limping, the victims still alive rise up "to follow" the vehicle, while "a cop stands idly swinging his club" and, as if in a dream, "No one screams/or speaks." This enigmatic silence is interrupted by an ecclesiastical retinue who recite their prayers, perhaps blessing and condoning this bizarre yet clearly quotidian incident, in a carnival atmosphere, where the dispensation of money is intended to right all wrongs, heal all wounds, and brings about the mock joyous air of festivity with which Ignatow ironically finishes:

> From the tail end
> of the truck, a priest and a rabbi intone
> their prayers, a jazz band bringing up
> the rear, surrounded by dancers and lovers.
> A bell rings and a paymaster drives through,
> his wagon filled with pay envelopes
> he hands out, even to those lying dead
> or fornicating on the ground.
> It is a holiday called
> "Working for a Living."

Preoccupation with violence, cruelty, and injustice continues into the next group of poems. "All Quiet" and "An American Parable" are incisive attacks on the Vietnam war and the financial investments of American foreign policy; there are individual pieces about Medgar Evers, Churchill's death, and Christ, followed by a harsh retaliation to the brutalities of militarism in "Soldier." But in the midst of these poems is placed the extraordinary and crucial "A Meditation on Violence," which must be understood, in the structure of *Rescue the Dead*, as a pivotal point for Ignatow's attitudes, bringing him some measure beyond the torment and hopelessness that invest so many of the pieces we have discussed. Starting in broken lines, as if to simulate or catch the poet's mind in its first groping motions of thought on the subject, the poem then develops, from the rather general sense of violence done to others—and the potential we possess for it—in fragmented images, toward a second stanza where Ignatow reflects on specific news reports from the war:

> On my birthday
> they knocked out
> two bridges
> a fishing boat standing at anchor
> and a forest
> defoliated with a napalm bomb
> on my fifty-first year

After another stanza, which comments on the official rhetoric of
" 'Peace,' " he looks at himself in his room, relaxing in thought
between the heat of the day and a breeze that tempers it; these
physical conditions supply analogies for rumination on men's heed-
less passions and their desirable but neglected capacities for rationality as a substitute for force:

> Through an open window
> facing the river
> the wind blows this hot day
> while I sprawl upon a bed,
> my skin cooled. Would
> that this were the fate of the world.
> a stream of cool reason
> flow serenely between hot shores
> into which steaming heads
> could dip themselves

Then, pointedly, with the initial line of the subsequent stanza,
Ignatow both recollects and reverses his concluding statement from
"Ritual Three," in which he had asserted that consideration for the
welfare of women and children must not prohibit us from thinking
how, perhaps, "we should no longer trouble/to live as human beings." Now, as he lies in his room enjoying the wind, it carries to
his ear the sounds of children at play outside; in their rapid shifts
of mood, their emotional flexibility and resilience, a lesson in human comprehension is to be learned. Recognition of the children's
liberty and elation breaks in upon his brooding over the war and
man's inclination toward violence, begetting a renewed feeling of
possibility. With serious intentness he gives himself up to these

young voices which seem like a nourishing rainfall for an earth
that urgently needs it:

> But the children, I think, should not be blotted out,
> as I sit listening to the rise and fall
> of their pleasures, the sudden change
> to bad temper quickly forgotten
> by the shift to joy,
> pleased with the world that lets them
> shout and jump and play at tantrums
> for this is freedom to understand
> until they wander off to bed.
> Shall I say their sounds are an intrusion
> when they show the meaning to my life
> is to celebrate, always to celebrate?
> I listen as I would to rain falling
> upon a field.

The potentiality for affirmation established in these lines does not
weaken again, though it can hardly avoid numerous challenges
from other poems. In the fifth section Ignatow starts out with a
brief poem, "The Signal," in which the intimations of forward
movement to his life, contained in the tacit message of the green
traffic light he studies ("It is when the signal turns red/that I lose
interest"), lend it a redeeming quality; faults become less significant when viewed against the new and changing:

> At night
> I am content to watch the blue-green
> come on again against the dark
> and I do not torture myself
> with my shortcomings.

This play of light in opposition to darkness occurs several times in
the imagery of poems immediately subsequent to "The Signal." A
number of the finest are love poems, beautiful, tender, and moving
declarations of affection for his wife, Rose Graubart, the painter,
and, of course, they more than offset the rigorous questionings of
his marital relationship in those poems preceding the "Rituals."

The central place she occupies in the pattern of Ignatow's life is
unmistakable from the citation of a passage or two:

> She is my love for everyday
> and darkness is the absence of her;
> and so it is enough for any man
> that he may do as much in this world
> as to have a Rose for his woman.
> —"Domestic Song"

> I need to see and touch
> and talk to you each day
> to assure myself
> I am not made happy with dreams.
> Then you become for me a tree
> of comforting shade, bellying
> where the branches bunch together
> full of leaves.
> I want a maternal world.
> —"For Nobody Else"

Intimations of harmony and a revived purpose for existence, in
spite of difficulties or obstacles which periodically loom up in for-
bidding aspect, emerge from these love poems and modify others
following them. Meditating on books and reading in "Against the
Evidence," Ignatow is compelled to examine his own mental habits
and processes, then to think about his isolation:

> I use books
> almost apologetically. I believe
> I often think their thoughts for them.
> Reading, I never know where theirs leave off
> and mine begin. I am so much alone
> in the world, I can observe the stars
> or study the breeze, I can count the steps
> on a stair on the way up or down,
> and I can look at another human being
> and get a smile, knowing
> it is for the sake of politeness.

"Estrangement" and loneliness, he realizes, are basic ingredients of man's situation, and books offer no correctives, for the reader consults them only by himself. With a gesture which recalls his attempt to gain reassurance and stability from tangible objects in "The Room," though here in a calm, thoughtful rather than high-pitched, nervous mood, the poet reaches out to touch his writing desk and settles down to work within the confinements of the dilemma he has perceived. Separateness still exists; he cannot alter the fact but may exorcize the demons haunting his inner life, to borrow Eliot's metaphor from *The Three Voices of Poetry*. The final line makes a positive declaration which puts behind him the substance of Ignatow's ordeal with the forces of negation, inhumanity, and degradation. Obviously, I am not implying that he can now simply dismiss those forces because he has faced them in favor of an easy optimism. On the contrary, he must always bear the scars and sense the strain of that journey through agonized suffering, of trial by fire; but if he was not to succumb to its vicissitudes in a manner which, logically speaking, could very well issue in death, then he had to pass through a nihilistic underworld and seek the means to go on. This closing passage reveals an intention to do just that and the strength of will supporting him:

> I stroke my desk,
> its wood so smooth, so patient and still.
> I set a typewriter on its surface
> and begin to type
> to tell myself my troubles.
> Against the evidence, I live by choice.

The sixth and last section of *Rescue the Dead* resonates with the poet's newly won energy and enthusiasm for living, visible in each of the marvelous, vital poems to be found there. But in order to secure the imaginative power for affirmation he desires, Ignatow must countenance openly the contesting negation of death and, without the solutions orthodoxy contributes and he cannot accept, refuse to be ruled by its ubiquitous, unpredictable presence. Something of what this struggle to salvage the human, mortal character of existence entails can be seen in the brief poems, already mentioned, on Medgar Evers and Christ; both of these exemplary sacrificial figures form in death an alliance with earth and so with the true prevailing spirit of existence—with life as it should be. This theme receives elaboration and amplification in the lovely poem "Six Movements on a Theme," which inaugurates and sets the tone for the entire sixth section. The piece at once establishes itself as a poem of reverie or waking dream; but if it exhibits characteristics and properties familiar to dreams, its progression can hardly be described as loose or random when, in fact, it moves increasingly in the direction of wakefulness and conscious aims.

The poem begins in the realm of Ignatow's consciousness, where desirable images of a temperate landscape and climate relax mind and body, drawing him toward sleep and actual dream. The dream itself is complex, consisting of several stages, the first of which discriminates between the poet's outward appearance—the way he looks to friends gathered round him as if to witness the end of his life—and the processes at work within him, or perhaps we should say, in his essential self or spirit:

> Thinking myself in a warm country
> of maternal trees under whose shade
> I lie and doze, I dream I am weightless.
> Magnified faces stare back at me—
> of friends wanting me to live
> to whom I am dying stretched out
> on the ground and barely breathing.
> Dead, they say as I hold my breath
> to close in and possess myself.

Reverie slides into dream, a dream of death which is neither feared nor resisted by the poet but seems deliberately sought, for he stops breathing by choice, so as to conclude the separation from his physical or bodily nature begun with his awareness of a levitated state, an airiness, in the third line. Whatever this death involves in terms of external reality, it does not bring extinction; instead, it precipitates or hastens that inward movement toward self-integration noted in the last line.

The dream continues with the second stanza, sinking deeper into the levels of creation, away from ordinary human concerns, and the poet experiences a corresponding transformation of a profound sort which locates him completely within the elemental context of the natural world:

> I dream my life to be a plant
> floating upon a quiet pool,
> gathering nourishment from water
> and the sun. I emerge
> of my own excess power, my roots
> beginning to move like legs,
> my leaves like arms,
> the pistil the head. I walk
> out of the pool
> until I reach my utmost weariness
> in a dance of the fading power
> of my roots—when I lie down
> silently to die and find myself
> afloat again.

A distinct contrast is evident in this imagery of a pacific existence in the pond, sustained by sun and water, with the preying crocodile, nosing through the swamp in "Ritual Three." But Ignatow has more in mind than such discrepancies between the gentle and the predatory, though we should do well to remember them. If the initial stanza can be considered—and I think it must be—as a purposeful abandonment of familiar human life and the preferred acceptance of a symbolic death and rebirth (contained within the progression of the poet's dreaming), then its basic motive, as the next stanza indicates, is a quest for that cast-off humanity in its pristine form which can be discovered only if approached in an evolutionary scheme from a lower species of life, in this instance, a water plant. The effort of the plant to leave its placid condition, its expenditure of strength to engage in the dance, to move as a man does, and finally to die in exhaustion and be returned to its original position in the pool can be understood both as a celebration of life's energies and, equally, as the compulsion to extend the effectiveness of those energies.

Yet this endeavor terminates in failure and results, with stanza three, in an apparent awakening from the dream, for Ignatow now meditates more consciously on the unlikeliness of ambitious evolutionary desires: "I see no fish crawling/to become man. The mountains/have been standing/without a single effort/to transform themselves/into castles or apartment houses." In other words, the nonhuman, whether animate or not, harbors no wish to become human or to be an instrument or production of the human: lesser creatures and things are content to remain themselves. Man alone aspires, and to his ideal of himself Ignatow turns in the following lines. "Amid silence," which signifies the otherness, the difference between man and the rest of creation, the poet erects "a statue/in my image" and directs his supplications to it:

> I love you, man,
> on my knees. To you
> I will address my pleas
> for help. You will save me
> from myself. From your silence
> I will learn to live.

The statue's lack of response puts the burden of aid on the poet himself; he may create and venerate an idealized image, request its help, yet it is merely an image, whose muteness enables Ignatow the better to hear his own questions, realize the humanity he must sustain for himself. The next stanza clarifies his responsibilities and designates the sole route he can travel. This way does not involve a thoroughgoing metamorphosis or transformation into something else; like the fish and the mountains, he will stay what he is, though he does not enjoy their natural integrity or self-unity and needs to search for that completion:

> I was shown my only form.
> I have no hope
> but to approach myself,
> palm touching palm.

The sense of touch, which Ignatow returns to in the stanza following, suggests how rudimentary and exploratory are the regions of experience he traverses here. His hand taps "on a wall," with the result that he gains an awareness of his "humankind" at the primal levels of the sensory order. Yet such awareness denotes a self-awareness which the wall, in its cold solidarity, never knows. The wall stands as an entity at one with itself, while the poet, as a man, has to bear the pain of division, of self-consciousness and individual isolation; others may touch his solitude as he touched the wall, simply confirming their and his separateness: "I feel my human-kind,/secretly content/to suffer./I too am a wall." This willingness to suffer, so crucial to Ignatow's final affirmation of existence, implies a resignation to the demands of necessity as the price of being human, of recognizing the array of possibilities available to a person and to nothing less. The poem closes with a night vision of cosmic proportions and the poet assumes, in an intense, exhilarated mood, the terms of his human life, including both its vitality and potentiality ("fire"), and its unavoidable end in death ("dumb"). Emphasis falls not on mortality as a defeat, but on the given span of existence as an essential bond with the universe and nature, in which death is incorporated:

> The stars are burning overhead.
> Excited, I understand
> from a distance:
> I am fire,
> I'll be dumb.

We should recall, in regard to these recent poems, Ignatow's references to a life without perspective and observe how, in spite of the odds, it becomes for him a viable, if always trying, form of being. The conclusion of "Six Movements on a Theme" proclaims the unity of a single existence; the poet remains inseparable from the most important and the least significant details of his existence, so that finally he must be identified with all of them as they shape a unique world of events, acts, dreams, loves, and pains, finishing in a death wholly his own. "Secretly," "The Life Dance," "Three in Transition," "For My Daughter in Reply to a Question," and "Walk There," among other poems, investigate, celebrate, and test in a variety of ways the relationship between self and the occurrences to which it is subject, in the interest of perceiving, comprehending, and preserving their bonds of attachment. Alone, in "Secretly," Ignatow indulges himself in the contemplation of his foot; his eye examines it scrupulously from every angle as if noticing it for the first time and absorbs its appearance in motion, while his mind elaborates its function in the journeying of his life. The surprising analogy he draws between this bodily member and a bird ("in profile shaped like a bird's head,/the toes long and narrow like a beak,/the arch to the foot/with the gentle incline/of a bird's body/and the heel thick and stubby/like a starling's tail") may also remind us how birds are associated in certain of his poems with freedom and independence, the potentiality for movement. Further, this likeness develops a double vision of his existence, the continuation of which seems fatiguing on the surface, yet, covertly, he is transported by the strength, resilience, and fleetness of his birdlike foot:

> The full weight of my body
> today walking on it
> supporting me in my weariness
> it can perform its flight,
> its shape delicate, light,
> swift-seeming, tense and tireless
> as I lie on a bed, my foot
> secretly a bird.

Looking even more closely at the mysterious ties which confer a true, personal intuition of authentic being-in-the-world (to borrow that familiar term from existential philosophy and psychiatry),

"The Life Dance" is a spontaneous exercise in joy derived from participation in the harmonious creative upwelling of nature's rich resources. Elated by the sight of a spring "bubbling out of the ground," Ignatow's "mind/too begins to spring," which then coaxes him into physical activity ("small hops"). Gradually, he abandons self-consciousness and engages in a vigorous dance whose motions and gyrations appear to dramatize a symbolic language he cannot himself translate:

> Is anybody watching?
> I care and don't care,
> as I hop, and soon
> because nobody is looking I'm leaping
> and twisting into awkward shapes,
> letting my hands make signs
> of a meaning I do not understand.

Abruptly Ignatow shifts inward to thought about his intense efforts, acknowledging in them a wish to strike far into the roots of existence, to seize and uncover by whatever means possible that underlying unity of origins which binds him to the reality of the world with the same intimacy as a hand clasped in friendship or the breath keeping him alive:

> I am absorbed in getting at what
> till now
> I had not been aware of.
>
> There is a feeling in the world
> I sometimes think I'm grasping.
> I find myself holding a hand or
> as I take a deep breath
> I think it is there.

This unity with earth is echoed in the ending of "Night at an Airport," written around 1940 but appropriately printed with these later pieces. Here the flux and form of our individual lives both originates in and imitates the patterns of recurrent turbulence and calm to be found in nature:

> We have our beginnings
> in breeze or storm, dancing or swirling;
> and are still when the wind is still.
> We have earth and return to it—
> everlasting as a thought.

Ignatow takes earth for our birthplace and our only home, the ground of our return and last repose. His statement and acceptance of this view certainly grow from the struggle toward affirmation of and union with existence he has maintained since departing the sinister void of the "Ritual" poems. In keeping with his commitment to a position of determined but gentle agnostic humanism— if such a phrase will do to describe what is a living response at every moment to the actualities of his experience—he desires also to adjust himself to the value of suffering and to the impending promise of death. He handles the first of these two requirements deftly and handsomely in his own brief moral coda to *The Divine Comedy*:

> Dante forgot to say,
> Thank you, Lord, for sending me
> to hell. I find myself happier
> than when I was ignorant.
> I am left helpless
> but more cheerful.
> Nothing could be worse
> than to start ignorant again.
> And so I look to you
> to help me love my life
> anew.

Such love proves to be everywhere in evidence in Ignatow's recent poems, but precisely for this reason the unavoidable termination of life requires assimilation into his total vision without simultaneously destroying it. In "Three in Transition," dedicated to the late William Carlos Williams, he muses on the enigmatic "beauty/in leaves falling" and wonders: "To whom/are we beautiful/as we go?" The seasonal passage into death he notes in the second stanza is a part of the very process of life, for as he gazes at the night sky from a field a sense that the rhythm of his respiration, of breath in and out of his lungs, is one of both living and dying overcomes him:

> Silently
> I breathe and die
> by turns.

The last portion of the poem focuses specifically on Williams's death, and, as in "Night at an Airport," Ignatow envisages this event as the entirely natural conclusion to an existence and perhaps as a release into the free, elemental energy of the universe. Nature or the physical cosmos is plainly asserted as the veritable location of human life and death:

> He was ripe
> and fell to the ground
> from a bough
> out where the wind
> is free
> of the branches.

With "For My Daughter in Reply to a Question" and "The Hope," as well as the two "Coffin" poems from the section of new work of the past decade which completes *Poems 1934–1969*, Ignatow persists in exploring various possibilities of this theme of death. The answer he gives to his daughter's query about human mortality rests finally on the indisputable uniqueness of each person; the singularity awarded to an individual, preserved and cherished by him, will secure his special place which the years to come cannot remove. (We can remark here an obvious contrast to the attitude taken in "The Song," discussed earlier, where time erases everything.)

> There'll never be another as you
> and never another as I.
> No one will ever confuse you
> nor confuse me with another.
> We will not be forgotten and passed over
> and buried under the births and deaths to come.

"The Hope," however, concentrates less on identity and more on conditioning, a toughening procedure that takes the poet into a natural setting at evening where he must do without the comforts and shields provided by civilization to insulate him from the inclemency of the elements. His intention is to endure the hardships of this situation, which threatens his life, and so achieve a new alliance with raw nature that indicates vigor and an ability to maintain himself in proximity to death:

> If I live through the night
> I will be a species
> related to the tree
> and the cold dark.

Some proof of the success of this venture for Ignatow can be discerned in the "Coffin" poems (the first in order of appearance bears no title in *Poems 1934–1969*, while the following piece is called "First Coffin Poem"). A kind of surrealist touch, the lightness of fantasy, rules his approach to mortality here, suffusing the dream-like quality of both poems with a strange humorousness. The initial, untitled piece steps directly into the realm of the irrational and absurd, its very lack of a designation adding to the reader's shock:

> They put a telephone in his coffin
> with an outside extension
> and were not surprised
> when the receiver was lifted
> and there were sighing sounds:
> Hair growing? Skin shrinking?
> Larvae coming into being?
> When those above asked for an answer
> they received none and went down
> and opened the grave. They found
> the receiver back in its cradle.

Our feelings of improbability are utterly vanquished by Ignatow's mastery of tone, atmosphere, and detail; we are captives of the same curiosity as his band of odd, anonymous investigators. The next stanza reveals them indefatigably at work, repeating the activities we have already observed but at last resorting to stricter measures as one member decides to remain in the grave "and peek through/ a hole bored in the wood" of the coffin. The others then enact their telephone routine once more and bring up their companion, whose news is unexpected. His succinct declaration needs to be understood in view of the fact that he has voluntarily stayed close to death, so that his descent into the grave, his "observations" there, and his return amount to a certain type of vicarious or symbolic death and rebirth motif which results in new knowledge for him, knowledge which takes the form of self-discovery. What he says to the rest of the group offers nothing to those avid for particulars yet is abundant in suggestiveness about man, the limits of whose being clearly cannot be fathomed or circumscribed:

> he stared long at his colleagues
> and said finally, as if to himself,
> I am a mystery.

If the sighs overheard from the coffin carry possible connotations of satisfaction, or of sleep and fulfillment—though they must, in the end, retain their air of ambiguity and resist strict definition—Ignatow's straightforward address in "First Coffin Poem" will not seem totally unexpected to the reader. He opens with a statement, however, as startling as the one with which the preceding poem began. In this instance death's presence and potentiality within an individual's existence, concretely realized as the coffin which, throughout the poem, is shifted about like ordinary furniture while the poet tries to incorporate it naturally into his daily affairs, is recognized and assimilated. The poem again aims at bizarre, surrealist evocations but does so deliberately to manipulate the reader into sharing the author's vision. Ignatow's speech marvelously mixes congeniality, practicality, and whimsy, which permits him to maneuver a bright surface of ideas and, at the same time, prove with genuine seriousness the relations between life and death:

> I love you, my plain pine box,
> because you also are a bench,
> with the lid down. Can you see
> my friends in a row seated
> at ease with themselves?
> I am in a coffin
> and it has been set against the wall
> of a living room. It is just before
> dinner and several friends are standing
> about with glasses in their hands,
> drinking to the possibilities
> that life offers.
>   The coffin also
> could be placed as a table
> in front of a grand sofa, with food
> and drinks served on it, and an ashtray.

Because death is inescapable it should be brought into the center of life's events, not ostentatiously but simply, pragmatically; the "possibilities" of an existence can only be valued and sought out by remembering its limited duration. Ignatow's outlook in this poem puts us in mind of the similar attitudes held by Wallace Stevens in "The Emperor of Ice Cream" and William Carlos Williams in "Tract," both poems containing funeral directions which treat death as a commonplace conclusion rather than a special occasion. As the poem continues, Ignatow replies to those who might find his various uses for the coffin "gruesome" and would prefer to substitute "an actual coffee table" by demonstrating that it

> . . . would prove
> how rigid we must be about ourselves
> and cause us to languish, caught
> in a limitation. We must make one thing
> do for another.

Whatever else these lines may imply, they point, as did the previous poem, to the constant aura of mysteriousness remaining, ineradicable, in human life and to the fluid borders between living and

dying. Ignatow enjoins us to be flexible, to allow death access to
the intimacy of our lives so that perhaps, like the sighs escap-
ing the coffin, life can somehow infiltrate death and humanize it.
If the two states remain compartmentalized, "rigid," we will never
enter fully into the realities of what we are now, and what we are
steadily and inexorably becoming:

> I am hope, in urging you
> to use my pine box. Take me to your home
> when I die imperceptibly. Without fuss
> place me against the wall in my coffin,
> a conversation piece, an affirmation of change.
> I am, sincerely yours.

Moods of determined persistence and of celebration dominate
several other poems at the close of *Poems 1934–1969*. Chief among
them are "Walk There," the final piece in *Rescue the Dead*, and
"While I Live," "Morning," and "Feeling with My Hands" from
the section of newer work. The recurrent metaphor of the walking
journey appropriately returns to finish *Rescue the Dead*, for as we
saw earlier in Ignatow's epigraph for the book ("I feel along the
edges of life/for a way/that will lead to open land") his entire
enterprise in the poems of this collection—in the complete body of
his writing as it exists up to the present moment, for that matter—
shapes into a personal quest conducted along the very boundary
lines of his existence, with all the attendant perils which threaten
nerves, vision, and seem to negate the prospect of going on, in
search of an honest, manageable means of being, a path that leads
toward a horizon. The route chosen circles down into darkness,
disorder, and bestiality, both as they appear in the prevailing as-
sumptions (frequently unconscious) of contemporary society and
as they break in upon and besiege the poet's own consciousness.
Ignatow makes this descent and climbs out again into daylight.
"Walk There" really needs no discussion; it dramatizes in sharp
detail the poet's continuing progress out of the "dark wood" which
will eventually result in his arrival at the "open land" of his epigraph, a place where life's possibilities still await him:

The way through the woods is past trees,
touching grass, bark, stone, water and mud;
into the night of the trees, beneath
their damp cold, stumbling on roots,
discovering no trail, trudging
and smelling pine, cypress and musk.
A rabbit leaps across my path,
and something big rustles in the bush.
Stand still, eye the nearest tree
for climbing. Subside in fear
in continued silence. Walk.
See the sky splattered with leaves.
Ahead, is that too the sky
or a clearing?
Walk there.

Just as Ignatow handles various objects in nature while passing, in the lines above, to feel a tacit kinship with them and refresh the awareness of his own solidity, so in "While I Live" he hears the language with which the physical universe—in trees, grass, and flowers, in the life-giving warmth of the sun—speaks to him. But he also recognizes "the darkness in language" and thus prepares to face the end that will come to him as to every living thing, "only that I may endure the necessary/ecstasy of my personal death." That conclusion, however, is not yet, he insists in the poem's strong, positive climax:

I am labor, I am a disposition to live.
Who dies? Only the sun
but you must wait
while I live.

Ignatow performs an act of human definition in "Morning," a longer, more detailed piece, delineating himself as a person apart from, though not alien to, the natural world he inhabits, represented here by the birds whose song he listens to as he awakens: "I am not their flesh and they sing." He proceeds to distinguish his brain as the agent bestowing "identity" on him, deciding his actions, carrying out the rapid processes of his thought, furnishing the words he employs ("where have I learned to know them/as quickly as you think them?") to name things, parts of his body, or to designate the kinds of emotions or states of being he experiences. Language further extends his potentialities by offering the opportunity for dialogue, for conversation with himself as well as with others:

> I am a talker, hearing myself
> and replying to myself. I have a companion
> and I am on my feet,
> walking where I can be heard.

And, not unexpectedly, we watch him moving again along the by now familiar track that opens out of the present into the unknown before him: "the road between the woods leading somewhere,/ sending its emptiness ahead." But this "emptiness" contains ominous overtones, for the birds are suddenly "silent" and the poet realizes how delicately constituted is his selfhood, how easily endangered with annihilation:

> Silent birds, are you listening to my voice
> giving me my self? Are you recording
> your listening to me? Are you birds then?
> And when will you sing again?
> My brain will have birds to record itself
> and it falls silent, my voice halts.
> There is silence
> and I could fade again.

Danger passes, however, and the final stanza starts on a climactic note in support of the poet's existence and that of the birds. Ignatow uses these closing lines to announce a fascination with basic sensory operations, with the fundamentals of experience in which mind and senses collaborate, as if here, at "the beginning," to borrow his words, the reality and worth of living as a man in the physical universe might be tried. Momentarily, he seems to adopt the guise of a second Adam; but rather than an innocent Adam

born into paradise, he is a man who has descended through all the
levels of a fallen or imperfect world and resolved to come back, to
initiate the venture once more:

> They live, I live,
> they sing, I hear them sing.
> No, this is not happiness.
> It is the beginning,
> it is curiousity,
> it is touch, by ear.
> It is sight,
> it is a coincidence of brain and body.
> I can be happy
> in this knowledge.

Characteristically, in his most recent statement in a poem of his
poetic convictions, Ignatow emphasizes both human movement
and sensory responsiveness, beginning with the title, "Feeling with
My Hands." Poetry must for him activate life and reply to it at
the very threshold of experience; it has to be an integral part of
the living flow and thus devoid of rhetoric or metaphysical pretensions. Ted Hughes, writing of East European poets such as
Vasko Popa (Yugoslavia), Miroslav Holub (Czechoslovakia), and
Zbigniew Herbert (Poland), speaks of certain human fundamentals from which they have tried to develop their work. Whatever
differences of circumstance and history may exist between them,
and between their situation and Ignatow's, something of what
Hughes says has unmistakable relationship with our poet's outlook and efforts:

The attempt these poets are making to put on record that man is
also . . . an acutely conscious human creature of suffering and hope,
has brought their poetry down to such precisions, discriminations
and humilities that it is a new thing. It seems closer to the common
reality, in which we have to live if we are to survive, than to those
other realities in which we can holiday, or into which we decay
when our bodily survival is comfortably taken care of, and which

art, particularly contemporary art, is forever trying to impose on us as some sort of superior dimension.[12]

Ignatow does not regard *Poems 1934–1969* as either a "collected" or definitive edition of his work; indeed, a supposition of this kind would allow some readers and critics to mark an end to his career. So, in spite of the extraordinarily rich, abundant achievement represented by this book, we must leave David Ignatow energetically, forcefully in process, with the words and images from "Feeling with My Hands" in which he depicts at once the poetic object he intends and himself active within it. His voice and gesture, compelling, unassuming, yet vibrant with earned humanity reach toward us as we read:

> Will this poem be able to think and breathe
> and have sex? Will it be able
> to lift a finger to call a waiter
> for the menu? Will it have hopes
> of a future life? Will it have friends
> among other poems? Oh yes, will it
> be able to write other poems?
>
> I do not want it to rest on its merits.
> I want others to look through it
> to see me breathing and taking food
> and embracing my wife, telling her
> she has lovely teeth. This poem
> should have an erection and everywhere
> should say hello and be a friend
> and not hesitate to tell other poems
> what it thinks about them. Be pleasant
> but be truthful. Be happy but fear not death.
> Here it is and I am still talking
> and feeling with my hands.

12. Introduction to Vasko Popa, *Selected Poems* (Harmondsworth, Middlesex, 1969), p. 9.

4   A Reading of Galway Kinnell

The little light existing in the mystery
that surrounds us comes from ourselves:
it is a false light. The mystery has never
shown its own.
> —Jules Renard

... le Rien qui est la verité
> —Mallarmé

All things are one thing to the earth ...
> —Kenneth Patchen

Galway Kinnell's first collection, *What a Kingdom It Was*
(1960), can be viewed in retrospect now as one of those volumes
signaling decisive changes in the mood and character of American
poetry as it departed from the witty, pseudo-mythic verse, apparently written to critical prescription, of the 1950's to arrive at the
more authentic, liberated work of the 1960's.[1] Our recent poetry
shows how closely and vulnerably aware of the palpable life of
contemporary society poets have become, for, increasingly during
the past decade or so, they have opened themselves as persons to
the complex, frequently incongruous, violence-ridden ethos of the
age in an effort to ground the poetic imagination in a shared, perceptible reality. This kind of openness—a sensitive receptivity in
which the poet, to borrow a phrase of Heidegger's about Hölderlin,
"is exposed to the divine lightnings" that can easily exact their toll

---

1. These changes were, of course, gradual but visible at widely varying points
on the American literary map from the mid-1950's on. Roethke, Patchen, Kunitz,
Eberhart, W. C. Williams, Weldon Kees, and others can be taken as forerunners.

on nerves and emotional balance—extends, in many instances, beyond matters of social and political experience to naked metaphysical confrontation: with the universe, the identity of the self, the possibilities of an absent or present God, or the prospect of a vast, overwhelming nothingness. In such poets as Theodore Roethke, Kenneth Patchen, John Berryman, Robert Lowell, James Wright, Anne Sexton, James Dickey, W. S. Merwin, and Sylvia Plath, for example, with all differences aside, the pursuit of personal vision often leads toward a precipitous, dizzying boundary where the self stands alone, unaided but for its own resources, before the seemingly tangible earth at hand with its bewildering multiplicity of life, the remoteness of space, the endless rhythms of nature, the turns of night and day, and within, the elusive images of memory and dream, the irrationality and uncertainty of human behavior, the griefs and ecstasies that living accumulates. Here the poet—and Galway Kinnell is certainly of this company—is thrown back upon his own perceptions. His art must be the authoritative testimony to a man's own experience, or it is meaningless; its basic validity rests upon that premise.

"Perhaps to a degree more than is true of other poets, Kinnell's development will depend on the actual events of his life," James Dickey remarked prophetically in a review of *What a Kingdom It Was*.[2] For what we encounter as an essential ingredient in his work as it grows is not only the presence of the poet as man and speaker, but also his identification, through thematic recurrences, repeated images revelatory of his deepest concerns and most urgent feelings, with the experiences his poems dramatize. In what follows we shall try to see how Kinnell, using the considerable imaginative and linguistic powers at his command from the beginning, explores relentlessly the actualities of his existence to wrest from them what significance for life he can. Through the compelling force of his art, we find ourselves engaged in this arduous search with him.

2. *Babel to Byzantium* (New York, 1968), p. 135.

With the advantages of hindsight we should not be surprised when we notice that the initial poem of *What a Kingdom It Was*, aptly entitled "First Song," is located out of doors—in Illinois cornfields with frog ponds nearby—and that in the course of its three stanzas there is a movement from "dusk" into night. A large proportion of Kinnell's poetry is involved with the natural world, for he is drawn to it in profound ways, has been since childhood, and it provides him with an inexhaustible store for his imaginative meditation, if that phrase will do to distinguish a kind of thinking through images and particulars that is integral to the poetic act. But Kinnell's images from nature will become increasingly stark and rudimentary, their bonds with the ordinary range of human sympathies ever more tenuous, as he matures. Indeed, his poems about killing a bird for Christmas dinner, shooting buffalo with a murderer for companion, mountain-climbing, camping out alone in the mountains during winter, examining fossils in the cliff above a frog pond, seeking to define himself by identifying with porcupine and bear, bring him finally to the contemplation of what it is to be human in an extreme, one might say primitive situation. Under such fundamental circumstances he faces himself and the conditions of the world simultaneously, without mediation or disguise. It should be said, however, that Kinnell employs other means than nature for cutting to the bone of existence, though intimate acquaintance with other living creatures and with the earth is of primary importance to his work.

Likewise, the imagery of darkness or blackness, mentioned above, plays a prominent part in many poems. The night with its infinite interstellar spaces reminiscent of those in Pascal or Mallarmé haunts Kinnell, heightening his sensitive awareness of immense emptiness and void in the universe. In "First Song," though, these stringent realities are softened, almost sentimentalized, by pleasant details of smoky, twilight cornfields, croaking frogs, and a small group of boys making "cornstalk violins" and "scraping of their joy" as night falls. Pleasurable nostalgia fills the poem, yet the final lines perhaps disclose something more, an indication of life's mixed blessings, a prediction of pain as well as exultation:

> A boy's hunched body loved out of a stalk
> The first song of his happiness, and the song woke
> His heart to the darkness and into the sadness of joy.

However muted this passage, however conventional its emotion, it does reflect, in the poet's backward look across time, a recognized moment of anticipation of those paradoxes of living which the years afterward must inevitably make manifest.

A number of the poems that follow enter more precipitously on the confusions and conflicts only hinted at in "First Song." At the risk of emphasizing the obvious, one should note how these poems dramatize through crucial incidents in the author's youth the passage from a state of ignorance and innocence into a state of experience which derives from a firsthand knowledge of guilt, violence, hypocrisy, and death.

Unavoidably, in treating this difficult awakening to experience, Kinnell comes up against the disturbing incongruities a boy senses between the spiritual or religious training he has received and the harsh facts of the world he begins to meet. "First Communion" and "To Christ Our Lord" explore this area but do not exhaust it for Kinnell; it is a major concern of his first book. The former poem focuses on the boy's estrangement from church religion. His remoteness from the formal pieties is evident in the opening lines, which start by defining the physical distance from home to church "way over in the next county" and move immediately to a completely secular recollection of having made "the same trip" the preceding year "carrying a sackful of ears to collect/The nickel-an-ear porcupine bounty." The contrast between the spiritual realities supposedly represented by the church and the tough-minded, earthy attitude of the porcupine hunters who slice off the ears of their prey to collect a reward hardly needs remarking, though it prepares for the manner in which the interior of the church and the sacrament of communion are conceived in the next lines—a totally material manner:

> Pictured on the wall over dark Jerusalem
> Jesus is shining—in the dark he is a lamp.
> On the tray he is a pastry wafer.

The perception here doesn't seem to get beyond the tangibility of the objects: all is what it appears to be and nothing more. But the picture of Jesus is described with an ambiguity and use of detail linking the lines with many later ones in Kinnell's poems. At first, the portrait has merely a material resplendence, the quality of the painting; then that resplendence plays upon the light/darkness imagery we associate with the prologue to St. John's gospel. Yet in terms of the kind of symbolic weight with which Kinnell continues to endow his images of light and lamps and flames, and his contrary images of darkness and night, the figure of Jesus is fundamentally implicated with human hopes and desires to escape the "dark Jerusalem" of the world. But these implications are cut short with the terse line reducing the communion wafer to a lump of perishable pastry. Kinnell next recounts the journey home from communion: the adults exchange pleasantries about the preaching but soon resort to local gossip of a slightly salacious kind. Once more the boy recalls the porcupine bounty and compares the worth of the two trips. His choice, never made explicit, seems indisputably the more verifiable value of the money: "The last time over/The same trail we brought two dollars homeward./Now we carry the aftertaste of the Lord."

The last stanza shifts to external nature and renders it, in part at least, in sacramental terms. The season is autumn; life flares forth in a final display of vitality; sunlight appears to lend the prairie grass intimations of "parable" to the observer, but one which refers to nature's unalterable cyclical pattern. Decline and death are sure to follow:

> The sunlight streams through the afternoon
> Another parable over the sloughs

> And yellowing grass of the prairies.
> Cold wind stirs, and the last green
> Climbs to all the tips of the season, like
> The last flame brightening on a wick.
> Embers drop and break in sparks. Across the earth
> Sleep is the overlapping of enough shadows.

The last line above functions obliquely, implying seasonal transition, the sinking toward winter, and at the same time serves to bring us away from external nature to the boy in his bed preparing for sleep and turning his final waking thoughts to the communion day just past. Addressed to Jesus, these thoughts constitute a rejection of the "disappointing shed" where "they"—doubtless the adults, minister included, whose professed beliefs and practices stir no feeling of the sacred in the boy—"hang your picture/And drink juice, and conjure/Your person into inferior bread." Christ is, then, both something less and something more than these parishioners believe. The poem ends with his resolution "not [to] go again into that place. . . ."

If Christ is not to be found in any truly apprehensible form in churches, His spirit and example still persist in the boy's mind, influencing the view he takes of his experiences and actions. The sharp discrepancy between what Jesus represents for the boy and the very different acts which existence seems to force upon him creates the inner tension of the beautiful poem "To Christ Our Lord." In the loveliness and terror of Kinnell's presentation of the winter landscape on which the poem opens there are evident at once the hard, puzzling contrarieties that compose life at any moment. Wolves hunt elk at Christmastime, tracking them over the frozen land, thus demonstrating an iron natural law of survival. Kinnell sketches the scene in swift strokes for the first three lines; then, without finishing his sentence, he offers a view of the Christmas dinner preparations. No comment is necessary for the reader to see that both man and wolf maintain themselves by adherence to the same law: "Inside snow melted in a basin, and a woman basted/A bird spread over coals by its wings and head."

The allusion to a crucified figure in the shape of the outspread bird is not accidental but is a particular instance of the cosmic image that brings the poem to its moving climax. The boy, listening to the grace said before this Christmas meal, wonders at the contradictions between his Christian and his human positions, for it is he who has been responsible for killing the bird. He remembers vividly how, as he hunted this creature, there alternated within him the dictates of conscience and the animal instinct of hunger which drives the wolves after elk. Hunger and the sense of necessity triumphed, causing him perplexity. Kinnell captures the feeling of pursuit, the winter dawn, the agonized choice and its result as they are recalled with the swiftness of the events themselves:

> He had killed it himself, climbing out
> Alone on snowshoes in the Christmas dawn.
> The fallen snow swirling and the snowfall gone,
> Heard its throat scream as the rifle shouted,
> Watched it drop, and fished from the snow the dead.
>
> He had not wanted to shoot. The sound
> Of wings beating into the hushed air
> Had stirred his love, and his fingers
> Froze in his gloves, and he wondered,
> Famishing, could he fire? Then he fired.

Though he repudiates the deed and wishes to love rather than kill, he has learned that, strangely, he harbors both impulses. But he is further disillusioned by the conventional prayer of thanksgiving which "praised his wicked act," an act that, in his mind, is opposed to everything Christ stands for. Finally, recognizing that there is "nothing to do but surrender" to the contradictions of the world and "kill and eat" as others do, he submits, though "with wonder." This "wonder" is an awe and puzzlement at the tragic mixture of love and death inherent in creation and brings on the expansive vision with which the poem concludes. In the closing stanza the boy again wanders "the drifting field" of snow (whose constantly changing shapes suggest the elusive, unstable character of reality) at night still searching for a meaningful reply to his questions. His querying of the black reaches of space, scattered as in Mallarmé's memorable phrase, with "la neige eternelle des astres," at first wins only silence, vacuity; but suddenly he sees the distant constellation of the Swan which, like the bird roasting outspread upon the coals, mimes the figure of the crucified Christ:

> At night on snowshoes on the drifting field
> He wondered again, for whom had love stirred?
> The stars glittered on the snow and nothing answered.
> Then the Swan spread her wings, cross of the cold north,
> The pattern and mirror of the acts of earth.

There can be little consolation or resolution in this image with its indications of death, but there is a certain understanding, possibly the beginnings of acceptance. A darkened universe returns to the watcher an enlarged symbol of the actuality he has so painfully met; the crucified figure, Christ or bird, is the proper image for the world's conditions.

I have discussed these poems in some detail not merely because they merit it for their obvious high qualities of language, imagery, and rhythm but because the experiences central to them are unquestionably of importance to Kinnell in his progressive stripping off of innocence, illusion, and his achievement of a hardened, stoic attitude. We catch an early glimpse of this attitude, or the need for it, in "Westport," a poem which ostensibly deals with a rugged westward journey, undertaken through some unavoidable compulsion. Not so oddly, if we consider what Kinnell has been saying in these other early poems; the speaker admits to the taxing and unpleasant aspects of the trip yet also confesses that these are its peculiar rewards as well:

> "Yes," I said, "it will be a hard journey . . ."
> And the shining grasses were bowed towards the west
> As if one craving had killed them. "But at last,"
> I added, "the hardness is the one thing you thank."

The travelers go their way, and in three brief lines finishing the poem they find darkness descending, listen to the desolate sounds of the landscape and wind. Their fate appears mysteriously implicated with the harsh but durable existence of nature:

> Now out of evening we discovered night
> And heard the cries of the prairie and the moan
> Of wind through the roots of its clinging flowers.

Obliquity is Kinnell's method here, a sign of even freer, more allusive writing to come. Like the travelers, the reader confronts the rich opacity of "night," the startling, potentially frightening "cries of the prairie" and wailing of the wind that readily remind him of pain; set against these dark or negative qualities there is that last phrase describing the tenacious hold on life of the "clinging flowers." These details are meant to remain suggestive but ambiguous, just as they would be in their actual setting, for the very possibilities in them to stir the imagination. Kinnell wishes such elements of experience to approximate the external circumstances of the world they mirror because he knows they cannot provide any meaning but what we read in them for ourselves. Or as Whitman says, "All truths wait in all things."

The chief poems in this first book, and those most relevant to Kinnell's development and more recent inclinations, are "Easter," "The Schoolhouse," "Seven Streams of Nevis," "The Descent," "Where the Track Vanishes," "Freedom, New Hampshire," "The Supper after the Last" (all of these but "Easter" appear in the third section of the volume), and the long poem "The Avenue Bearing the Initial of Christ into the New World." I do not intend to slight the other poems, but those named are clearly the most notable for range and vision, and in several instances for manner and technique. Also apparent in these poems is Kinnell's preoccupation with the larger metaphysical themes previously in evidence and now increasingly at the forefront of his interests. Death, suffering, the will to elude the body's mortality, and the brute facts of the actual world: Kinnell's imagination turns these themes over and over, dwelling on the insoluble enigmas of life's significance or lack of it as these emerge in the process of his own living.

"Easter,"[3] the most conventional in form with its rather neat quatrains, rhymes and off-rhymes, again, as in "First Communion" and "To Christ Our Lord," separates what the poet takes for the shallowness of official Christianity from what he perceives as the true meaning of Christ—that He is symbolic of the ubiquitous pain, victimization, and death of man and all other living things. Just as the hunted bird of "To Christ Our Lord" was transformed into an emblem of the sacrificed Jesus, so in the present poem the "virgin nurse," who has been "Raped, robbed, weighted, drowned" in the river, exemplifies His death yet another time. The poem is crowded with subtle ambiguities, resonances, and ironies, for Kinnell elicits effects from the particulars he uses on both literal and metaphorical levels at once. The second stanza, for example, begins in a matter of fact way: "To get to church you have to cross the river,/First breadwinner for the town. . . ." And for the banal, unspiritual townspeople, satisfied with the comforts of thoughtless, routine belief, the statement has merely literal application. But in terms of the victim whose body rides in its depths, the river is reminiscent of the Jordan and likely the Styx, too; throughout the poem it symbolizes a dimension of death beyond the reach of the living. The myopic sight of the townspeople, who view these waters only with the eyes of commerce and gain, fails to comprehend them, as the poet's vision does, as the means of redemption, though a natural rather than a supernatural one: "its wide/Mud-colored currents cleansing forever/The swill-making villages at its side."

In contrast to the muddy river which purifies the towns along its banks and the lives within them, there is heard the "disinfected voice of the minister" preaching his Easter sermon. But his remarks are irrelevant; he speaks to his parishioners neither of their deaths nor of the nurse's murder, "he is talking of nothing but Easter,/Dying so on the wood, He rose." The story is too familiar so the

3. A good discussion of this poem appears in Glauco Cambon, *Recent American Poetry* (Minneapolis, 1961), pp. 33–36. Necessarily, I echo some of his observations.

congregation, inattentive, put their minds to something more immediate, a "gospel" from the headlines which at least quickens
their pulses—"Some of us daydream of the morning news." Others,
more distracted or uncomfortable in hard pews, are rendered by
Kinnell wittily, though a bit pretentiously, in parody of Easter's
original significance:

> Some of us lament we rose at all,
> A child beside me comforts her doll,
> We are dying on the hard wood of the pews.

After a stanza commenting on death's omnipresence, the poem
returns to the river where, with the ironic reminder that many of
Christ's disciples were fishermen, "with wire hooks the little boats
are fishing" to recover, in a spurious attempt at resurrection, the
body of the nurse. The last five stanzas are addressed by the poet
to the dead woman and convey his own notion of her redemption.
If her corpse is not hauled up from the river, she must find her
true communion in the sacrament of its muddy currents (". . .
drink well of the breadwinner") and be carried by them in what
seems a movement toward liberation that is also an identification
with water as an element of both death and purification. Surprisingly, Kinnell urges her not to regret "That the dream has ended,"
to reflect on her life and see it for what it was, what she dimly,
when alive, thought it actually might be—a kind of hell. Only in
death is there the hope of serenity or repose:

> Turn
> On the dream you lived through the unwavering gaze.
> It is as you thought. The living burn.
> In the floating days may you discover grace.

In "Easter" and the poems following it Kinnell contemplates
human experience against the silent, puzzling background of earth,
universe, and death, particularly as it can be witnessed in the
character and fate of others. In "The Schoolhouse," a learned
but isolated country schoolmaster who once taught the poet and
who wrestled with problems of knowledge and belief; in "Seven

Streams of Nevis," the seedy, outcast lives of seven individuals through whom the poet seeks the seven virtues and the purpose of human affliction; in the death of a friend while mountain-climbing in "The Descent"; in the implications of the path to a deserted Alpine cemetery in "Where the Track Vanishes"; in the death of his brother in "Freedom, New Hampshire"; in the tragic, desperate but resilient lives of the poor Jews and Negroes in the New York ghetto in "The Avenue Bearing the Initial of Christ into the New World." A single exception is "The Supper after the Last," a complex poem of a fierce, apocalyptic sort which assumes the aspect of hallucinated vision.

By comparison with most of these poems "Easter," in spite of its subject, appears cool, detached, objective, for Kinnell's approach to his material grows more personal and intense as he continues to write. In a stanza such as the following from "Seven Streams of Nevis" the formal structure strains outward under the tremendous emotional force generated from within, so that, as in certain poems by Baudelaire, Yeats, Lowell, or Kunitz, for example, the language seems barely able to contain its pressure:

> O Connolly! O Jack! O Peaches!
> When you fall down foaming in fits
> Remember with your scrawny wits
> And knee up laughing like leeches:
> You are just flesh but you will be
> —One rainy day—faith, hope, and charity.

The second section of this poem departs somewhat from the strictness of the first to develop one long stanza rising to its own powerful climactic lines but more suited to the meditative nature of Kinnell's vision as he nears a symbolic source from which the uncontrollable energies of life spill forth. Leaving behind the horror and suffering of the seven lives he has examined in the opening part, the poet, alone, climbs Ben Nevis in western Scotland, the highest peak in England, which takes on in the poem the features of a sacred mountain, soaring into the heavens, fixing a metaphysi-

cal center point in the universe with access to the divine world and
to the infernal regions.[4] At this locus some knowledge of the ultimate origin and design of existence should be obtainable; that is
the motive behind the poet's climb. But the knowledge that is forth-
coming can only be called somber and chilling awareness; there is
no mystical revelation or illumination. The entire stanza abounds
in the imagery of darkness and blackness, only occasionally con-
tradicted by images of light. The poet starts the ascent of Ben Nevis
"in darkness" reflective of his own ignorance of final answers, as
well as indicative of the literal time of day. Climbing, he comes
upon the seven streams, "well foreknown," that in their separate
courses and movements suggest the terrible headlong rush toward
disaster of the seven persons already portrayed:

> One sang like strings, one crashed
> Through gated rocks, one vibrated, others
> Went skipping like unbucketed grease across
> Hot stones, or clattered like bones, or like milk
> Spilled and billowed in streamers of bright silk,
> Irises glimmering a visionary course—
> Me grimping the dark, sniffing for the source . . .

The "source," discovered in the next lines, turns out to be a still,
"dark" pool "Whose shined waters on the blackened mountain/
Mirrored the black skies." And stressing again the darkness that
seems less a temporary absence of light than the very negation of it
distilled from mountain, water, and sky, the poet carries his search
forward to the middle of the pool, the calm eye of the world's hur-
ricane, the heart's chaos:

> . . . I rode out on
> Dark water under the darkness of the skies,
> And the waves ringing through the dark were the rings
> Around the eye itself of the world, which,
> Drawing down heaven like its black lid, was there
> Where merely to be still was temperate,

4. For a discussion of sacred mountains, see Mircea Eliade, *Patterns in Compara-
tive Religion* (New York, 1958).

> Where to move was brave, where justice was a glide,
> Knowledge the dissolving of the head-hung eyes;
> And there my faith lay burning, there my hope
> Lay burning on the water, there charity
> Burned like a sun.

The primary revelation as the poem moves toward its climax and conclusion is that the cosmos, and thus men's lives, is dominated by darkness. The poet arrives at a midpoint, a place of recognitions which is his version of Eliot's "still point of the turning world," but what he recognizes is the sheer human strength and virtue that the acts of living demand. He discovers no divine source as Eliot does. Darkness surrounds men, the pool and the empty black heavens above; it is Kinnell himself who bestows the light there is in his "faith," "hope," and "charity" with regard to the human situation. A person apparently must create his own virtue by traveling to the center of himself, accepting himself, and realizing his isolation in the world. We are close, I think, to Yeats's recommendation at the finish of "A Dialogue of Self and Soul" when he proclaims himself rightful judge of his own acts:

> I am content to follow to its source
> Every event in action or in thought;
> Measure the lot; forgive myself the lot!

Kinnell ends with a request that approaches prayer, asking the "pool of heaven" to give "the locus of grace"—which I presume to be a condition of awareness similar to the one the poet has achieved —to

> seven who have
> Bit on your hearts, and spat the gravels of
> Tooth and heart, and bit again; who have wiped
> The thumb-burst jellies of sight on a sleeve
> (The visions we could have wrung from that cloth)
> And sprouted sight like mushrooms—O seven
> Streams of nothing backgazing after heaven,
> In the heart's hell you have it; call it God's Love.

The seven in their agonized lives, so powerfully and graphically asserted throughout the poem, are allied here to such great tragic figures as Oedipus and Lear, whose suffering and blindness result in another kind of penetrating vision of reality. They are brought to knowledge of their nothingness which still thirsts for meaning, solace, transcendental resolution ("backgazing after heaven"). The "locus of grace" offers, in the last line, a shocking disclosure that echoes in part the conclusion of "Easter," where life is referred to as infernal: "In the heart's hell you have it; call it God's Love." These words can be interpreted variously. One might say Kinnell implies that God wills the suffering of individuals out of the paradox of a divine love whose goal is their purification and salvation. If we isolated the line and elicited from it a Christian meaning, we could indeed say something of that sort. But I cannot locate anything else in the poem, or in the rest of Kinnell's work for that matter, which would sustain this reading. It appears more likely that, severe though it may be, Kinnell extends to us "the heart's hell" as the fundamental human reality we have to live with, and from which we must summon our own virtue. Heaven is an illusion, looked on with nostalgia, which worsens our state by measuring it against an impossible ideal. Poetry, Kinnell tells us later, in the second of his "Last Songs" from *Body Rags* (1968), should incorporate the specifically human faults, the things that make man part of this world, not an eternal or paradisiacal one (there are some resemblances in this, of course, to Rilke and Wallace Stevens):

> Silence. Ashes
> In the grate. Whatever it is
> that keeps us from heaven,
> sloth, wrath, greed, fear, could we only
> reinvent it on earth
> as song.

Obviously, neither in "Seven Streams of Nevis" nor "Last Songs" is Kinnell praising man's fallibility, but he continues to insist on realizing it as integral to what man is. If we return to the phrase

"God's Love," the final words of the poem, I think we find it suggests first of all the poet's bitterly ironic criticism of the idea of a benevolent Creator who could will misery and death for His largely helpless creatures; further, it emphasizes his conviction that the love and value to be found in the tumult of earthly existence are in man's ravaged breast: God's love is simply what man makes it.

In "The Descent" and "Where the Track Vanishes" Kinnell gets nearer the looser structures of more recent poems. The two pieces juxtapose or alternate various scenes and incidents as the means for tracing out the theme of death and the pattern of ascent and decline which he perceives in all the particulars of nature and in man. More and more, in line with European poets such as Rilke or Yves Bonnefoy (whose poems he has so beautifully translated),[5] he envisages death as something like a negative presence, awaiting its appointed moment to emerge from beneath the surface of each individual life. This vision extends to the whole creation; it cannot be denied but must be faced with strength and tenderness, as this passage from "Where the Track Vanishes" points out:

> My hand on the sky
> Cannot shut the sky out
> Any more than any March
> Branch can. In the Boston Store
> Once, I tried new shoes:
> The shoeman put my feet
> In a machine, saying Kid
> Wrig yer toes. I
> Wrigged and peered:
> Inside green shoes green
> Twigs were wriggling by themselves
> Green as the grasses
> I drew from her
> Hair in the springtime

5. Yves Bonnefoy, *On the Motion and Immobility of Douve*, trans. Galway Kinnell (Athens, Ohio, 1968). Bonnefoy's epigraph from Hegel is perhaps significant: "But the life of the spirit is not frightened at death and does not keep itself pure of it. It endures death and maintains itself in it." (Translated by Kinnell.)

> While she laughed, unfoliaged
> by sunlight, a little
> Spray of bones I loved.

It is no more possible for the poet, as a man, to avoid participation in the life of nature than it is for a tree: both are wedded indissolubly to earth. Under the green light of the now old fashioned X-ray machine used to test the fit of shoes Kinnell watches, with a boy's fascination and an adult's understanding, the skeleton beneath the skin, his own mortality; suddenly, movingly, it recalls for him a girl whom he once loved and an affectionate gesture they shared. She takes form not in any ordinary description of her features but as an image of delicate, almost frail being lifted momentarily from the world like the season and surroundings in which he remembers her. The elegiac quality implicit in the last lines strengthens the impression of the evanescence of affection and, more emphatically, of personal identity, which also occupy Kinnell in "Freedom, New Hampshire."

The place "where the track vanishes" in this poem is a ruined mountain graveyard, "a heap of stones/Mortared with weeds and wildflowers—/The fallen church." Though everything here decayed long ago, and there would seem to be little chance of visitors, still a track is worn through the grass, ending among the gravestones. Perhaps, the poet muses, it is the crippled French peasant, leading his twelve goats up the mountainside to pasture, who has cut this path, but it is far from certain. Kinnell proceeds to another section filled with mythologies of the cosmos, the constellations, and finishes with a stanza opening out to the vastnesses of space. If the symbolic implications of herdsman, goats, cemetery, and ruined church were not quite pinned down for the reader till now, this last stanza does not permit him to mistake their purpose, though of course they remain essential as specific, literal details of actuality too, in keeping with Ezra Pound's belief that "the natural object is always the *adequate* symbol." At this point the peasant becomes the "Herdsman," doubtless referring to the northern constellation Bootes but likewise certainly representative of Christ with His twelve disciples (somewhat ironically presented here as goats) ascending the night sky toward the stars, riddlingly described as "A writing of lights," in search of the ever elusive "fields" of paradise. The stanza introduces both Christian supplication and pagan goddesses of fertility and renewal to delineate the ceaseless human desire for transcendence or rebirth. Looking back on the cemetery, where Kinnell imagines the dead merging with one another in the common soil, and the "fallen church," we note how they reinforce the main interests of the poem by indicating the universality of death and absorption into the earth, and by implying that creeds grow outworn. Nonetheless, the longing to go beyond the confines of mortality endures, the track climbs up. The three closing lines possess a dark ambiguity. They hint at a primal level of being which is associated with the earth, is at once the state of origins and the state of return; the poet conceives this as the source of our lives and mythologies and their conclusion. Existence begins to manifest itself constantly in Kinnell's work as unerringly cyclical in form:

> Fields into which the limping Herdsman wades
> Leading his flock up the trackless night, towards
> A writing of lights. Are they Notre Dame des Neiges
> Where men ask their God for the daily bread—
> Or the March-climbing Virgin carrying wheat?
> Where the track vanishes the first land begins.
> It goes out everywhere obliterating the horizons.
> We must have been walking through it all our lives.

Similarly, "The Descent" is constructed upon the symbolic pattern of human aspiration or ascent and the inevitable gravity of nature and fate that compels man downward to conclude in death and the earth. Designed in four parts, the poem alternates between a mountain-climbing expedition that results in tragic death and two moments in the Seekonk Woods—one the poet's recollection of childhood, the other a visit to the same location years later. All of these events demonstrate aspects of the cyclical scheme Kinnell intuits. At the outset he says of the string of mountain-climbers, seeing them on the slopes as if from below though he is really in their company: "it must have seemed/A lunatic earthworm headed for paradise"—already emphasizing the basic urge for transcendence the poem unfolds. One climber, Jan, a former member of the Resistance, tries to shortcut by jumping a crevasse and falls, mortally injured. Through some oddity or dimming of the dying man's vision he mistakes the declining moon before him for the rising sun behind, a misconception the symbolic properties of which Kinnell puts to use:

> Then he whispered, "Look—the sunrise!"
> The same color and nearly the same size
>
> But behind his back, the new sun
> Was rising. When the moon he was
> Staring at set in the mountains
> He died. On the way down the ice
> Had turned so perilous under the sun
> There was no choice: we watched while he went down.

The confusion of Jan's vision becomes for Kinnell a dramatic way of introducing into the poem the theme of human illusion in conflict with the undeviating cyclical pattern of sunrise and moonfall, ascent and decline, or birth and death, to which man and nature alike are subject. The conflict arises because the individual longs to retain his identity by rebirth or resurrection elsewhere; for while renewal occurs in the sense that new lives begin, death destroys each unique being, disperses the self into the undifferentiated whole again. As Kinnell writes near the close of "Freedom, New Hampshire," meditating on the loss of his brother, "But an incarnation is in particular flesh/And the dust that is swirled into a shape/And crumbles and is swirled again had but one shape/That was this man." So within the context Kinnell establishes in "The Descent" both mountain-climbing and what Jan thinks he sees are signs of man's wishes and illusions, while Jan's fall and consequent death, the sinking of the moon, and the fact that the sun's heat melting the ice makes the slopes treacherous, forcing the climbers to let Jan's body sled down the mountain alone, are actualities which complete the cycle. This pattern recurs in the second section, where the poet remembers lying hidden in grass "In Seekonk Woods, on Indian Hill" when someone fired a shotgun at nearby crows. His reaction was instantaneous, boyishly impulsive, and touching:

> Two crows blown out from either hand
> Went clattering away; a third
> Swam through the branches to the ground.
> I scooped it up, splashed the ford,
> And lit out—I must have run half a day
> Before I reached Holy Spring. (Anyway,
>
> I thought it was holy. No one
> Had told me heaven is overhead.
> I only knew people look down
> When they pray.) I held the dying bird
> As though, should its heartbeat falter,
> There wouldn't be much heartbeat anywhere.
>
> After a while I touched the plumes
> To the water. In the desert
> By the tracks I dug a headstart
> Taller than myself. I told him,
> "Have a good journey, crow. It can't be far.
> It'll be this side of China, for sure."

Thus the boy's childish but shrewd thought that heaven must be beneath the ground because the dead are laid to rest there and the praying head inclines this way contributes to Kinnell's symbolic scheme, as does the simple baptismal gesture the boy bestows as an unconscious allusion to rebirth. The poet is led to think again of his dead friend Jan, of the possibility that he might have kept a grip on life: had he been turned "to the sun/Might not the sun have held him here?" He replies to his own query with a rhetorical question stressing the contrarieties that work upon a person, pulling him in opposite directions:

> Or did he know the day came on
> Behind, not glancing back for fear
> The moon was already dragging from his bones
> The blood as dear to them, and as alien,
>
> As the suit of clothes to a scarecrow
> Or the flesh to a cross?

At this moment he can comprehend his friend's "descent," announced in the poem's title and grasped naively by the poet in his boyhood, for what it is, the unavoidable rounding off of the course of existence: "To his valleys/Rivers have washed this climber to the sun/The full moon pestled into earth again." Then the last two stanzas of this section play upon the important thematic suggestiveness of height and depth, light and darkness. The paradisiacal realm, however, is no longer located where boyhood had it, underground; the poet has learned what men believe, or imagine, that it is a luminous celestial dimension ("Heaven is in light, overhead,/I have it by heart"). By way of contrast, the realities of death, burial, nightfall, and the earth to which life is joined are brought forward:

> Yet the dead
> Silting the darkness do not ask
> For burials elsewhere than the dusk.
> They lie where nothing but the moon can rise,
> And make no claims, though they had promises.

Formal religion makes these "promises," yet from this sleep comes no awakening; only nature, contained in the image of moonrise, continues its eternal circle. The milkweed seen growing at the start of the second stanza puts us in mind of the hopes and plans of men who try to launch themselves beyond the graveyard soil of their beginnings but become merely "drab," don't succeed in resolving the enigmas of existence or rising above them, and fulfill their lives only by extinction. New life springs from the deaths of others and progresses toward the same goal, that is the clear assertion emerging from the abundant detail of Kinnell's writing:

Milkweed that grow beside the tombs
Climb from the dead as if in flight,
But a foot high they stop and bloom
In drab shapes, that neither give light
Nor bring up the true darkness of the dead;
Strange, homing lamps, that go out seed by seed.

The final portion discovers Kinnell back at the scene of the crow
shooting, attempting to recapture something of that moment in
the past which is for him still redolent with grace. He seeks the
spontaneous, honest feeling for the numinous that was his as a boy,
but it has vanished beyond recovery. Instead, he looks upon a
changed landscape; Indian Hill has turned into a subdivision, the
crosslike TV aerials on the rooftops exhibit the secular interests
now presiding over this once (for the poet) sacred spot. When he
tries to find his "Holy Spring" he faces the blunt, incontrovertible
facts of nature:

Fields lying dark and savage and the sun

Reaping its own fire from the trees,
Whirling the faint panic of birds
Up turbulent light. Two white-haired
Crows cried under the wheeling rays;
And loosed as by a scythe, into the sky
A flight of jackdaws rose, earth-birds suddenly

Seized by some thaumaturgic thirst,
Shrill wings flung up the crow-clawed, burned,
Unappeasable air. And one turned,
Dodged through the flock again and burst
Eastward alone, sinking across the wood
On the world curve of its wings.

With these lines Kinnell draws together the echoes, parallels, and
recurrences of his poem. One can say that in a certain sense its construction reflects the cyclical pattern of existence which is everywhere so plain to him and dominates his imagination. When he
attempts to revive the experience of his youth, he is answered only

by nature with its fertility and its alternating creative and destructive energies. (The scene is reminiscent though hardly imitative of
those in Richard Eberhart's "The Groundhog," and there are thematic affinities with Dylan Thomas.) The actions of the crows and
jackdaws, moreover, do not really differ from those of humans. We
are all "earth-birds," like the "earthworm" mountain-climbers of
the poem's opening, vainly scaling the heights or searching for the
sacred of which we were once confident. Our desires are no different from the birds' instinctive climbing through the air; we are
obsessed with the miraculous, the supernatural that will free us of
death and preserve us. The lone bird flying eastward, away from its
flock, follows the line of "descent" to earth, recalling Wallace
Stevens's "casual flocks of pigeons" at the close of "Sunday Morning" who "make/Ambiguous undulations as they sink,/Downward
to darkness, on extended wings." This jackdaw is the counterpart
among unself-conscious creatures of Jan, who, dying, believes he
sees the sunrise of renewal; the "world curve of its wings" proclaims unmistakably the universality of death, the return to earth.
So we are "Strange, homing lamps, that go out seed by seed."

But Kinnell goes beyond these resolutions of imagery, parallel-
isms of quest and incident, to introduce the figure of Christ at the
poem's end, once again clothing Him in an image from the natural
world yet symbolically appropriate. He appears, then, as a "fisher-
bird," who still speaks in the voice of His suffering and despair
upon the cross; His cry articulates the agony of every living being,
of all who feel the torment of mortality. Concentrating on the idea
of the Incarnation, Kinnell sees Christ as the exemplary sufferer
in whose speech, passion, and death the pain of others is embodied,
manifested as the supreme, heartrending instance of man's "thaumaturgic thirst" for immortality—and its defeat:

> Nor do we know why,
>
> Mirrored in duskfloods, the fisherbird
> Seems to stand in a desolate sky
> Feeding at its own heart. In the cry

> *Eloi! Eloi!* flesh was made word:
> We hear it in wind catching in the trees,
> In lost blood breaking a night through the bones.

Once more Christ's presence occupies a central position in Kinnell's poetry, and that is in "The Supper after the Last," which is also the piece he selected for inclusion in Paul Engle and Joseph Langland's anthology *Poet's Choice*. His accompanying comment has a special relevance to his imaginative preoccupations at that time, and since:

> It is from this poem, "The Supper After the Last," that I want to make a fresh start, and I chose it for this reason. I mean towards a poem without scaffolding or occasion, that progresses through images to a point where it can make a statement on a major subject.[6]

"A poem without scaffolding or occasion, that progresses through images. . . ." Kinnell might have been speaking here about the poetry of Robert Bly, Louis Simpson, W. S. Merwin, Frank O'Hara, Donald Hall, or John Ashbery, among others, and certainly about much of the most important contemporary European and Latin American poetry—in fact, about almost any poetry whose roots lie in the Surrealist or Expressionist traditions of twentieth-century literature. A common concern of such poets is the creation of a poetry which relies less and less upon logical or narrative structure, upon the representation of external events (surely, these are the types of things Kinnell means by "scaffolding or occasion"), but which develops around a highly suggestive grouping of images whose source is inward experience, memory, dream, or vision. The purpose of this technique is to increase the authenticity of poetic statement, to dispense with artificiality, to free poetry from any ties that would prevent it from approximating as closely as possible its sources. Of course, this is not the only kind of poem Kinnell will write in the future, and he does not seem to have converted himself so completely to these artistic strategies as, say, Merwin or Bly; but there can be no doubt that this new direction to his efforts has

6. *Poet's Choice* (New York, 1962), p. 257.

strengthened, purified, and quickened the poems of his two later collections.

"The Supper after the Last" can best be approached as a culmination of a sort as well as a new start. Themes we have noted in considerable detail in previous poems are not only quite apparent in this one but also reach a fierce, shocking resolution: a ruthless visionary statement that assimilates its predecessors, abolishes the hesitations, hopes, defeated yet renewed desires so evident before. The poem has near-surrealist qualities in its opening lines which bring forward mirage, illusion, and hallucination; but the particulars of water, sky, dragonfly, the bather and his shadow, however puzzling at first, must not be overlooked, for they will reappear charged with meaning. A scene is offered at the start that is deliberately indefinite, that doesn't permit the reader to settle securely on a specific landscape, for land and sea obscurely mingle while the sky overarches them in the mirage; then a brightly colored dragonfly floats down to the desert floor and a bather comes into view, wading in what has already been called both "illusory water" and "The sea [that] scumbles in" and trying without success to destroy that dark reflection of himself which is his shadow. The atmosphere is mysterious, confusing. Kinnell has, in accordance with his prose remarks, confined himself to a mental occasion. The landscape before us has been formed by the inner eye:

> The desert moves out on half the horizon
> Rimming the illusory water which, among islands,
> Bears up the sky. The sea scumbles in
> From its own inviolate border under the sky.
> A dragon-fly floating on six legs on the sand
> Lifts its green-yellow tail, declines its wings
> A little, flutters them a little, and lays
> On dazzled sand the shadow of its wings. Near shore
> A bather wades through his shadow in the water.
> He tramples and kicks it; it recomposes.

Once we begin to read carefully, examining the recurrence and expansion of various details from this scene later in the poem, our bearings grow more distinct. The "illusory water" already seen returns as water reminding us of baptism or the waters of life, both implying faith or renewal. Such significance gains support by the assertion that this water "Bears up the sky," that is to say, metaphorically speaking, it animates or sustains a belief in the transcendent, the otherworldly. This notion of the passage seems less strained when we recall that the poem's title entertains the notion of resurrection: we can assume that it refers to a meal Christ eats after His return from the dead. In part two water is an essential element in another scene that discloses a "whitewashed house" while "Framed in its doorway, a chair,/Vacant, waits in the sunshine." We are not told for whom this chair waits, but undoubtedly it has been prepared for the risen Christ. The next stanza reveals the water in a container, and the invisible world hovers on the verge of visibility:

> A jug of fresh water stands
> Inside the door. In the sunshine
> The chair waits, less and less vacant.
> The host's plan is to offer water, then stand aside.

The anonymous "host," one who awaits the coming of Christ, and so one of the faithful, places the water as a sacramental gesture signifying new life or resurrection and as a token of his belief that it will come through Him. Thus far, the poem establishes an almost hypnotic stillness; the one violent act of the bather kicking in the first stanza is absorbed by the vagueness and fluidity of the mirage. As we observed, the second part opens on a stark, simple arrangement of house, doorway, sunlit chair, and jug of water; but as the host removes himself to make way for his expected guest the poem reaches a turning point that, with the beginning of part three, shatters the calm and jolts the reader's complacency. Suddenly we are shown "the supper after the last" carried on with savage gusto:

> They eat *rosé* and chicken. The chicken head
> Has been tucked under the shelter of the wing.
> Under the table a red-backed, passionate dog
> Cracks chicken bones on the blood and gravel floor.

As this section continues, so does the ferocity of the meal increase. The unidentified figure devouring chicken is, I take it, a particularly brutal portrait of Christ as Death, the universal destroyer whose ravenous jaws and digestive system are transformed into a horrifying image of the Styx down which everything must pass. The message of this Christ, who apparently has been robbed by His suffering and death of the illusion of His teachings, His promises at the Last Supper, is mortality without reprieve. This supper has nothing sacred or life-renewing about it; plainly it is a feast of sheer annihilation:

> No one else but the dog and the blind
> Cat watching it knows who is that bearded
> Wild man guzzling overhead, the wreck of passion
> Emptying his eyes, who has not yet smiled,
>
> Who stares at the company, where he is company,
> Turns them to sacks of appalled, grinning skin,
> Forks the fowl-eye out from under
> The large, makeshift, cooked lid, evaporates the wine,
>
> Jellies the sunlit table and spoons, floats
> The deluxe grub down the intestines of the Styx,
> Devours all but the cat and dog, to whom he slips scraps,
> The red-backed accomplice busy grinding gristle.

This "emptying" of the eyes can be understood, I think, as one instance in Kinnell's work of the deprivation of spiritual significance from existence, a demythologizing of life and the cosmos we have observed in various poems which here assumes a more stringent character, for it refers to Christ's loss of His transcendental vision. At the outset of part four even the host, the man of faith, falls victim, his "bones . . ./Crack in the hound's jaw" as if to herald the wild man's speech, which begins with ironic reversals of the Gospels. His words inform men of their fundamental nothingness, describe them as creatures of dust who long for immortality, who form from these deep-seated wishes pictures of the eternal, the entirely compassionate and merciful, and insist on the veracity of the pictures because they have imagined them:

> I came not to astonish
> But to destroy you. Your
> Jug of cool water? Your
> Hanker after wings? Your
> Lech for transcendence?
> I came to prove you are
> Intricate and simple things
> As you are, created
> In the image of nothing,
> Taught of the creator
> By your images in dirt—
> As mine, for which you set
> A chair in the sunshine,
> Mocking me with water!
> As pictures of wings,
> Not even iridescent,
> That clasp the sand
> And that cannot perish, you swear,
> Having once been evoked!

With the poem's closing part we look again on the desert mirage of the beginning. The vision of Christ trembles, blurs, "begins to float in water" as everything now seems illusory, uncertain. Christ is finally named as He is on the point of disappearing, but His voice continues while His figure blends into the liquid fluctuations of the atmosphere: "Far out in that mirage the Saviour sits whispering to the world,/Becoming a mirage." The words of His parting statement bring back the images of dragonfly, light and darkness. Man strives, He says, to ascend "from flesh into wings," an effort indicative of the will to escape his fate, and He admits that "the change exists." But it is not a permanent change, and obtains only within the boundaries of mortal life, though man wishes it to endure beyond them: "But the wings that live gripping the contours of the dirt/Are all at once nothing, flesh and light lifted away." So the Saviour proclaims Himself the *idea* of God or the eternal, the objectification of man's desires—"I am the resurrection, because I am the light"—thus recalling, in "The Descent," a similar expression of the human will to survive: "Heaven is in light, overhead,/I have it by heart." But the fading Christ, introducing again the dragonfly we first saw laying "the shadow of its wings" on the sand, asserts that man's destiny is analogous to that small creature's downward flight; the earth is his last home, to vanish is his end. At the poem's finish the Saviour appears in the dual role of a phantasmal god of unattainable worlds and the architect of man's death. In spite of his metamorphoses, his struggles toward the "light," a man's final transformation brings him to the ground from which he came:

> I cut to your measure the creeping piece of darkness
> That haunts you in the dirt. Steps into light—
> I make you over. I breed the shape of your grave in the dirt.

That moving "piece of darkness" is an individual's shadow, the reflection of his death inseparable from his existence which the bather at the poem's outset tries unsuccessfully to dispel. The poem concludes in the absoluteness of death, an assurance for Kinnell that holds little promise for appeal.

With "The Supper after the Last" Kinnell has not only arrived at decisive technical changes that will influence many of his later poems, but he has also brought a course of thematic exploration to an end. This exploration, concerned with man's spiritual compulsions and aspirations, the forms they take in concrete experience, the illusory convictions they foster, derives its impulse from sources deep within the poet's own psyche, his inner and affective life. By exposing what he believes to be the hopeless falsity of these longings for eternity, and by confronting death as an unconditional fact in a tough, unremitting way, he prepares as the ground for his future writing certain limitations of existence within which his poems must be created. We can surmise, I think, that Kinnell has purged himself in the poems we have discussed of personal anxieties and questionings with regard to death, Christ, the purpose and goal of existence. This is not to say he does not ponder still the elusive, mysterious nature of human life and its stubborn refusal to yield the explanatory meanings for it we seek; but hereafter the realms of transcendence remain a dark void, an inscrutable blackness on which he can cast no illumination, and the person of Christ, as might be expected, no longer occupies him with a few incidental exceptions. He takes a new grasp on the world at hand, on his life here and now in all of its immediacy, or engages himself with the particulars of other lives and surroundings present to him. The poem "Last Spring," from *Flower Herding on Mount Monadnock* (1964), can be read as a statement of his altered interests. The first part describes his dreaming through "a dark winter" and losing his hold on the physical substance of things, accepting their "glitter" as substitute; but this mode of dreaming leads to death, or at least to a loss of contact with actuality. His mind is invaded by "the things/Whose corpses eclipse them,/Shellfishes, ostriches, elephants." But with the movement of seasons into spring and new life the sun's brightness and clarity dissolve the poet's private fancies, his "keepsakes . . . inventions,"

> It left me only a life
>
> And time to walk
> Head bobbing out front like a pigeon's
> Knocking on the instants to let me in.

This attentiveness to being in the world in its full temporal and tangible immediacy is a striking attribute of the long, ambitious poem "The Avenue Bearing the Initial of Christ into the New World." Composed freely, without linear or narrative structure, in a series of fourteen sections focusing on a variety of moments and figures in the life of Avenue C in New York with its teeming ghetto population of Jews, Negroes, and Puerto Ricans, the poem evokes, through myriad impressions of the particulars of daily experience interspersed with the poet's imaginative projection into individual lives and his allusive imagery, provocative ironies, a comprehensive vision of people existing under circumstances of destitution, pain, persecution, and death in a country that supposedly extends promises of refuge, security, equality, and oppor-

tunity for those who flee to her shores. Christ does not appear in
the poem except in a brief, glancing reference; Kinnell simply uses
Him in the title to point up the victimization of persons who had
come to America in the hope of achieving a better sort of life.
Throughout the poem there is an insistence on the element of
betrayal, especially of the Jews—though the application is obviously
much wider—first by God, who is treated with disgust and rejection because He deceived Abraham (doubtless Kinnell means
all the Jews as well) and has nothing but cold indifference to human feelings; He is reduced in a simile from omnipotent deity to
repellent insect:

> A child lay in the flames.
> It was not the plan. Abraham
> Stood in terror at the duplicity.
> Isaac whom he loved lay in the flames.
> The Lord turned away washing
> His hands without soap and water
> Like a common housefly.

Then they are betrayed by America, the new world to which they
have voyaged in desperate flight from poverty, pogroms, concentration camps, only to find themselves still imprisoned; in spite of
this disappointment and constant hardship they exhibit a sturdi-
ness, a will to endure, which is the inherited strength of ages and
draws the poet's admiration:

> The promise was broken too freely
> To them and to their fathers, for them to care.
> They survive like cedars on a cliff, roots
> Hooked in any crevice they can find.

Behind Kinnell's poem stand Whitman's *Leaves of Grass*, Hart
Crane's *The Bridge*, and Williams's *Paterson*, along with something of *The Waste Land* and *The Cantos*. Like those poets, ours
immerses himself in the rich welter of life and does so with sympathy and understanding. As a result, the poem abounds in images
rendering with vigorousness and exactitude the very feel of this

street, the lives thronging it, from "the eastern ranges/Of the wiped-out lives—punks, lushes,/Panhandlers, pushers, rumsoaks" to the old Jew who "rocks along in a black fur shtraimel,/Black robe, black knickers, black knee-stockings,/Black shoes"; or where

> The old women peer, blessed damozels
> Sitting up there young forever in the cockroached rooms,
> Eating fresh-killed chicken, productos tropicales,
> Appetizing herring, canned goods, nuts;
> They puff out smoke from Natural Bloom cigars
> And one day they puff like Blony Bubblegum.
> Across the square skies with faces in them
> Pigeons skid, crashing into the brick.
> From a rooftop a boy fishes at the sky,
> Around him a flock of pigeons fountains,
> Blown down and swirling up again, seeking the sky.

Such a burst of energy and exaltation, the abrupt takeoff of the pigeons, wakens thoughts of escape—"To fly from this place"—but these deteriorate rapidly into nightmare images of failure and death: "To run under the rain of pigeon plumes, to be/Tarred, and feathered with birdshit, Icarus,/In Kugler's glass headdown dangling by yellow legs." Indeed, death pervades this poem, making itself felt just the other side of the hard, marginal lives Kinnell portrays on this city street, in the seedy rooms and restaurants, in the market, in the memory of a dead friend, in the figure of the "ancient Negro" who sings "Over Jordan" outside "the Happy Days Bar & Grill," in the frightening persons of "Bunko Certified Embalmer,/Cigar in his mouth, nose to the wind" and the owner of the fishmarket who "lops off the heads,/Shakes out the guts as if they did not belong in the first place,/And they are flesh for the first time in their lives," in the occasional reminders of the concentration camps and the extermination of Jews. But perhaps most resonant with meaning because they touch a more fundamental symbolic level are the parallel images of the Avenue itself and the East River. Both are implicated with the flux of life, the current that draws everything toward annihilation, in the arterial flow of blood through the body which ends thus: "The lungs put out the light of the world as they/Heave and collapse, the brain turns and rattles/In its own black axlegrease." The final section of the poem begins with suggestions of an absent God and the inexorable passage of life into death, here embodied in the details of the fish:

> Behind the Power Station on 14th, the held breath
> Of light, as God is a held breath, withheld,
> Spreads the East River, into which fishes leak:
> The brown sink or dissolve,
> The white float out in shoals and armadas,
> Even the gulls pass them up, pale
> Bloated socks of riverwater and rotted seed,
> That swirl on the tide, punched back
> To the Hell Gate narrows, and on the ebb
> Steam seaward, seeding the sea.

In succeeding stanzas the street reappears with its desolation, violence, and irrationality. Then Kinnell resorts to a highly suggestive interweaving of light and dark, familiar because of earlier applications in "The Descent," "Where the Track Vanishes," "The Supper after the Last," and elsewhere. Momentary luminescence is always swallowed in darkness. Even more cruelly paradoxical is the glow of a corpse in the night waters of the river, which has now become one with the Avenue and the sea into whose depths life empties:

> It is night, and raining. You look down
> Towards Houston in the rain, the living streets,
> Where instants of transcendence
> Drift in oceans of loathing and fear, like lanternfishes,
> Or phosphorus flashings in the sea, or the feverish light
> Skin is said to give off when the swimmer drowns at night.

This identification compels the poet to a stanza of summary proportions that makes explicit the poem's crushing ironies, the human frustration and waste, the sacrifice linking the Avenue's population with the murdered Christ, and the cosmic injustice behind these realities:

From the blind gut Pitt to the East River of Fishes
The Avenue cobbles a swath through the discolored air,
A roadway of refuse from the teeming shores and ghettos
And the Caribbean Paradise, into the new ghetto and new paradise,
This God-forsaken Avenue bearing the initial of Christ
Through the haste and carelessness of the ages,
The sea standing in heaps, which keeps on collapsing,
Where the drowned suffer a C-change,
And remain the common poor.

If there is something strained about "C-change," so that it seems
rather gimmicky for so serious a passage, the meanings it generates, both with respect to crucifixion and to the irony of Ariel's
song in this context, are anything but slight. Yet for all of its grim-
ness, which continues into the closing stanzas with their renewed
emphasis on the fugitive and outcast person, on persecution and
death, the poem is completed on a note that combines lamentation,
hardiness, and a kind of resignation to life's inequities and miseries
which even allows, in the face of oblivion, a corrosive laughter:

> In the nighttime
> Of the blood they are laughing and saying,
> Our little lane, what a kingdom it was!
>
> oi weih, oi weih

A considerable number of the poems from Kinnell's next two
volumes, *Flower Herding on Mount Monadnock* and *Body Rags*,
adhere closely to the lineaments of a specific experience; rather
than enlarging on it as some previous pieces do, they attempt to
seize it through a literal concreteness or through the more oblique
progression of images referred to in *Poet's Choice*. Quite often the
two approaches are joined in the same poem, as, for example, in
"Middle of the Way." In any event, the desire to articulate what
the poet sees, hears, thinks, and dreams with undeviating accuracy,
with as little departure from the quality of the original experience
as possible, causes him to tighten his language even further; imagery becomes sharp, spare, precise and is set down with an ad-

mirable directness that enhances the effect of lyric purity. And the
relationship to nature we have observed throughout Kinnell's work
increases in importance for him. Like Roethke or Gary Snyder, he
is attracted to the nonhuman world, not as a field for intellectual
conquest but as the basic context of man's living—the only one he
really knows—in which other forms of life manifest their being
together with him. This perception comes alive variously in many
poems, nowhere with a more moving sense of participation than
"In Fields of Summer":

> The sun rises,
> The goldenrod blooms,
> I drift in fields of summer,
> My life is adrift in my body,
> It shines in my heart and hands, in my teeth,
> It shines up at the old crane
> Who holds out his drainpipe of a neck
> And creaks along in the blue,
>
> And the goldenrod shines with its life, too,
> And the grass, look,
> The great field wavers and flakes,
> The rumble of bumblebees keeps deepening,
> A phoebe flutters up,
> A lark bursts up all dew.

In such poems as "Tillamook Journal (2nd version)," "On Hard-
scrabble Mountain," and "Middle of the Way" he carries his own
human solitariness far into forest and up mountainside, there to
assimilate whatever he can of nature's existence, separate in its
magnitude, its awesome age, its unity that excludes man with his
unique self-awareness: "I love the earth, and always/In its dark-
nesses I am a stranger." "Middle of the Way," from which these
lines come, demonstrates, as do other poems, Kinnell's persistent
use of the imagery of darkness to connote the unfathomable aspects
of the universe and his own temporary being within it. This period
of isolation in the wilderness, at night by a dying fire "under the
trees/That creak a little in the dark,/The giant trees of the world,"

elicits the beautiful meditative stanzas concluding the poem. The progression of Kinnell's thought is convincingly set forth in images which realize the total experience:

> The coals go out,
> The last smoke weaves up
> Losing itself in the stars.
> This is my first night to lie
> In the uncreating dark.
>
> In the heart of a man
> There sleeps a green worm
> That has spun the heart about itself,
> And that shall dream itself black wings
> One day to break free into the beautiful black sky.
>
> I leave my eyes open,
> I lie here and forget our life,
> All I see is we float out
> Into the emptiness, among the great stars,
> On this little vessel without lights.
>
> I know that I love the day,
> The sun on the mountain, the Pacific
> Shiny and accomplishing itself in breakers,
> But I know I live half alive in the world,
> I know half my life belongs to the wild darkness.

Not only do we get the impression of being *there*, of the immediacy of Kinnell's reflections under the circumstances, but we also witness the quite personal flow of his thoughts and feelings. While it is sensitive to external setting—the middle section preceding these stanzas is cast in the abbreviated form of a prose journal recording the day's events in the mountains—the poem moves rapidly into the poet's mind in the first lines above, away from the facts of the dead fire, the final wisp of smoke, toward the center of consciousness where specific elements from the outer world (the stars, the worm, the black-winged butterfly, the sun, the mountain, the Pacific) are charged with hidden implications drawn from the non-rational psyche and the emotions to enter into new combinations. Behind them lies the effort to uncover covert impulses, ties, tendencies of the inner self that pass unnoticed while an individual is occupied with daily affairs; in these stanzas they are released to convey the poet's mind on a kind of dream-journey of associated images which culminates in his realization of the double urge in him toward a world of radiance, clarity, and order, and toward a world of impenetrable darkness, chaos, and oblivion. Of course, what I am claiming for this passage in the way of meaning remains implicit in the images themselves, in accordance with Kinnell's wish for a poem lacking logical structure, "scaffolding or occasion," and such images as he offers are not readily exhausted but prove continuously stimulating to the reader's imagination.

"Middle of the Way," however, is only one of many meditative poems from *Flower Herding on Mount Monadnock* and *Body Rags* in which the poet employs linked groups of images, metaphorical statements, and specific details of observation or recollection to speculate on the self's identity, its relationship to nature, time, and, as always, death. Through most of these pieces runs Kinnell's recurrent alternation of night and day, physical actuality and the possibility of nothingness. Occasionally, accompanying these opposing conditions of being and nonbeing, we find the waters of flux and change, the river that glides toward death. In "Poems of Night," a sequence of brief lyrics, the poet quietly, gently traces the features of his beloved as she sleeps, moving his "hand over/ Slopes, falls, lumps of sight,/Lashes barely able to be touched,/Lips that give way so easily." Finally, in the last two poems, he perceives a portion of his own existence embodied in the contours of her familiar form; her self has been so deeply bound up with his for a time that in holding her body in his arms he feels he is embracing something fundamental to his own nature: "I hold/What I can only think of/As some deepest of memories in my arms,/Not mine, but as if the life in me/Were slowly remembering what it is." Yet the next poem, which brings morning, fails to provide confidence or hope in these discoveries because the day itself is seen as fragile and doomed, a vessel we float perilously and, at last, in vain upon the darkened flood:

> And now the day, raft that breaks up, comes on.

> I think of a few bones
> Floating on a river at night,
> The starlight blowing in place on the water,
> The river leaning like a wave towards the emptiness.

Kinnell frequently reflects in recent poems on wreckage, either that of the human body, as above, or the ruins of houses, sea wrack scattered along deserted beaches, fossils, burnt out stretches of timber. For him such sights constitute the residue of lives lived, human or otherwise, and so prove worthy of contemplation. Though they are perceptible reminders of perishability, sometimes of suffering, they can reveal as well an innate dignity and strength that confirm the value of what they have been. It should be noted too that the universe as Kinnell now represents it contains destructiveness as a perpetual native element, no less a part of the underlying design of things than the wind, which he often makes a symbol for it:

> The wind starts fluting
> In our teeth, in our ears,
> It whines down the harmonica
> Of the fingerbones, moans at the skull . . .

> Blown on by their death
> The things on earth whistle and cry out.
> Nothing can keep still. Only the wind.
> —"Tree from Andalusia"

At the outset of "Spindrift" the poet's attention is fixed on what the sea has washed ashore: "old/Horseshoe crabs, broken skates,/ Sand dollars, sea horses, as though/Only primeval creatures get destroyed." Later, in a ritual gesture, Kinnell draws "sacred/Shells from the icy surf,/Fans of gold light, sunbursts"; one of these he is to raise to the sun, source of life and light, and pledge himself to go "to the shrine of the dead." Performing this natural religious ceremony, with its implicit veneration for the principle of life in the cosmos, he enjoys briefly its sudden manifestation as the sunlight strikes the shell:

> And as it blazes
> See the lost life within
> Alive again in the fate-shine.

But we can only assume the "shrine of the dead" is here, or any place where a man turns his thoughts upon the dead, which Kinnell proceeds to do during the rest of the poem. Section after section, he shifts from one object of reflection to another, apparently at random, yet all the while skillfully accumulating force, particularly through the repetition of key images of wind, light, and shell, as he aims toward a final comprehensive statement. Kinnell studies the iconography (to borrow a term he suggests) of nature's forms, trying to extract the meanings worked by the world into a seashell, a worn root, the motion and sound of the surf; in the latter he reads a message lying beneath every detail of the poem: "It is the most we know of time,/And it is our undermusic of eternity." The waves' recurrence, the sea in its seemingly contradictory aspect of stable sameness and ceaseless change, reminiscent of Valéry's "La mer, la mer, toujours recommencée!", indicates metaphorically for the poet the rhythm which holds together the life of creation. He is then able to remember the death of a friend or relative in the ambiance of that imagery of light and shell given a sacred significance previously:

> I think of how I
> Sat by a dying woman,
> Her shell of a hand,
> Wet and cold in both of mine,
> Light, nearly out, existing as smoke,
> I sat in the glow of her wan, absorbed smile.

The "lost life," glimpsed earlier as the shell was held to the sun, appears now in this memory of an existence about to be abandoned, a light darkened, revived here as the poet lifts it up to the human warmth of his thought. In the next part we find him "Under the high wind" already mentioned as the sign of flux and destruction "holding this little lamp,/This icy fan of the sun," which is, we recall, his Golden Bough, the token of his permission to visit the dead. The first of the two stanzas shows the fateful wind as it "moans in the grass/And whistles through crabs' claws," and in the second its ominousness grows more immediate to the poet himself: his life is threatened, lies under the same sentence:

> Across gull tracks
> And wind ripples in the sand
> The wind seethes. My footprints
> Slogging for the absolute
> Already begin vanishing.

Existence is, then, constantly being consumed; it vanishes like the smoke, the gull tracks and footprints, into the surrounding, the hurling, eroding wind. The last section introduces an anonymous old man who might be anyone, including a projection of the poet into old age; his "wrinkled eyes" are "Tortured by smoke," which would seem, as in the instance of the dying woman, to specify the minimal amount of life left in him. Physically crippled by his years, what can this man "really love," the poet wonders. Other creatures not endowed with this self-consciousness or the capacity for this type of affection simply exist to the end by instinct and without advance knowledge of death:

> The swan dips her head
> And peers at the mystic
> In-life of the sea,
> The gull drifts up
> And eddies toward heaven,
> The breeze in his arms . . .

Kinnell's answer to his inquiry amounts to a compassionate declaration of acceptance that asks nothing further but binds man to temporal creation. At the close the image of the shell returns,

symbolic of all life, refined and polished by its travels through
time, sacred because it is what we know, possess for a while, and
value supremely:

> Nobody likes to die
> But an old man
> Can know
> A kind of gratefulness
> Towards time that kills him,
> Everything he loved was made of it.
>
> In the end
> What is he but the scallop shell
> Shining with time like any pilgrim?

A more detailed version of this acceptance occurs at the finish
of "Flower Herding on Mount Monadnock," where the poet locates in the forest a flower corresponding to his desire early in the
poem for one "which cannot be touched," that is, which will be
permanent and inviolable. But the flower he discovers is quite
mortal. Its life burns up and disappears much as the lives in "Spindrift," though here Kinnell examines its pretensions to durability—
in effect, to immortality of the spirit—but these are discounted
when death affirms its reality and life's single appeal is to itself. The
end of the poem puts us squarely in front of the observable facts,
dismisses the unseen aura with which we are tempted to surround
them. "No ideas but in things," insisted William Carlos Williams,
and Kinnell surely agrees:

> In the forest I discover a flower.
>
> The invisible life of the thing
> Goes up in flames that are invisible
> Like cellophane burning in the sunlight.
>
> It burns up. Its drift is to be nothing.
>
> In its covertness it has a way
> Of uttering itself in place of itself,
> Its blossoms claim to float in the Empyrean,
>
> A wrathful presence on the blur of the ground.

> The appeal to heaven breaks off.
> The petals begin to fall, in self-forgiveness.
> It is a flower. On this mountainside it is dying.

The poems of *Body Rags* do not alter the direction Kinnell's work has taken thus far, nor do they exhibit any changed attitude toward an existence whose horizon is ringed by death, though the intensity with which he enters into his experience has never been greater. In the haunting meditations of "Another Night in the Ruins" he recalls a night flight over the ocean during which his dead brother's face appeared to him shaped from storm clouds, "looking nostalgically down/on blue,/lightning flashed moments of the Atlantic." These "moments" have their counterparts in the other imagery of light and flame remarked before as significant of the vital energy which is life breaking forth and yet consuming itself, finishing at last in smoke, ashes, darkness. Kinnell's image of his brother catches him brooding on this paradoxical principle and revives the dead man's words:

> He used to tell me,
> "What good is the day?
> On some hill of despair
> the bonfire
> you kindle can light the great sky—
> though it's true, of course, to make it burn
> you have to throw yourself in . . ."

True to the obliquity of his technique, he proceeds away from the demanding implications of this statement and provides a stanza emphasizing harsh, ruinous change and a nearly hallucinatory intuition of ultimate vacuity with "the cow/of nothingness, mooing/down the bones." But the return to his brother's idea begins with the unexpected appearance of a rooster who "thrashes in the snow/for a grain"; when he uncovers it, he "Rips/it into/flames," an act that matches exactly, in meaning and imagery, the gesture of self-sacrifice (so full of echoes of Christ's death) required by his brother's reasoning to bestow on an existence an importance beyond itself. The symbolic rooster in this metaphysical barnyard, "Flames /bursting out of his brow," urges Kinnell to a point of recognition we have watched him arrive at before: namely, that man is no phoenix ("we aren't, after all, made/from that bird which flies out of its ashes"), there is no rebirth. But he goes further than he has in previous instances by regarding as valid his brother's word and seeing the necessity for the self to assimilate its destiny and death:

> . . . for a man
> as he goes up in flames, his one work
> is
> to open himself, to *be*
> the flames . . .

"Another Night in the Ruins" is the first poem in *Body Rags*, and with good reason, I think, since many of the pieces which follow reflect the terms of recognition given there. So in "Lost Loves" the poet can "lie dreaming" of women he has cared for, moments in the past, while time heads him "deathward." In spite of these losses and the eventual outcome of his life, he finds it possible to take pleasure in perpetual alteration and to identify himself with the many "lives" and selves passed through in the course of one existence:

> And yet I can rejoice
> that everything changes, that
> we go from life
> into life,
>
> and enter ourselves
> quaking
> like the tadpole, his time come, tumbling toward the slime.

Poetry, when it is written, is the product of this existence and consequently will bear the marks of the self's struggles, transformations, failures, escapes. Like the scarred hill of the world in which the layers of time past lie fossilized, it contains whatever its author has done or been:

> The poem too
> is a palimpsest, streaked
> with erasures, smelling
> of departure and burnt stone.
>   —"The Poem"

The last four poems in the collection, however, to my mind best demonstrate Kinnell's bold and powerful attempt to integrate himself with his experience, and to do it without mediation or protection, exposing himself completely to a direct encounter with his perceivings. The resulting poetry has a stunning force and uncompromising toughness that sometimes leave the reader gasping. Of course, these pieces, which include the long poem "The Last River," "Testament of the Thief," "The Porcupine," and "The Bear," differ from one another in various ways, too, though the latter pair are close in spirit.

"The Last River" shows an evident kinship with "The Avenue Bearing the Initial of Christ into the New World," not merely because of its length but because both poems are concerned with large, specifically American areas of experience. As he did in the earlier poem, Kinnell here employs juxtaposition and collage to accommodate a wide range of material; now, however, the atmosphere is more fluid and indeterminate. The two poems are held together simply by the focus of the poet's consciousness, but in "The Last River" he makes himself felt more definitely as a presence, a person in the poem to whom everything there is happening, than he does in "The Avenue . . . ," where he prefers occasionally to be anonymous. So it is his consciousness in "The Last River," shifting and sliding through images and memories, ever changing, dropping below to the levels of dream and nightmare, following the course of the Mississippi southward and, at the same time, floating down the waters of the Styx into the underworld with his Virgil a boy named Henry David, visiting the damned in their torments, and returning to achieve, through the agency of another version of Thoreau, a prophetic vision of national destiny, that is the locus of the poem.

Kinnell starts off by mingling details from his travels in the South and his work with black people in a voter registration program with impressions of a jail cell at night into which he was locked, presumably for this activity among Negroes, or something related to it. An air of sombreness, futility, and malevolence dominates the poem but is alleviated by sudden flashes of grace, instances of dignity and love, usually revealed through images of lightning, fire, or sunlight. The effect of such passages, when they occur, can be startlingly beautiful, implying a kind of revivification, a rebirth into life in its plenitude that comes close to a religious affirmation of living for Kinnell.

> A girl and I are lying
> on the grass of the levee. Two
> birds whirr overhead. We lie close,
> as if having waked
> in bodies of glory.
>
> And putting on again
> its skin of light, the river
> bends into view. We watch it, rising
> between the levees, flooding for the sky,
> and hear it,
> a hundred feet down, pressing its long weight
> deeper into the world.
>
> The birds have gone,
> we wander slowly homeward, lost
> in the history of every step . . .

Then too one must remark the achievement of the descriptive portions of the poem, in which Kinnell, writing in a line of descent from Whitman and the Roethke of *North American Sequence*, catches with a richness and precision of language the strange, poignant lyricism of American rivers:

> the Ten Mile of Hornpout,
> the Drac hissing in its bed of sand,
> the Ruknabad crossed by ghosts of nightingales,

> the Passumpsic bursting down its length in spring,
> the East River of Fishes, the more haunting for not
>   having had a past either,
> and this Mississippi coursing down now through the silt of
>   all its days,
> and the Tangipahoa, snake-cracked, lifting with a little
>   rush from the hills and going out in thick, under-
>   nourished greenery.

In the midst of these changing scenes, memories and perceptions sharp with pain, nostalgia, disgust, and intermittent joy, Kinnell centers his imagination on a journey to Hell, hunting some revelation about the life of this country among the condemned dead: "The burning fodder dowses down,/seeking the snagged/bodies of the water buried. . . ." A different sort of Aeneas, he takes "a tassel of moss from a limb" and starts on his way, led by the boy Henry David "over the plain of crushed asphodels" to meet a horrendous scarecrow Charon, who ferries them to the inner precincts of the underworld. Subsequent sections, dramatizing the punishments of such offenders against individual and society as Northern and Southern politicians, the Secretaries of Profit and Sanctimony, and even a well-meaning liberal, whose appearance in this place greatly disturbs the poet, struck me at times as both excessive and too derivative, their immediate ancestor being not Dante but the Ezra Pound of the "Hell" *Cantos* XIV and XV. For all the likely justice done here to those who deserve it, these tortures do not realize the effect Kinnell wants; the reader turns aside finally with no sense of moral triumph or fulfillment but with feelings of revulsion:

> On the shore four souls
> cry out in pain, one lashed
> by red suspenders to an
> ever-revolving wheel, one with
> red patches on the seat of his pants
> shrieking while paunchy vultures
> stab and gobble at his bourbon-squirting liver,
> one pushing uphill

> his own belly puffed up with the blood-money
> he extorted on earth, that crashes back
> and crushes him, one
> standing up to his neck
> in the vomit he caused the living to puke . . .

Journeying on, the poet and his guide pass "The Mystic River," where crowds drink Lethean waters that run down "from Calvary's Mountain," and an enigmatic "Camp Ground," whose character is not disclosed, for the mists of the underworld close about Kinnell and his mind lapses into unconsciousness. When he awakens, it is to "a tiny cell far within" his brain, a jail cell as well, and there he envisages an anonymous man "of noble face," identifiable as Thoreau, who in anguish and self-torment, "wiping/a pile of knife-blades clean/in the rags of his body," tries to expiate the sins of American history:

> "Hard to wash off . . .
> buffalo blood . . . Indian blood . . ." he mutters,
> at each swipe singing, *"mein herz! mein herz!"*

Confessing that he had sought a love above the human, unencumbered by the flesh, and that he really "only loved [his] purity," Thoreau fades out, leaving Kinnell with "a letter for the blind" which places upon him his own guilt, the burden of his obligations as a man. The poem ends with a vision of "the last river" dividing a black man on one side from a white man on the other; between them, in the middle, stands a symbolic figure whose qualities not only erase the obvious differences of pigmentation in the other two men but also radiate, through the now familiar imagery of lightning and flame, suggestions of a nearly divine power, harmony, grace. (One recollects, reading this passage, lines which occur early in the poem: ". . . then lightning flashed/path strung out a moment across the storm,/bolt of love even made of hellfire/between any strange life and any strange life . . ."):

> a man of no color,
> body of beryl,

> face of lightning,
> eyes lamps of wildfire,
> arms and feet of polished brass.

The figure speaks, prophesying a national agony, a crisis of relations that will tax citizens extraordinarily; but as he begins his appeal to men's virtues, in a horrifying instant, this visionary idol crumbles and is transformed into the hideous scarecrow Charon, on whose ferry Kinnell previously entered Hell. Ironically, the "last river" has become that of the underworld:

> . . . he is
> falling to pieces,
> no nose left,
> no hair,
> no teeth,
> limbs dangling from prayer-knots and rags,
>
> waiting by the grief-tree
> of the last river.

The possible implications of this conclusion are numerous, and Kinnell allows the reader to tease them out for himself. One can say, nonetheless, that this collapse of the ideal into the vicissitudes and mortality of the real, like Thoreau's recognition in the poem of the necessary taint of the physical, the humanly imperfect in existence, conforms with the attitude toward experience Kinnell has developed so forcefully in his work. It is noteworthy that both Thoreau and the "man of no color" finish clothed in "body rags," the tattered evidence of their encounters with the rough actualities of the world. Inasmuch as Kinnell identifies himself with his vision and can "choke down these last poison wafers" bequeathed him in Thoreau's parting message (*"For Galway alone./I send you my mortality./Which leans out from itself, to spit on itself./Which you would not touch./All you have known."*), the words and images of this poem, lifted from his own deep-felt moments of experience, are "the prayer-knots and rags" of his life. Though there are a few spots where the poem weakens, especially in parts of the Hell episode, as a whole it leaves, like most of its author's writing, a profound impression, as of something lived through.

"Testament of the Thief," "The Porcupine," and "The Bear" create similar indelible effects but do so with, if anything, more raw violence, undisguised, earthy matter-of-factness—in short, whatever means will permit Kinnell to shortcut poetical niceties and cleave to the bare truth of his perceivings. The truth or vision contained in these poems cannot be readily abstracted; it is extremely personal —indeed, the poems seem to me the most personal Kinnell has written—yet it involves no more than a continuation of his quest for the fundamentals of existence. Each poem of the three appears composed at the very frontiers of experience, the imagination working against any restraints in order to achieve the shocking dimensions of its discoveries. So it is that Kinnell identifies in the poems with fierce, hardened, alienated creatures—thief, porcupine, and bear—shares their mania "for the poison fumes of the real," endures their bodily suffering and death to arrive at a knowledge of himself in them.

"Testament of the Thief" opens with the thief already dead on the gallows. The poem progresses by jumping to two other outcasts—a coolie and a beggar—who sit nearby, undisturbed by the swinging corpse, and then to another pariah, the keeper of an opium den, a specialist in supplying illusions and dreams in which members of society take refuge from reality, and whose attitude involves no moral scruples, only practical business considerations. From section to section stress falls on the elementals of life, on the creative/destructive processes ruling man and beast that have long been a feature of Kinnell's work:

> Under the breeze, in the dusk,
> the poor cluster at tiny
> pushcarts of fire, eating
> boiled beets,
> gut,
> tongue,
> testicle,
> cheeks, forehead, little feet.

Life feeds on life to save itself: it is this hard but basic law of earth on which many of the poem's images concentrate. In the environment of the poor, whose lives are pared to the rudimentary bone, the thief once wandered; the ground where he slept retains the imprint of his body. Kinnell halts the reader here, admonishes him of the basic realities of daily life, and hints, with perhaps an indirect rejection of Yeats's exalted, courtly conception of the poet's role at the end of "Sailing to Byzantium," that the true sources of poetry more properly lie in this place:

> Stop a moment, on his bones' dents,
> stand without moving, listen
> to the ordinary people
> as they pass. They do not sing
> of what is gone or to come, they sing of
> the old testaments of their lives,
> the little meals,
> the airs,
> the streets of our time.

These lines keep to the spirit of Verlaine's "tout le reste est littérature" or Henry Miller's declaration at the outset of *Black Spring*: "What is not in the open street is false, derived, that is to say, *literature*." Surely, Kinnell's grappling in these three poems with the very blood and bones and guts of creatures, with life and death in their blunt material aspects, demonstrates his imaginative drive to gain utter authenticity in the essentials of his vision. This intention shows up plainly in the actual "testament" the thief leaves, "items" addressed respectively to the keeper of the opium den, the beggar, the coolie, and "the pewk-worm" of torment and mortality who "lives all his life in our flesh." To each of them his legacy must come as an education in harsh reality, the dispersal of hope or illusion; only the "pewk-worm" fits into a different category, and this is indicated by putting the stanza about him in a final, separate section. The "opium master/dying in paradise," a world of inhaled, manufactured dreams, receives the thief's nose, in a key statement we have already seen, "in working disorder,/crazed/ for the poison fumes of the real." For the beggar who lies asleep, wallowing in erotic dreams of the "girl friends/of his youth," he offers "their/ iron faithfulness to loss." And to the coolie, whose life is hard labor and "whose skeleton/shall howl for its dust like any other" in the common fate of death, he gives, in a burst of extravagant language, "this/ultimate ruckus on the groan-meat," which is to say, the rending chaos of the body. The poem concludes with the thief's legacy to the "pewk-worm," inhabiting man's flesh and slowly boring away at him, consuming him from within, whom "you can drag forth/only by winding him up on a matchstick/a quarter turn a day for the rest of your days," so inseparable has he become from the person of his victim. This worm is, in fact, the determined principle of corruption bred into man's nature; therefore the thief's gift to him, "this map of my innards," signifies a recognition and acceptance of this inevitable condition, infused with wry, grim humor. Giving final, unquestionable support to this testament of the thief is the remembered brutal concreteness of death, his "thief-shadow lunging by the breeze" at the end of a rope and presiding over the entire poem.

Kinnell moves from description through analogy to conclude finally in identification with the porcupine in the poem of that title. First presented as a voracious creature, the porcupine is afterward linked, in the bold, outspoken manner of these recent poems, with humans:

> In character
> he resembles us in seven ways:
> he puts his mark on outhouses,
> he alchemizes by moonlight,
> he shits on the run,
> he uses his tail for climbing,
> he chuckles softly to himself when scared,
> he's overcrowded if there's more than one of him per five acres,
> his eyes have their own inner redness.

This extravagance of tone and statement increases and the porcupine emerges as a fantastic, obsessed animal whose single devotion is to "gouge the world/empty of us, hack and crater/it/until it is nothing if that/could rinse it of all our sweat and pathos." So he is addicted to everything man's flesh has touched and soiled, "objects/steeped in the juice of fingertips/ . . . surfaces wetted down/ with fist grease and elbow oil," and in an exuberant fashion Kinnell claims him as an "ultra-/Rilkean angel," one in whom the tarnished things of the world find an honest measure of their value, one

> for whom the true
> portion of the sweetness of earth
> is one of those bottom-heavy, glittering, saccadic bits
> of salt water that splash down
> the haunted ravines of a human face.

In contrast to the imagined creature he has built up thus far, Kinnell turns suddenly in the fourth part to give a straightforward but quite grisly account of the shooting of a porcupine by a farmer. But it grows clear that in this episode, as in the earlier parts of the poem, we are being treated to a display of persistence, a dogged tenacity toward life which exists to the point of annihilation. In the end the furious efforts of the dying animal seem no less astonishing than the poet's previous depiction of his curious inclinations:

> A farmer shot a porcupine three times
> as it dozed on a tree limb. On
> the way down it tore open its belly
> on a broken
> branch, hooked its gut,
> and went on falling. On the ground
> it sprang to its feet, and
> paying out gut heaved
> and spartled through a hundred feet of goldenrod
> before
> the abrupt emptiness.

After a brief stanza in which Kinnell announces that the sacred books of the ancient Zoroastrians reserve a place in Hell for those who destroy porcupines, the poem shifts its center to the poet's own life. Lying sleepless and disturbed, he envisages himself as undergoing metamorphosis, "the fatty sheath of the man/melting off." With the disappearance of his human features, the inward torments of self-consciousness also vanish; whatever pained his thoughts and feelings before changes into outward aggression. The transformation complete, he has become the porcupine: "a red-eyed, hardtoothed, arrow-stuck urchin/tossing up mattress feathers,/pricking the/woman beside me until she cries." Having identified himself thoroughly with this animal, he can see the aptness of the alteration in terms of his past experience. Pierced with the arrows of his quills, he has suffered, in the woundings and dyings imposed by existence, like a "Saint/Sebastian of the/scared heart," indeed, has felt himself disemboweled like the porcupine shot from

> And fallen from high places
> I have fled, have
> jogged
> over fields of goldenrod,
> terrified, seeking home,
> and among flowers
> I have come to myself empty, the rope
> strung out behind me
> in the fall sun
> suddenly glorified with all my blood.

The dramatic horror of such remembrance is matched by the desolate mood with which the last stanza begins. Here Kinnell maintains his altered identity, which should be interpreted not as subhuman but as the human reduced by lacerating acquaintance with life to a level of fierce struggling to keep a hold on it under narrowed, unaccommodating circumstances. In the final sense, his tenacious fight for survival, his determination to forage the world for sustenance in spite of a crippling feeling of personal emptiness, wins respect for this poet-turned-porcupine. And beyond this basic impulse to stay alive, to keep on going, the images of thistled and thorned flowers, so close to the sharp, bristling porcupine quills,

imply something more: a rough, wild beauty of bloom and blossom
—or translating these into terms of Kinnell's life as the effort to
create poems—which the rude contest for existence may yield:

> And tonight I think I prowl broken
> skulled or vacant as a
> sucked egg in the wintry meadow, softly chuckling, blank
> template of myself, dragging
> a starved belly through lichflowered acres,
> where
> burdock looses the arks of its seed
> and thistle holds up its lost blooms
> and rosebushes in the wind scrape their dead limbs
> for the forced-fire
> of roses.

From this dark condition of the spirit, then, there rises an affirming gesture which, rather characteristically for Kinnell, is glimpsed
through analogies with nature. What the private implications of
the attitude taken at the end of the poem are for him we cannot
say, nor is it a matter of importance for the reader. What does matter is that the severe, at times repellent, poetic myth created in "The
Porcupine" incarnates a view of ourselves that, left to our own devices, we should probably not be hardy or unflinching enough to
formulate. The same must be said for "Testament of the Thief,"
and certainly for "The Bear." In the latter the quest for identification with the beast is even more urgent, violent, and terrifyingly
absolute; the whole poem possesses the aura of symbolic nightmare
in which the meaning may prove elusive but the details are dread-
fully realistic. The poet goes off at once on the track of the bear;
no hesitations or deliberations are involved, for every step proceeds
with a predetermined and frighteningly rigid logic, while, nonetheless, nothing appears reasonable or humane. The manufacture
of the fatal bait with its vicious sharpened wolf's rib for the bear to
swallow marks the first stage in a hunt of ever more agonizing,
distasteful, yet necessary proportions. As he follows the track of

blood from its hemorrhage, the poet gradually adopts some of the beast's behavior. The quest is evidently preparing him through initiatory processes for his last transformation, and these can be both repulsive and hardening:

> On the third day I begin to starve,
> at nightfall I bend down as I knew I would
> at a turd sopped in blood,
> and hesitate, and pick it up,
> and thrust it in my mouth, and gnash it down,
> and rise
> and go on running.

With the exactitude of ritualized dream the hunter-poet, "living by now on bear blood alone," after seven days sights the dead animal, "a scraggled,/steamy hulk," and soon, with a ruthlessness and a ravenous hunger that would do credit to the bear, he is devouring its flesh, assimilating its strength and nature. At last he opens its hide, merges his identity with the bear's, and falls asleep in its skin. But the process has not been completed. If this poem exhibits the qualities of some awful dream from its beginning, then the sections immediately subsequent to the one in which he enters the bear's body compose a dream-within-a-dream that brings the hunter-poet closer to the goal of his quest. For now, wrapped in the flesh and fur of the animal, sated with its blood and meat, he must dream as he sleeps there that beast's agonizing death journey, of which he is the cause, as if it were his own. Once again, in these fifth and sixth sections, Kinnell engages the most brutal sufferings the self can tolerate:

> 5
> And dream
> of lumbering flatfooted
> over the tundra,
> stabbed twice from within,
> splattering a trail behind me,
> splattering it out no matter which way I lurch,
> no matter which parabola of bear-transcendence,

which dance of solitude I attempt,
which gravity-clutched leap,
which trudge, which groan.

6
Until one day I totter and fall—
fall on this
stomach that has tried so hard to keep up,
to digest the blood as it leaked in,
to break up
and digest the bone itself: and now the breeze
blows over me, blows off
the hideous belches of ill-digested bear blood
and rotted stomach
and the ordinary, wretched odor of bear,

blows across
my sore, lolled tongue a song
or screech, until I think I must rise up
and dance. And I lie still.

The pain and the persistence resemble what we saw in "The Porcu-pine." In neither poem can the suffering creature elude its cruel destiny, its torturous death; such are the inexplicable premises of existence which Kinnell's poetry probes relentlessly from the start. But in his recent work he not only takes these realities as they come; he even searches them out with the intention of living them through to the finish, reaching toward the extreme, the rock-bottom of existence, so to speak, in order to find some final principle of being, a hard kernel of self that endures, and turn it to poetic ac-count. So, out of the hideous torments he undergoes in dreaming the bear's death as his own, comes the possibility of poetry—though one almost shies from the word "art" under the circumstances—more than the primitive "song or screech" blown from his ex-hausted mouth, or the sudden desire to perform a dance of death; it is a deeper, more personal sense of the poem and what animates it that emerges in the closing stanza after the hunter-poet awakens. He sees again the known landscape of winter, yet he further realizes

that now he is the bear, and has his own journey to make, strangely
nourished by the painful myth he has enacted:

> And one
> hairy-soled trudge stuck out before me,
> the next groaned out,
> the next,
> the next,
> the rest of my days I spend
> wandering: wondering
> what, anyway,
> was that sticky infusion, that rank flavor of blood, that
>   poetry, by which I lived?

This powerful dream-poem of the poet's initiation, which seems
to me in spite of its harshness to be ultimately quite strong in its
affirmation of existence, completes Galway Kinnell's latest book.
It also puts us in mind once more of the indivisibility for this fine
poet of "the man who suffers and the mind which creates"—a reversal of Eliot's well-known dictum. This indivisibility is a distinguishing mark of the work of many of the most important and
forceful younger American poets during the past fifteen years,
poets whose "poems take shape from the shapes of their emotions,
the shapes their minds make in thought."[7] Kinnell's growth as a
poet has traced such a pattern in close congruence with the events
of his life, his most fundamental perceptions and emotions, the
themes and images, obsessing his consciousness. As even a cursory
reading of his work would indicate, he is one of the most substantial, accomplished poets of a very talented generation. His future
poems should not be predicted but awaited with anticipation.[8]

7. Foreword to *Naked Poetry*, ed. Stephen Berg and Robert Mezey (Indianapolis and New York, 1969), p. xi.

8. Just as this volume of studies was completed, Kinnell published his extraordinary new *Book of Nightmares* (Boston, 1971), which continues through a
group of ten profoundly linked poems many of the preoccupations with existence,
death, and nothingness discussed above. Poetically speaking, it is a striking accomplishment and must stand as one of the imaginative landmarks of the 1970's.

There is something essential of Kinnell himself and of his poetry in
these memorable lines he wrote for Robert Frost:

> Who dwelt in access to that which other men
> Have burnt all their lives to get near, who heard
> The high wind, in gusts, seething
> From far off, headed through the trees exactly
> To this place where it must happen, who spent
> Your life on the point of giving away your heart
> To the dark trees, the dissolving woods,
> Into which you go at last, heart in hand, deep in . . .

5 Donald Hall's Poetry

I wake to sleep, and take my waking slow
—Theodore Roethke

Je ferme les yeux simplement
pour mieux voir
—Philippe Soupault

The recent appearance of *The Alligator Bride*, a volume of new and selected poems, provides a good occasion for looking at the development in Donald Hall's writing, where his work began, and the important alterations it has subsequently undergone. Of the poetic generation of the 1950's Hall is one of the most interesting and influential figures. As an editor, anthologist, and sometime critic, he has helped to shape a sense of current poetic history, its multiple ideas and aims; he has been an open proponent of pluralism in contemporary poetry and opposed to established critical theories and dogmas. Nowhere does he declare his attitudes more clearly and succinctly than in the admirable introduction to his anthology *Contemporary American Poetry* (1962). There he starts by noting the gradual downfall of the New Criticism as the "orthodoxy" dominating American poetry from "1925 to 1955," and then rightly observes that "typically the modern artist has allowed nothing to be beyond his consideration. He has acted as if restlessness were a conviction and has destroyed his own past in order to create a future. He has said to himself, like the policeman to the vagrant, 'Keep moving.'"

For present purposes I should like to shift attention from the general applicability of this statement and regard it instead as perfectly suitable to Hall's own career as a poet. Indeed, he has, in his own writing, and certainly in the life of imagination and feeling which lies behind it, charted the kind of course he detects in the work of many of his contemporaries, a course that demands at some crucial juncture radically decisive gestures, the destruction of a "past in order to create a future." That past in Hall's case becomes quite evident in his first two collections, *Exiles and Marriages* (1955) and *The Dark Houses* (1958), though the latter reveals tangible growth and the desire for change. The initial book, however, shows how closely he adhered to the then prevailing requirements of—in his own words—"symmetry, intellect, irony, and wit" derived from Eliot's criticism and the thought and practice of various modern critics. In a recent lecture, *The Inward Muse*, Hall remarks that he "grew up in the thick of the new criticism" and as he worked on his early poems "could sometimes hear the voice of Mr. Ransom" (whom he did not know) reminding him to be appropriately ironic; he adds that "it took ten years to get rid of that voice."[1] Doubtless, other poets of Hall's generation have known the same or similar experiences. In the later 1950's, however, the break with the critical establishment began, first with the arrival of Ginsberg and the Beats, but soon rejections came from every quarter. As it appears now, this movement has delivered poetry back into the hands of poets.

Hall's early poems, of which he wisely retains only a few—and these usually revised—in *The Alligator Bride*, are not wholly devoid of interest, especially since the reader can glimpse in them some of the areas of experience most meaningful to the poet and certain themes persisting in his work. But one can dismiss without regret, as Hall does, the slick, witty pieces such as "The Lone Ranger," "A Novelist," "Conduct and Work," "Apology," "Syllables of a Small Fig Tree," "Some Oddities," "Carol," "Cops and

1. I am greatly indebted to Mr. Hall for allowing me to use, in addition to published essays, various unpublished lecture and broadcast materials, and for permitting me to read manuscript versions of his new book, *The Yellow Room Love Poems.*

Robbers," "Nefas Tangerine," "Six Poets in Search of a Lawyer,"
"Lycanthropy Revisited," and various others, including the long
poem "Exile" (winner of the Newdigate Prize at Oxford), which
does reappear in the later collection, only reduced from one hundred to six lines. Formal skills, dexterity, irony, and intelligence
are all on view here, along with occasional echoes of mentors, but
the best one can say for these poems is that they exhibit a gift for
knowledgeable, polished versifying; today they seem dated and
very slight.

More support can be mustered for several other poems which
must have emerged from deeper sources in the poet and, corre-
spondingly, touch profound, truly sensitive chords of feeling in the
reader. Some of these are poems of New Hampshire, where Hall
spent summers on his grandparents' farm from the time he was a
small boy. The annual visits, the farm labors, his love for his grandparents and complex attachment to the slowly dying way of life
they knew provide material for quite a few poems in his first book
and after. It is also instructive, as well as pleasurable, to read the
fine prose memoirs of these farm experiences, published in 1961 as
String Too Short to Be Saved; from this book the background and
many of the details in a poem such as the moving "Elegy for Wesley
Wells" (his grandfather) become clear. That poem and "Old
Home Day"—both of them shortened and revised—are the best of
the early New Hampshire pieces and the only ones Hall has sal-
vaged. In the first version the "Elegy" lost something of its force
through lengthiness; in its present form it is still long, but the dead
farmer, his past, and the history of the region he inhabited have
become more intimately and vitally related. We realize soon after
the poem's beginning that Hall is writing from England; his distance from his home country not only increases the sense of loss
but also offers the perspective of exile which sharpens his vision of
the contours of Wesley Wells's life and inheritance, finally confirming his solidarity with it. The opening effectively renders the
atmosphere of absence and deprivation death creates which has
now descended upon the farm:

> Against the clapboards and the window panes
> The loud March whines with rain and heavy wind,
> In dark New Hampshire where his widow wakes.
> She cannot sleep. The familiar length is gone.
> I think across the clamorous Atlantic
> To where the farm lies hard against the foot
> Of Ragged Mountain, underneath Kearsarge.
> I speak his name against the beating sea.
>   His dogs will whimper through the webby barn,
> Where spiders close his tools in a pale gauze
> And wait for flies. The nervous woodchuck now
> Will waddle plumply through the world of weeds
> Eating wild peas as if he owned the land,
> And the fat hedgehog rob the apple trees.
> When next October's frosts harden the ground
> And fasten in the year's catastrophe,
> The farm will lie like driftwood,
> The farmer dead, and deep in his carved earth.

Following this passage, Hall shifts to historical considerations, to the richness of this region before the Civil War, which "took off the hired men" who cultivated the fields, so that in time these lands returned to their original state "thick with ashy pine." The poem continues by recounting the steadily worsening fortunes of the inhabitants—those who remained—and through the bizarre, disturbing image of an abandoned railroad and locomotive evokes the departure of progress and prosperity. (A more detailed description of this engine and its setting occur in *String Too Short to Be Saved*.)

> Deep in the forest now, half-covered up,
> The reddened track of an abandoned railroad
> Heaved in the frosts, in the roots of the tall pines;
> A locomotive stood
> Like a strange rock, red as the fallen needles.

Recalling the daily and seasonal routines of the farm that formed the basis for his grandfather's existence for so many years, the poet achieves an essential, durable picture of the man to be retained in memory, one which incorporates the honesty, stability, and unobtrusive heroism of that life:

> I number out the virtues that are dead,
> Remembering his soft, consistent voice,
> His gentleness, and most,
> The bone that showed in each deliberate word.

The poem's closing portions show Hall keeping a solitary vigil "on England's crowded shore" and realizing that his ties are to that "place and people" far off "in dark New Hampshire"; he ends envisaging his grandfather's body carried to the cemetery for burial.

"I cannot see the watch on my wrist/without knowing that I am dying," Hall writes in a poem from his second collection, *The Dark Houses*; and that acute sensitivity to time and mortality, acquired in part at least from his New Hampshire experience, develops into a constant element of his work. The most accomplished of the early poems seem possessed by intimations of death, loss, isolation, and guilt. In the shortened, rearranged version of "Old Home Day" the initial stanza blends images of man and landscape in a condition of general decay:

> Under the eyeless, staring lid,
> And in the pucker of a mouth,
> Gullied hayfields cave together
> And crumble in the August drouth.

And from the lengthy, rather tedious original text of "Exile," once a poem of four pages, Hall has extracted what were three parenthetical couplets set in the middle of different stanzas to make brief yet highly suggestive summaries of personal dilemmas. Each stanza designates a relationship valued by the poet which has now been violated, either through death, through the poet's own betrayal, or through the changing circumstances that influence an individual's life. None of the violations is elaborated in much detail; instead, a simplicity of language and description stimulates the reader's imagination, permitting him to tease out the possibilities and to discover similarities in his own experience. The final couplet, while it depicts a particular moment of knowledge, the realization that a person grows away from even his deepest roots and that he will return to the place of his origins only to find it alien and strange because he has himself altered, should not be understood merely as a third instance of perplexing loss in the poem. For if we view the three stanzas in sequence, we comprehend a certain kind of movement. In the first couplet death deprives the poet of a good friend, still in his boyhood. In the second, and most complex, he breaks off a relationship with a girl while he yet loves her—out of what hidden motives we are not sure—and suffers a period of remorse, then dismisses the incident from consciousness, though it obviously has not vanished since he must include it at the center of the poem (this experience turns up elsewhere in Hall's early poetry). Finally, in the concluding stanza, he visits his birthplace and thinks it has changed completely. What appears of primary importance in the poem, I believe, is that all of these events cause alterations in the poet, and the last couplet with its rhyme of grew/ new emphasizes the continuity of change in each life. The exile of the title denotes an unavoidable, recurrent aspect of existence: time and death exile us, and we even exile ourselves from others, yet we grow and mature from such experiences, always impelled forward by the promise of what is yet to come. Loss, then, creates the possibility of gain, and so, in this light, the third couplet slides ambiguously between estrangement and potentiality:

> A boy who played and talked and read with me
> Fell from a maple tree.

> I loved her, but I told her I did not,
> And wept, and then forgot.

> I walked the streets where I was born and grew,
> And all the streets were new.

"Wedding Party," a poem Hall uses to begin both *Exiles and Marriages* and *The Alligator Bride* (though in a shorter, improved form in the latter volume), takes up this theme of temporal change

and erosion and treats it in a slightly fantastic manner, especially
as the irrational elements are allowed to dominate in the new, condensed version with its total abandonment of verisimilitude. At the
very start imaginative vision dictates the order of details, which are
not given as we might expect, for the focus falls at once upon somewhat ominous figures rather than the bridal couple:

> The pock-marked player of the accordion
> Empties and fills his squeeze box in the corner,
> Kin to the tiny man who pours champagne,
> Kin to the caterer. These solemn men,
> Amid the sounds of silk and popping corks,
> Stand like pillars.

This odd group, ruling over the occasion as it turns out, mutes and
qualifies the conventional gaiety from the outset. The bride appears
after these men, in the last line and a half of the stanza, in a bizarre
analogy to the Virgin or some other female saint carried in effigy
by a religious procession through a throng of worshipers:

> And the white bride
> Moves through the crowd as a chaired relic moves.

Certainly, the phrase "chaired relic" induces a feeling of strange-
ness and also—quite importantly—first implies the ideas of time,
aging, and death so central to the poem's climactic vision. With
the end of the initial stanza, then, unpleasant expectations, though
as yet indefinite, have been established. In his original version Hall
included a middle stanza which identified the poem's speaker as
a guest invited at the last moment, a "friend to the bride's rejected
suitor," added further unnecessary filler, and finished with "summer twilight" and the threat of an approaching storm. This stanza
merely dissipated the curious atmosphere generated by the preceding one and made concessions to ordinariness or normalcy which
the reader, intent upon the irreality of the situation, couldn't care
about less. Now, with such externals removed, the last stanza immediately picks up and magnifies the disquieting details. The ac-

cordionist suddenly assumes the gigantic, terrifying proportions of a god or fate presiding over these ceremonies. Under his spell, as if in a hallucination, the bride's marriage and future life are envisaged as already completed, transformed into a few faded memories, and, by implication, nearing death. (It is perhaps worth noting that in neither version is the groom mentioned.) The storm which breaks, no longer related to the thundershower of the omitted stanza, thus can be understood metaphorically as the tempest of time striking the bride and, I believe, her guests as well, ravaging their lives, while above them looms the accordionist-god, his instrument directing the rhythms of existence, of air in and out of lungs:

> Now all at once the pock-marked player grows
> Immense and terrible beside the bride
> Whose marriage withers to a rind of years
> And curling photographs in a dry box;
> And in the storm that hurls upon the room
> Above the crowd he holds his breathing box
> That only empties, fills, empties, fills.

In *The Dark Houses* Hall's work develops along lines similar to those distinguishing the better pieces in his first book. There are fewer poems that seem all skill and fancy, and more that try to reach those concealed roots of experience on which imagination thrives. Once again, as with most of the superior poems from *Exiles and Marriages*, there is an obvious concern with death, time's passage, and with the missed opportunities for a full existence. In "Christmas Eve in Whitneyville," an elegy for his father, the poet reveals an incisive social awareness which draws ironic pictures of middle-class isolationism on this feast day; each family is locked in its home as if it were a cell:

> Each car is put away in each garage;
> Each husband home from work, to celebrate,
> Has closed his house around him like a cage,
> And wedged the tree until the tree stood straight.

Hall proceeds to summarize his father's business career, how after success he could afford trips to Europe, where, unable to forget work, he "took the time to think how yearly gains,/Profit and volume made the business grow." Now, dying early at fifty-two, he has acquired money but has seen little of life or the world; his comment, recalled by the poet, discloses the regret and ambivalence he feels toward the close of his fatal illness:

> "The things you had to miss," you said last week,
> "Or thought you had to, take your breath away."
> You propped yourself on pillows, where your cheek
> Was hollow, stubbled lightly with new gray.

Reflecting on this devotion to acquisitiveness, Hall comes again to the image of enclosure; the house which resembled a "cage" becomes synonymous with a mode of living that is itself a form of imprisonment. The poet looks elsewhere for liberation and reward:

> This love is jail; another sets us free.

Without anger but in a mood of determination, Hall leaves his father buried among the people who still pursue the same ends he has rejected. For the poet it is a moment of farewell and departure in search of a different, more abundant existence. The imagery of darkness links the town's sleeping inhabitants with the dead who lie in its cemetery. In different ways all of them are denied life:

> The lights go out and it is Christmas Day.
> The stones are white, the grass is black and deep;
> I will go back and leave you here to stay,
> While the dark houses harden into sleep.

Certain other poems in this second collection also exhibit social interests and criticism;[2] the best of these are "1934," which treats effects of the Depression in New Hampshire, and "The Foundations of American Industry," a sharp, ironic depiction of wasted

---

2. For a perceptive discussion of the social dimensions of Hall's poetry, see "Crunk" [Robert Bly], "The Poetry of Donald Hall," *The Fifties*, 3 (1959), pp. 32–46.

life among auto workers whose fathers had labored in government projects during the 1930's. Their jobs are mechanized by assembly line techniques, their leisure is aimless and empty:

> In the Ford plant
> the generators
> move quickly on
> belts, a thousand now
> an hour. New men
> move to the belt when
> the shift comes.
>
> For the most part
> the men are young, and
> go home to their
> Fords, and drive around,
> or watch TV,
> sleep, and then go work,
> towards payday;
>
> when they walk home
> they walk on sidewalks
> marked W
> P A 38;
> their old men made
> them, and they walk on
> their fathers.

Notable here is the entirely successful adoption of a deliberately flat, conversational manner, coupled with the type of observation and rhythmical movement associated with William Carlos Williams and, later, David Ignatow. One senses the attempt on Hall's part to "make it new," in Pound's phrase, to look beyond the formal confinements of most of his writing up to this point and reduce the margin between the poet and his material, or to put it in terms of the Imagists, again borrowing from Pound: "Direct treatment of the 'thing' whether subjective or objective." While his later poems—with striking exceptions such as "Woolworth's" and "Crew-cuts" from *The Alligator Bride*—rarely venture into areas of social or political commentary, the present piece offers strong hints of the kind of freedom, economy, simplicity, and directness of statement (even when the implications of the imagery are strange or oblique) Hall will arrive at six years afterward with *A Roof of Tiger Lilies* (1964).

A few more poems in *The Dark Houses* are quite effective in their individual ways and prepare for further achievements. These include "Religious Articles" (shortened, revised, and called "'I Come to the Garden Alone'" in *The Alligator Bride*), "Three Poems from Edvard Munch," "The Three Movements," "Waiting on the Corners" (reduced to the first of seven sections in its later version), "The Presences of Death," and "Revelations, Contradictions" (the last two omitted from *The Alligator Bride*). In each of these poems Hall struggles toward a greater degree of self-knowledge or seeks a more penetrating intuition of the circumstances of human existence; gradually he is breaking away from the superficial intelligence that rules his previous writing. The conclusion of "Religious Articles," in which the poet visits an old church he attended in childhood and thinks about the dead members of his family lamenting the deprivation and loss of their lives, urges on him an agnostic, skeptical attitude, but one which will also force him to take up the burden of his own life. The voices of the dead, he realizes, are voices he lends them; as they speak all pretense is stripped away:

> "We who do not exist make noises
> only in you. Your illusion says
> that we who are cheated and broken
> croon our words to the living again.
> You must not believe in anything;
> you who feel cheated are crooning."

And in "Revelations, Contradictions" Hall scrutinizes intently his alternating perceptions of order and disorder, of fragmentation and nothingness with symmetry and fullness of being; between them stands the perceiving self. At the end he is compelled to accept contrariety as a fundamental principle: "Things are their opposites. To understand/Today's solution makes tomorrow's lie."

Pressing further beyond the surfaces and the barriers of false appearance and convention with which experience is frequently masked, the poet confronts emptiness, cruelty and violence, metaphysical terror, and death in the poems inspired by Munch's three pictures, "The Scream," "Marat's Death," and "The Kiss" (the later, shortened versions are most satisfactory), and in "Waiting on the Corners." What Hall says in "The Scream" is true for all of these poems: "Existence is laid bare," and it is an existence turned back upon itself, without spiritual appeal. "The blood not Christ's,/ blood of death without resurrection,/winds flatly in the air," Hall observes of the surging background to Munch's agonized figure, and concludes that this picture has "not even the pause,/the repose of art that has distance." Distance. It is exactly such emotional and experiential spacing we have already seen Hall beginning to eliminate from his poetry. The third poem of the original sequence "Waiting on the Corners" brings a new lucidity and intimacy of vision to bear upon the poet himself. In keeping with one of the main themes of the sequence, the poem finishes on a level of psychological and spiritual vacancy, but prior to that conclusion it enters a highly subjective area of the speaker's life, probing and dramatizing vividly in pulsing rhythms a crisis of the self, an excruciating symbolic death and rebirth in the psyche which leaves its victim changed but also emptied out. In its own fashion this poem displays affinities with some of Theodore Roethke's work, "The Return," for example, and with the intense poetry of self-revelation written by Anne Sexton and Sylvia Plath. But it is chiefly significant in terms of Hall's efforts to increase the depth and authenticity of his poetic experience:

> At least once before
> my skin has felt rough fingers
> pull my eyelids down,
> my body laid
> on the floor like clothes.

I struggled against the pit
like a bull in the yards.
I tried
to lift myself out by willing,
for I knew
what I hated the most.
After I died, my eyes
opened to find the colors
as bright as knives.
It was necessary to die,
for a few moments only
to give up
whatever I owned, and all
I might become, and the sight,
taste, touch, and smell
of the particular world.
There, in the pit,
all willing gone from me,
no more an animal
in hatred,
"You" (I heard a voice)
"who have lost everything
want nothing."

The interior concentration of this poem and its reading of a baro-
meter of hidden emotional stresses and dilemmas place it as prophetic of the deliberate turning Hall's work will soon take.

The final poem in *The Dark Houses* is "The Three Movements,"
and through irregular lines and phrasing, suggestive of the uncertain, searching efforts of the poet's mind, it also leads him toward
the brink of anticipated changes in his writing. The poem involves
a poetic or imaginative quest to replenish his art, but it cannot be
achieved simply by looking to tradition, learning from others:

It is not in the books
that he is looking, nor for
a new book, nor
documents of any kind . . .

The lack of desire for "a new book" indicates, I think, a wish to reach beyond the restrictions of literary convention. But what he seeks is not available to the poet effortlessly either, occurring like a sudden event in nature:

> ... nor
> does he expect it to be like the wind,
> that, when you touch it, tears
> without a sound of tearing, nor
> like the rain
> water
> that becomes
> grass in the sun.

The image that comes to him when he envisages his goal is that of a person, alert, sensitive, resolute, attentive to experience; and it is difficult not to see this figure as a re-creation of the poet's self, in the sense in which, say, Whitman, Yeats, Rilke, or Neruda make themselves over in their art to assimilate more life, more of reality into poetry. In short, Hall recognizes that he must make himself over in order to transform his writing; or, as Robert Bly remarks, "Since the country [America] has no image of a poet as a poet, a poet to develop must learn to imagine himself":

> He
> expects that when he finds it,
> it will be
> like a man, visible, alive
> to what has happened and what
> will happen, with
> firmness in its face, seeing
> exactly what is, without
> measure of change, and not
> like documents,
> or rain in the grass.

In a second stanza he entertains his doubts and hesitations; perhaps what he requires "is not/for the finding," and the previously dismissed alternatives must be accepted as the only possibilities after all. But in the last stanza he acknowledges that he has slighted "the movement/that intrigues/all thinking," a process whereby the covert, the oblique, the unconscious aspects of the mind are drawn into focus; from this "movement" will emerge the startling, unexpected image of the poetic self whose identity is exact, unmistakable:

> It is
> the movement which works through,
> which discovers itself
> in alleys, in
> sleep, not
> expected and not
> in the books of words and phrases
> nor the various paints and edges
> of scenery.
> It is, he says,
> familiar when come upon,
> glimpsed
> as in a mirror
> unpredicted,
> and it appears
> to understand. It is
> like himself, only visible.

With the awareness of new imaginative resources announced at the close of "The Three Movements" Hall's poetry departs from past practices and sets out for unexplored territories of experience. The areas into which he moves after his own fashion are regions of inwardness, the preconscious, the peripheries of sleep, the moods of reverie and daydream, which is to say, wherever the energies of the interior life, the life of images and dreams rich with association, persist, and what Hall has termed "the vatic voice" can speak and be heard. In this endeavor he has some remarkably illustrious modern predecessors such as Whitman, Rilke, Lawrence, Breton, Trakl, Desnos, Neruda, Vallejo, Eluard, and Roethke, among others, and certain of his more immediate contemporaries—Robert Bly, James Wright, W. S. Merwin, for example—who began to create a poetry which, as Bly noted in an interview printed in *The Sullen Art* (1963), "simply disregards the conscious and the intellectual structure of the mind entirely and, by the use of images, tries to bring forward another reality from *inward* experience." Meanwhile, several New York poets, John Ashbery, Kenneth Koch, and the late Frank O'Hara, closely linked with the influential painting *avant garde* (and, oddly enough, originally students at Harvard at the same time as Hall and Bly), were introducing their own modes of irrationalism and surrealist techniques into poetry.

In various essays and lectures Hall discusses the creative process in himself and in the work of other poets (see, for instance, his introduction to *A Choice of Whitman's Verse*, 1968), and he observes that the critical and technical powers operate instinctively upon the flow of images, intuitions, and details which the mind offers in moments of inspiration. Thus he rejects, in *The Inward Muse*, the "theoretical dualism of *creation* which provides material, and *criticism* which shapes it." But in a later lecture on *The Vatic Voice: Waiting and Listening* (printed in the *Michigan Quarterly Review*, Fall 1969) he tries to describe the passive attendance on creativity, the coming of words and images in a sudden release, and the nature of this expression from far within ourselves. Hall begins by seeking a fundamental principle:

> A premise: within every human being there is the vatic voice. *Vates* was the Greek word for the inspired bard, speaking the words of a god. To most people, this voice speaks only in dream, and only in unremembered dream. The voice may shout messages into the sleeping ear, but a guard at the horned gate prevents the waking mind from remembering, listening, interpreting. It is the vatic voice (which is not necessarily able to write good poetry, or even passable grammar) which rushes forth the words of excited recognition, which supplies what we call inspiration. And inspiration, a breathing-into, is a perfectly expressive metaphor: "Not I, not I, but the wind that blows through me!" as Lawrence says. Or Shelley's

"Ode to the West Wind." We are passive to the vatic voice, as the cloud or the tree is passive to the wind.

For the poet, indeed for any man, it is necessary in Hall's opinion to hear this voice, to listen for it, away from the strictures of logic or reasoning, the demands of practicality, the noise and distraction of our urbanized society, "not only to make poems, or to invent a new theory of linguistics, but because it feels good, because it is healing and therapeutic, because it helps us to understand ourselves and to be able to love other people." Attention to this voice revives and animates the imaginative life, the apprehension of the world, as Hall says, children know and the poet, among others, needs to rediscover if his work is to achieve depth, resonance, true poetic quality. A few paragraphs devoted to Hall's personal habits, deliberate reliance on dream and reverie as a means of stimulating the imagination and stirring the vatic voice to speech (he notes that the "Two characteristics that distinguish the vatic voice from normal discourse are that it is always original, and that we feel passive to it. We are surprised by it, and we may very well, having uttered its words, not know what we mean.") are of particular interest for the light they cast on experiences in back of much of the poetry included in *A Roof of Tiger Lilies* and *The Alligator Bride*. Then too these disclosures may remind us, as Gaston Bachelard remarks, how in order to comprehend what a poet has formulated from his creative reverie we must join him in dreaming it as we read. One can likewise see resemblances between Hall's intentions and the investigation and experimentation with sleep, dreams, and their imagery conducted by André Breton, Robert Desnos, and other Surrealists.

Sometimes I have tried to keep in touch with this vatic voice by sleeping a lot. Taking short naps can be a great means of keeping the channel open. There is that wonderful long, delicious slide or drift down heavy air to the bottom of sleep, which you touch for only a moment, and then there is the floating up again more swiftly, through an incredible world of images, sometimes in bright colors.

I come out of these fifteen or twenty minute naps, not with phrases of poetry, but wholly refreshed with the experience of losing control and entering a world of apparent total freedom. I wake with great energy. On occasion, I remember phrases or scenes from dreams—either night dreams, or nap dreams, or waking fantasy dreams—take these phrases or images directly into a poem. That happens, but it is not the only virtue of dream. Dream is the spirit dying into the underworld, and being born again.

There is also the deliberate farming of daydream. There is a way in which you can daydream quite loosely, but also observe yourself. You watch the strange associations, the movements. These associations are frequently trying to tell us something. The association is always there for some reason. Listen. When you hum a tune, remember the words that go with the tune and you will usually hear some part of your mind commenting on another part of your mind, or on some recent action.

There is something I want to call peripheral vision, and I don't mean anything optical. If you talk about a dream with an analyst, and there is an old battered table in the dream that you casually mention, he may well say, "What about this table? What did it look like?" Often these little details are so important. When I am listening to something passively speaking out of me, I don't attempt to choose what is most important, I try to listen to all of it. I never know what is going to be the most important message until I have lived with it for a while. Very frequently, the real subject matter is something only glimpsed, as it were out of the corner of the eye. Often the association which at first glance appears crazy and irrelevant ultimately leads to the understanding, and tells what we did not know before.

With these observations of Hall's before us we can better understand the nature of that "movement" of the mind in the act of discovering the materials of a poem. And these materials, whose sources lie in subterranean levels of the self, when gathered and shaped into the final form of the completed poem, will result in a poetry of dream and inward vision, a kind of surrealism already familiar in modern European and Latin American literature, "ultimately a poetry of the deep mind all men share," in Hall's words about Whitman. Emphasis shifts from the techniques of verse-making, the outside or external aspects of the poem, to "spirit" or vision, the force within the poet animating and relating his images. Obviously, this does not mean that formal considerations are dispensed with altogether—one still finds Hall employing various prosodic devices; but the general tendency is toward greater looseness or openness of form, away from iambics and rhyming. The strength of such poetry depends to a considerable degree on the phrasing, the rhythm and movement of lines as both imaginative *and* musical units within the whole, as well as on diction, imagery, and intensity or authenticity of vision. Its aim is finally, in a paradoxical phrase, to awaken the reader to dreams, which is to say, turn him away from the superficialities that consume his outward existence and indicate the immense hidden reservoirs of life within him. Poetry of this order rehabilitates the powers of imagination, of dreaming on the world, and may even be said to revive a sense of the sacred, as it certainly does in some poems of Hall's, Merwin's, Bly's, Dickey's, and Wright's, though there is no specifically orthodox theological framework involved. The mysterious range of poetic possibilities disclosed to Hall through this transformation of his art is best described, however, by the poet himself briefly but evocatively in "The Poem," placed in the first section of *A Roof of Tiger Lilies*:

> It discovers by night
> what the day hid from it.
> Sometimes it turns itself
> into an animal.
> In summer it takes long walks
> by itself where meadows
> fold back from ditches.
> Once it stood still
> in a quiet row of machines.
> Who knows
> what it is thinking?

What this kind of poetry is thinking is a question readers coming upon it for the first time may well ask, for unlike, say, a Metaphysical poem of witty conceits and learned allusions, it yields little to rigorous logical analysis—a reason perhaps why Surrealism, Expressionism, the contemporary poets of France, Germany, Spain, Italy, and Latin America, with a few exceptions such as Valéry and Rilke, never engaged most of our important critics of the past three decades, while European critics have long been studying them. If that situation in America is being revised now, it is chiefly due to the prose writings of poets themselves and to the extraordinary increase in the enterprise of translation. Hall's "The Poem" stands both as a statement of the sources and procedures of his new work and as an example of it. We understand that this is so, yet at the same time we cannot "translate" the substance of the poem from its images into a more rational and readily assimilable prose paraphrase—that is, to borrow a phrase of James Dickey's, *use up* the imaginative or creative matter which is the poem by the process of exegesis. Just as this type of poetry originates in the interior life and evokes that life, so the imagery and implications draw inward in the poem, and the reader must follow them toward the center rather than try to pull them away from the poem for inspection and explanation. Of course, I am not saying that the poem means nothing, but that the meaning is implicit, inherent in the particular arrangement of images and movement of lines bearing them. To be sure, this is true of virtually all poems, but we are dealing here with a kind of poem that is purposively irrational, within whose imaginative context meaning emerges only by suggestion, evocation, indirection, or obliquity. Only by living within the body of images, or floating on them, to use Hall's own description, do we approach a point of comprehension; then themes and motifs make themselves felt, patterns of emotion are revealed. As the opening lines of "The Poem" imply, the poetic imagination looks to the "night" world of dream, reverie, the preconscious and the unconscious in preference to the daylight world which demands lucidity, not mystery; rational coherence, not indefiniteness or suggestion.

This poem also exhibits what might be called the infinite capacity of the poetic imagination for extending itself, for rejecting any kinds of restriction upon the realms of experience it can partake of—animals, summer meadows, machines: the strange evocativeness of these possibilities for the poem tells the reader something of how such poetry should be apprehended.

In correspondence with these remarks, the dominant mood or atmosphere of the majority of poems in *A Roof of Tiger Lilies* is that of reverie, daydream, or the more enigmatic narrative of the night dream which displays characteristic qualities of ellipsis, condensation, and displacement. Frequently, a poem starts off with an external, objective situation or observation; then gradually, as the poet's mind loosens its narrow or rigid focus, barriers fall, and associations, memories, images begin to assert themselves: the poem thus slips inward, unfolding its interior drama. The themes of these poems remain close to those of Hall's earlier writing, but now they are explored from within; their roots in the psyche of the poet become essential material for his work. "The Snow," the first poem in the collection, provides an introductory illustration. In the beginning stanzas the speaker watches snow falling outside his window. As it takes over his perceptions, memories are stirred, then hidden affective resonances until, at the close of the second stanza, his sight seems blurred, as if he were physically outside in a blinding snow, though he has really moved inside himself, to the border of his inner world and its vision:

> Snow is in the oak.
> Behind the thick, whitening
> air which the wind drives,
> the weight of the sun
> presses the snow
> on the pane of my window.
>
> I remember snows and my walking
> through their first fall in cities,
> asleep or drunk
> with the slow, desperate falling.

> The snow blurs in my eyes
> with other snows.

In his lecture *The Inward Muse* (*Michigan Quarterly Review*, Winter 1967), Hall notes how the poem got started, where it led him, and what he tried to accomplish during its composition:

> Poems begin any number of ways, but here is a frequent way. It is snowing, the first snow of the year. I become sleepy with the snow, I relax, daydream, enter that sleepy and almost hallucinating state I recognize as preluding a poem; my spirit wanders out of myself into the snow, and phrases come into my head. Suddenly, I realize that snow does this to me, every year, especially first snow. I must write about it in order to understand it. Snow is, in psycho-analytic language, over-determined for me. It is burdened with affect, heavy with a nameless emotion. Being over-determined, it must have multiple sources. I try to keep my attention diffuse and responsive to suggestion, my pen moving, as one thing leads to another down the page. I am trying to reach, be true to, exploit—the multiple sources of this over-determination.

It must be added that Hall continues by denying that he is merely taking "dictation of [his] unconscious mind" here, for he insists that such dictation is too rapid and prolific to be recorded verbatim; instead, the trained critical instincts busily accept and reject words and images as they appear. But we recognize in Hall's descriptive remarks the first stages of the poem: the initial direct statement ("Snow is in the oak."), the details ending with the irrational perception that the "weight of the sun" is forcing the snow against the speaker's window, and the drop away from perception into recollection, finally into an indistinct blend of memories unified by snow. The third stanza inaugurates a quest for the implications and associations in the interior or psychic life of the poet; this search leads back to the origins of existence before the poem concludes. At the outset, Hall sees snow as representative of the phase of decline to which all things are destined, and this significance discloses in turn a deep-seated obsession with mortality already evident, as we noted, in the earlier poetry:

> Snow is what must
> come down, even if it struggles
> to stay in the air with the strength
> of the wind. Like an old man,
> whatever I touch I turn
> to the story of death.

Following this passage, snow is viewed as an agent of reversal and transformation, endowing everything it covers with "the substance of whiteness." But the last three stanzas of the poem perform an analysis, after their own fashion, of the poet's response to snow in the attempt to trace the origins of that response at the beginnings of his life. The inevitable fall of snow toward the earth, which previously aroused submerged associations and the fear of death, is now linked to a birth trauma; an individual resists birth as a fall into the world culminating at last in death in the same way as a sick and dying man fights against his end. Hall's method of analysis does not employ rationalistic or logical means, for again he proceeds by reverie, reaching back along connecting strands of emotions and memories to revive within himself the child's sense of reality:

> So the watcher sleeps himself
> back to the baby's eyes.
> The tree, the breast, and the floor
> are limbs of him, and from
> his eyes he extends a skin
> which grows over the world.
>
> The baby is what must
> have fallen, like snow. He resisted,
> the way the old man
> struggles inside the airy tent
> to keep on breathing.
> Birth is the fear of death.

The final stanza makes at once a flat assertion of perishability—the fate of man as well as of snow—and the poet declares his inability to find what amounts to a pattern that includes survival or revivification. The poem finishes with the removal of the sun and its life-giving rays, and the return of falling snow, accompanied in the last line by a general statement of descent that may recall Rilke's poem "Autumn," with its haunting lines, "We are all falling. This hand's falling too—/all have this falling-sickness none withstands." But the "One whose gentle hands/this universal falling can't fall through" (J. B. Leishman's translation) seems precisely the saving God whom Hall cannot discover behind the locked "door/to the cycles of water";

> Snow is what melts.
> I cannot open the door
> to the cycles of water.
> The sun has withdrawn itself
> and the snow keeps falling,
> and something will always be falling.

"We want to regress in the service of the ego, we want to become as children," Hall affirms in *The Vatic Voice*, and it is exactly such a regression he undertakes in "The Snow" and a variety of other poems. "The Grass," a poem thematically allied with "The Snow," likewise starts with a visual perception which rapidly leads to a hidden chain of thoughts compelling the poet's imagination to merge with the essences of nature. Like Roethke in his greenhouse poems and his childhood sequences of *The Lost Son* and *Praise to the End!* Hall wishes to uncover the identity and significant relation of things with himself in the intimacy of an imaginative or visionary union with them.

> When I look at the grass
> out my window in rain,
> I know that it happens
> again. Under
>
> new grass,
> among stones and the downward
> probe of trees,
> everything builds

or alters itself.
I am led
through a warm descent
with my eyes covered,

to hear the words
of water. I listen, with
roots of
the moist grass.

The process of identification with the earth, grass, and roots of trees simultaneously initiates a fall toward sleep, the lapsing into a reverie or daydreaming state ("I am led/through a warm descent/with my eyes covered") which successfully blocks the ordinary rational operations of the conscious mind and permits the poet to listen for a more fundamental voice within himself, a voice that will disclose his relationship with the natural world. The speech he wants to hear is formed from "the words/of water," and when we recall the traditional associations of that liquid element with birth, purification, fertility, and renewal, the character of Hall's search in the poem becomes more obvious. "For things as for souls," Gaston Bachelard writes in *The Poetics of Reverie*, "the mystery is inside. A reverie of intimacy—of an intimacy which is always human— opens up for the man who enters into the mysteries of matter." So the dream which engages the poet here draws him into a profound participation in the life of the elemental cosmos, where he may learn its secrets of rebirth for himself. In the poem's final image he has felt himself to be a living part of nature, his nerves and sensibilities resemble the roots of grass vibrant with expectancy, waiting for the life-renewing voice of water to fill them. Unlike "The Snow," then, "The Grass" pursues a course of descent which concludes without any definite resolution but hints strongly at the imminent arrival of animating energies, potentialities for existence.

Water, that element containing such affective stimulus for Hall, has some of its central attributes enumerated in "The Sea," where, in this expanded form, it appears as the universal feminine, womb of life, image of serenity or repose, identified also with earth, and is a destroyer as well—in short, something possessing the qualities of the paradoxical figure of Durga:

> She is the mother of calms
> and the hot grasses;
> the mother of cliffs
> and of the grinding sand;
> she is the mother of the dead
> submarine, which rolls
> on a beach among gulls.

No wonder that in his poem "The Child" Hall envisages a boy whose inner ear waits for the whispers and stirrings—as the mature poet does in "The Grass"—of the primal waters. His recommendation in *The Vatic Voice* of the reanimation of childhood's uninhibited imaginative modes of perception and invention—a recommendation which has, of course, been made and put into practice by a considerable number of modern poets and painters—and the desire to accomplish it finally brings him to the persona of that boy, whose actual existence was long ago terminated in time and personal history but who has yet remained an inhabitant of the unconscious life of the adult. In "The Child" that lost figure of the poet's youth revives. Hall's interest, however, plainly does not consist in awakening particular memories, scenes, or incidents from his past; such details of recollection as one finds in the poem are generalized. The awakening here is an arousal of the latent sensibilities and imaginative powers of the child Hall was, recognizing them now for what they are and can offer. Suddenly, this boy's way of seeing and feeling the world, his essential but acutely sensitive solitude on which the impressions of experience register with purity, his primitive, unspoiled awareness of a proximity to the roots and origins of his being (in the image of the cave and the repeated image of the pool)—and I think to non-being too—are necessary to Hall as a poet. By delving into himself far enough to carry the child in him back from sleep, he has acquired the gift of that child's fresh mental and perceptual faculties:

He lives among a dog,
a tricycle, and a friend.
Nobody owns him.

He walks by himself, beside
the black pool, in the cave
where icicles of rock

rain hard water,
and the walls are rough
with the light of stone.

He hears some low talking
without words.
The hand of a wind touches him.

He walks until he is tired
or somebody calls him.
Then he leaves right away.

Later when he plays with his friend
he stops suddenly
to hear the black water.

From the discussion of these few pieces in *A Roof of Tiger Lilies*
("The Grass" and "The Child" are slightly revised in *The Alligator
Bride*) we begin to notice recurrent motifs or thematic patterns
that occupy Hall in a large proportion of the poems. Speaking ab-
stractly—for each specific poem is a different, concrete realization
the contours of which a statement of theme merely traces—the
scheme visible in these poems is the familiar universal one of descent or death and rebirth or recovery. As I suggest, this symbolic
scheme appears in a unique form in each poetic instance; the entire
pattern is not always in evidence in a single poem. We can credit
the manifestation of such themes, I think, to the kind of poetry of
psychic exploration which Hall starts to write with this book. While
the imagery of reverie or the unconscious as it is used in Hall's
poetry helps to create a sense of objectivity, of a general validity,
the watchful reader also perceives the poet's personal engagement
with the themes and materials of his work—in other words, a sub-

jective necessity which is already clear enough in "The Snow," "The Grass," and "The Child."

Consequently, the figure of the self stands squarely at the center of this recurrent scheme, for the pattern of change or transformation involved in the poems results ultimately in an alteration of the speaker who has experienced the inner dramas they portray. We have observed in "The Child" how the poet has descended into himself to awaken the dormant childhood figure resident there. In such poems as "Cold Water," "At Thirty-Five," "Digging," "Sleeping," "Wells," "Self-Portrait, as a Bear," "The Days," "The Tree and the Cloud," and "The Stump" Hall also presents phases or versions of an inward journey, psychic crisis, or symbolic dying, all in the interest of attaining a regenerated condition, a new mode of apprehending the realities of the world and the possibilities of his existence—in effect, gaining entrance to a new dimension of being. (His two elegies, "O Flodden Field" and "The Old Pilot's Death," project the vision of a new integration or wholeness beyond mortality but are not specifically religious.) While occasionally we are given a few details or incidental aspects of the outward portions of the poet's experience, these poems largely focus on the interior processes and responses to his external life. "Sleeping" serves as a paradigmatic poem for these psychic ventures because it is both an embodiment of them and a comment on their character. In the poem's second section Hall, napping briefly, is startled by a momentary vision of death and dissolution:

> I was lying on the sofa to rest, to sleep
> a few minutes, perhaps.
> I felt my body sag into the hole of sleep.
> All at once I was awake and frightened.
> My own death was drifting near me
> in the middle of life. The strong body
> blurred and diminished into the dark waters.
> The flesh floated away.

As before, water has the aspect of a primal source and also of death. Here the threatening dream of personal destruction and annihila-

tion prepares for Hall's convictions about the descent into the unconscious life of the self in the closing stanza:

> The shadow is a tight passage
> that no one will be spared
> who goes down
> to the deep well.
> In sleep, something remembers.
> Three times since I woke
> from the first sleep,
> it has drunk that water.
> Awake, it is still sleeping.

These final lines disclose the poet's persistence in his explorations,
and the waters which at first seemed to promise nothing but death
have become waters to be drunk and suggest healing or renewal.
The "shadow," in Jungian or analytical psychology, is an unconscious opposite of the ego or conscious self and contains qualities
consciousness has repressed, "aspects," in the words of M.-L. von
Franz from *Man and His Symbols* (edited by Jung), "that mostly
belong to the personal sphere and that could just as well be conscious. In some aspects, the shadow can also consist of collective
factors that stem from a source outside the individual's personal
life." In this poem it is clear that Hall continues his efforts to probe
the recesses of his inner world so that an experience which initially
appears both negative and terrifying may be turned to more positive account in the end. Confrontation with the shadow is an
ordeal, a rite of passage within the self which must be undergone
before the way of integration can open; the last line of the poem
implies that what the shadow concealed has been brought to consciousness, recognized, and assimilated.

Several poems locate changes in nature which inaugurate or pro-
mote changes in the self. In "The Tree and the Cloud" Hall remarks the differences between them: when the tree is cut down it
becomes various other things, while the cloud goes through metamorphosis, "becomes other clouds." Consequently, the tree teaches
us the solidity of matter, but the elusive quality of the cloud taxes,

and thus develops, our sensibilities—or so I understand the poem's conclusion:

> The tree is hard to the hands.
> To touch the cloud
> hardens the touching.

"The Stump" and "Digging," more ambitious poems, exhibit an intimate relationship, a communion really, between the person of the poet and the life of nature. Both pieces achieve visionary experience, though in quite separate ways, for in "The Stump" it is earned as the result of the poet's gradual approach to and contemplation of the object, while "Digging" starts almost immediately on the plane of dream or surrealist vision. Beginning descriptively in "The Stump," Hall offers details of the cutting down of a dead oak tree on his lawn in mid-winter. Nothing unusual occurs in this first section until the last stanza, where an odd mood of exultancy suddenly seizes the poet at the thought of the felled tree. This elation is, of course, indicative of the responses of the unconscious, affective being to a seemingly routine external event; in his inward self what is taking place assumes for the poet the preliminary stages of a symbolic drama:

> Yet I was happy that it was coming down.
> "Let it come down!" I kept saying to myself
> with a joy that was strange to me.
> Though the oak was the shade of old summers,
> I loved the guttural saw.

With the second section the "nude trunk" is reduced by a man with a saw to the stump of the poem's title. But, strangely perhaps, the stump is resistant to his attempts to plane it down to smooth wood, even with the ground, and at last he abandons the task, leaving in section three only the poet to observe, then draw near the stump, with his imagination dilating upon the latter's properties:

> Roots stiffen under the ground
> and the frozen street, coiled around pipes and wires.
> The stump is a platform of blond wood

in the gray winter. It is nearly level
with the snow that covers the little garden around it.
It is a door into the underground of old summers,
but if I bend down to it, I am lost
in crags and buttes of a harsh landscape
that goes on forever. When the snow melts
the wood darkens into the ground;
rain and thawed snow move deeply into the stump,
backwards along the disused tunnels.

Now the stump's altering appearances, whether viewed close-up as an infinitely extending and rugged topography or seen in the larger perspective of the effects of seasonal change, dominate the poet's mind. The imagery of "rain and thawed snow" penetrating the wood "along the disused tunnels" can only recall Hall's frequent employment of water symbolism with its cycle of recurrence and renewal. If the last section of the poem remains descriptive at the outset, certain phrases there prepare us, as does the reference to water, for the imaginative leap into another dimension of experience taken in the two closing stanzas. Weathering blackens the "edges of the trunk," but at the center of the stump's upper surface "there is a pale overlay,/like a wash of chalk on darkness." Next we are told that "the desert of the winter/has moved inside" the stump. In the first passage the trace of chalky whiteness is set against the darkness in a manner highly suggestive of both purification from and resistance to the negative or deathly connotations of the encroaching dark. The second passage, which shows the sterility of winter passing far into the stump, implies its absorption by the tree—a step that precedes any possibility of rebirth.

At this point a radical break occurs in the poem's continuity. Suddenly we are witnesses not of the familiar stump in the yard, but of an exotic visionary world, abundant with new life, rich with the magical promise of voyages like those of Baudelaire or St.-John Perse, filled with an exquisite dream detail reminiscent perhaps of parts of Rimbaud's *Illuminations*. Only in the final lines does the stump emerge again, but transformed forever by the vision of which it has been the focus:

> There is a sailing ship
> beached in the cove of a small island
> where the warm water is turquoise.
> The hulk leans over, full of rain and sand,
> and shore flowers grow from it.
> Then it is under full sail in the Atlantic,
> on a blue day, heading for the island.
>
> She has planted sweet alyssum
> in the holes where the wood was rotten.
> It grows thick, it bulges
> like flowers contending from a tight vase.
> Now the stump sinks downward into its roots
> with a cargo of rain
> and white blossoms that last into October.

In the terms of Hall's imaginative transfiguration the stump takes on the form of the crippled ship which, planted with flowers by the mysterious, anonymous fertility goddess of the concluding stanza whom we can best simply identify as a revitalizing principle of nature or existence, is rendered capable of making its voyage to an "island" of unknown character. What matters here, anyhow, is not an explanation of the voyage or its end but the transforming, life-giving energies that underlie the poet's dreamlike images. The entire pattern of descent and renewal is contained in the last three lines, where the stump, heavy with water, "sinks downward into its roots," and by doing so sends up durable "white blossoms." By recognizing this cyclical pattern of death and rebirth, the poet has uncovered the meaning of his own strange desire early in the poem to see the tree cut down; thus we comprehend that attention to these processes or events in nature has its correspondences in the "deep mind," where similar patterns are followed.

In "Digging" the poet imagines himself returned home in the middle of the night after a long day of ecstatically pleasurable work

in his garden. The atmosphere of the day and the garden exude
potentiality and fecundity: "when lilies/lift themselves out of the
ground while you watch them." From here on the poem assumes
the aspect of a symbolic dreaming which concentrates explicitly on
the transformation of the speaker through his assimilation by and
participation in the fundamental cycles of nature. Shrunk to the
size of a seed, he is carried by a South wind until he falls "in cracked
ground." Death, the way back into water, and an awakening that
partially reminds us of Adam's after Eve was created follow this
imagery of sexuality and fertilization. The luxuriant blossoming
consequent upon these separate stages is directly explained as the
integration of the self, which might lead the reader to think of
the "green shoot" rising from the poet's side in Jungian fashion
as the Anima, the female principle within the male, which needs
to be in harmonious balance with the Animus in order to achieve
wholeness:

> The dirt will be cool, rough to your clasped skin
> like a man you have never known.
> You will die into the ground
> in a dead sleep, surrendered to water.

> You will wake suffering
> a widening pain in your side, a breach
> gapped in your tight ribs
> where a green shoot struggles to lift itself upwards
> through the tomb of your dead flesh

> to the sun, to the air of your garden
> where you will blossom
> in the shape of your own self, thoughtless
> with flowers, speaking
> to bees, in the language of green and yellow, white and red.

"The well is an archetype, one of the gravest images of the human
soul," Bachelard writes in *The Poetics of Reverie*; Hall's "Wells,"
with its obviously quite personal significance, certainly bears out
the French philosopher's remark. In this poem, as in "At Thirty-

Five" and "Cold Water," there is considerable evidence of private dilemmas—the implications are at once sexual, domestic, and spiritual—which cannot be circumvented (indeed, a situation of impasse seems indicated) but must be lived through, endured, and finally gone beyond in the effort to rescue the self from stultification or oblivion. "Wells" also shares with "The Stump" and "Digging" the imagery of nature's effloresence as a means of expressing a new flowering of the self and reestablished bonds with earth or the world. The initial stanzas create the impression of withdrawal, fear, and impotence; the ladder may be interpreted both as a phallus (as can the tree, partially, in "The Stump" and the head of the musk-ox and the boat in "The Long River," for example) and as the way of ascent from the self's isolation, of communication with external reality and the being of others:

> I lived in a dry well
> under the rank grass of a meadow.
>
> A white ladder leaned out of it
> but I was afraid of the sounds
>
> of animals grazing.

Help, when it comes, arrives in the form of sexual love and brings with it a blossoming of life, a revived fertility which draws the speaker out of his solitude into new relationships; he has found a well of sustaining waters that is not his alone:

> I crouched by the wall ten years
>
> until the circle of a woman's darkness
> moved over mine like a mouth.
>
> The ladder broke out in leaves
> and fruit hung from the branches.
>
> I climbed to the meadow grass.
> I drink from the well of cattle.

(It is also possible to view the well in its first appearance as an image of entrapment in a domestic or sexual relationship which has deteriorated, become sterile, but from which the speaker hesitates to escape until another affection frees him.)

"At Thirty-Five" and "Cold Water" are the concluding poems in *A Roof of Tiger Lilies*. They make sense of the poet's inner drama, the problems he must come to grips with in his private life, when read in sequence; though on the surface, except for the fact that they are both expressive of affective or psychic states, there is no close resemblance between them. With "At Thirty-Five" we find Hall in the middle of his life confronting his own dark wood of failures and losses, as well as the prospect of death; the imagery is harsh and violent, filled with overtones of sexual frustration, misdirection, and final destruction:

> At the edge of the city the pickerel
> who has lost his way
> vomits and dies. The river
> with its white hair staggers to the sea.
>
> My life lay open like a smashed car.

The movement or progression of this poem depends upon lightning-like flashes of thought and imagery, sudden jumps in association; it is the kind of poem, as Hall says in a recent essay (*Michigan Quarterly Review*, Fall 1969), that gives us "the expression without the song," where song is taken to signify "the old baggage of ostensible content which, as Eliot says, is never the true content" and so can be ignored. As a result, "images set free from realistic narrative or from logic grow out of each other by association, and poems move by an inward track of feeling." We have already noted such qualities in Hall's work, but it is worth recalling them as we look at this poem, which in its loose, associative arrangement, its "anti-narrative" story (Hall's term), anticipates later pieces such as "The Alligator Bride," "Apples," and "Swan."

The next phase of "At Thirty-Five" constitutes a shift backward, so to speak, first into the decline and ruin of a domestic or amatory relationship, then further back into images of past family life, all linked with the death and decay of relationships and households. Finally, as in the instance of the destroyed auto above, a single line serves both to summarize and punctuate the preceding portion of the poem. If we are puzzled by the interposed, separate lines with their image of a Boeing 707 airliner submerged in the sea yet oddly "intact" after its crash, Hall remarks in his BBC broadcast comments that an image similar to this was so obsessive with him at one time in his life he believed it to be the memory of an actual scene. He adds: "My poetry's full of crashed airplanes anyway, usually having to do with women somehow or other." In the present instance the plane clearly refers to the anonymous woman whose countenance undergoes hideous metamorphoses in the nightmare of the opening stanza of this stage of the poem. The lucidity and calm of the plane's setting suggest, I believe, that she has, after all, survived her agonies and disruptions:

> Windows barred, ivy, square stone.
> Lines gather at her mouth and her eyes
> like cracks in a membrane.
> While I watch, eyeballs and tongue
> spill on the tiled floor
> in a puddle of yolks and whites.
>
> The intact 707
> under the clear wave, the sun shining.
>
> The playhouse of my grandfather's mother
> stands north of the shed; spiders
> and the dolls' teacups of dead women.
> In Ohio the K-Mart shrugs;
> it knows it is going to die.
>
> A stone, the closed eye of the dirt.

We then proceed to discover the poet freed from the confines of his house (so closely identified with the woman above that, as the concentrated imagery implies, the collapse of one is the collapse of the other), walking the streets "before dawn" and receiving un-

expectedly a vision of possibilities, perhaps even of the patching of
broken bonds, though the images point to an ambivalence, particularly since the resurrected houses are still designated as "wrecks":

> A door clicked; a light opened.
> Houses sailed up
> like wrecks from the bottom of the sea.

Musing on the nature of dreams—of which this vision of restored
houses is perhaps one—he reminds himself that lechery, greed, and
vulgarity must be counted parts of the world even "if the world is
a dream." This chain of thought forces an abrupt, stark view of the
existence of the single man, deprived of love and sexual compan-
ionship, living in a terrible futility and isolation comparable to the
situation evoked at the outset of "Wells." The stanza's importance
is magnified once we realize that the poet can imagine this barren
condition as his own potential future. Again, Hall follows his
stanza with a single line, indicating here that the course of his
thinking in this direction has reached termination:

> There are poor bachelors
> who live in shacks made of oilcans
> and broken doors, who stitch their shirts
> until the cloth disappears under stitches,
> who collect nails in tin cans.
> The wind is exhausted.

The poem has moved into a dead-end passage where hope and
strength appear to be utterly abolished (the collecting of nails in
cans is surely an image of complete sexual futility and despair);
only some surge of vitality, a marked change in the perspective of
life, can salvage the poet. True to the patterns we have discerned
in Hall's poetry, this revivification does occur, for the last stanza
reverses the negativism, desperation, and deathward leaning of the
first. The lost route of the dying pickerel and the river staggering
toward the sea become, as the poet awakens from the horrendous

dreams of his recent past, a visible path of his destiny on which he can proceed, aided by the surprising surrealist vehicle of the trolley car that carries him rapidly to the forest of "new pine" where another life awaits him (in "The Dump" from *The Alligator Bride* a similar trolley leads to a colony of old men like the bachelors above):

> In the middle of the road of my life
> I wake walking in a field.
> A trolley car comes out of the elms,
> the tracks laid down through an acre of wheat stubble,
> slanting downhill. I board it,
> and cross the field into the new pine.

From its very opening, "Cold Water" may be read as a deliberate continuation of "At Thirty-Five," with its setting the forest of pine into which the poet disappears. It is a poem that in its early details, as well as in the startling turn it takes in the two closing stanzas, is devoted to a search for abandoned beginnings. Unlike its immediate predecessor, "Cold Water" follows a perfectly straightforward narrative line, broken only by the sudden appearance of the Iroquois elders and the realizations and decisions their coming generates in the poet. As we have seen so often in Hall's poems, however, and can observe equally in the work, say, of James Wright, Louis Simpson, W. S. Merwin, William Stafford, or Galway Kinnell, natural details, objects, or gestures accumulate a significance beyond themselves, become expressive or symbolic in terms of their poetic context, that is, but do so unobtrusively. In this instance the "dammed stream," the shoe full of "cold water," the "shade/of a thicket, a black pool,/a small circle of stunned drowsing air," when looked at within the structure of the entire poem, seem necessary stages in the kind of initiatory ritual process thematically proposed there. That we find ourselves engaged more with some deep layer of the poet's thought than with a literal landscape becomes rather obvious in the second and third stanzas where the imagined act of fishing turns suddenly real:

I step around a gate of bushes
in the mess
and trickle of a dammed stream
and my shoe fills with cold water. I
enter the shade
of a thicket, a black pool,
a small circle of stunned drowsing air,

vaulted with birch which meets overhead
as if smoke
rose up and turned into leaves.
I stand on the roots of a maple
and imagine
dropping a line. My wrist jumps
with the pain of a live mouth hooked deep,

and I stare, and watch where the lithe stripe
tears water.
Then it heaves on my hand: cold,
squaretailed, flecked, revenant flesh
of a Brook Trout.
The pine forests I walked through
darken and cool a dead farmer's brook.

While it would be a mistake, I think, to insist too strenuously on the symbolic properties of various particulars in these stanzas, they still remain enormously suggestive, especially in view of what is yet to come. The dammed river, the unpleasant experience of the soaked shoe, the black pool (which, of course, evokes the other pools, wells, and subterranean waters in Hall's work), and the atmosphere of lassitude and stagnation surrounding the pool combine to create an impression of withdrawal to the vicinity of origins, the beginnings of existence, though at first it may appear to be a *cul de sac*, a place of stultification. But if we remember that at the finish of "At Thirty-Five" the poet went off into the forest, presumably to begin his life anew, then the situation described above can be understood as the regression required if an individual is to reach the starting point of self-transformation. This sort of journey backward which precedes the self's purification and integration recalls familiar instances in such poems as Frost's "Directive" and Roethke's "The Lost Son." Strangely enough, too, the forest clearing in Hall's rendering has something of the shape and character of a cathedral, but not a man-made one—a cathedral formed by nature ("vaulted with birch which meets overhead") and thus the appropriate location for the consecration of the self to its true destiny.

The imagined gesture of casting a line which quickly and enigmatically turns into the physical act of catching a fish can perhaps best be comprehended as the initiatory movement by the poet that breaks the spell of torpor dominating the forest clearing and, more pointedly, his inner being. Certainly, this effort and its success call forth the Indian elders; having satisfied a preliminary requirement, the poet has readied himself to be led by them, in spite of hardships, to the heart of "the mystery," and so to a confrontation of the possibilities of achievement or defeat in the struggle to win rebirth:

> I look up and see the Iroquois
> coming back
> standing among the birches
> on the other side of the black pool.
> The five elders
> have come for me, I am young,
> my naked body whitens with cold
>
> in the snow, blisters in the bare sun,
> the ice cuts
> me, the thorns of blackberries:
> I am ready for the mystery.
> I follow them
> over the speechless needles
> of pines which are dead or born again.

We may ask why Hall chooses an American Indian initiation ritual, which introduces a boy into men's tribal activities and their religious significance, as the means for presenting aspects of his own psychic procedures. A primary answer would probably be that he did not choose it in the sense of a rationally calculated selection, but that such images originally came unbidden and recommended themselves for their imaginative implications. We can obtain a further answer from Hall's comment on two passages from poems by Robert Bly and Louis Simpson in the introduction to his *Contemporary American Poetry*; he could as easily be talking of his own poem as of theirs when he says, "This new imagination reveals through images a subjective life which is general, and which corresponds to an old objective life of shared experience and knowledge." The mythic and religious attitude toward life, which was once (with Indians and medieval Christians alike) a common property of the outward existence of the community, and thus had all its members as participants, has been abolished from the external world of modern man by science, technology, urbanization, and widespread agnosticism. But since this attitude corresponds with and reflects the fundamental nature of the self, it cannot be completely vanquished; instead, it goes underground to become an active part of a person's unconscious mind and dream life. The conclusion of Hall's poem acquires strength and conviction as a result of these images of trial and rite of passage, for we can feel that he is engaged, in an inner way, with a progression of the self which is not merely his alone but a central feature of the larger life shared by humans in all times and places.

The twenty-five recent poems gathered in *The Alligator Bride* continue in the vein of the work we have examined in *A Roof of Tiger Lilies*; indeed, as we might expect, certain themes and imaginative preoccupations, because they are charged with personal meaning for Hall, declare themselves again. "The Blue Wing," for example, links the relationship with women to the crash of a plane; the final stanza with its wreckage and residue of bones implies a symbolic dying which is survived through the parabolic arc of death and rebirth which the last three lines describe:

> The tiny skeleton inside
> remembers the falter of engines, the

cry without
answer, the long dying
into
and out of the sea.

Similarly, "The Dump" and "The Train," using the imagery of
trolley lines and railways, are poems of movement away from the
past. The first of these, mentioned previously, terminates sombrely
in a "graveyard of trolleys," populated by old men, "in narrow
houses full of rugs,/in this last place," where quite obviously they
wither into death. In "The Train" memory presents itself as "a long
shape/of darkness, tunnel/huddled with voices, hunger/of dead
trees, angels" from which a train emerges gliding off into the distance. A woman's head and arm, growing less and less discernible,
extend from a window in gestures of farewell:

The train curves tightening
the light hair to itself
and diminishes
on a Sunday morning down
the track forever,
into memory, the tunnel
of dead trees.

Death, metamorphosis, the abolition of or escape from the past,
and renewal or ascent into a fresh, hitherto unknown dimension
of being form the thematic concerns of most of Hall's new poems,
so that they constitute a distinct extension of the preceding work,
sometimes overlapping it but also breaking into further territories.
Close in feeling to the poems of departure, division, and the death
of relationships which entails the abandonment of a whole segment
of life is the negative continuation of these experiences of severance
into static situations, terrible in their desolation and lack of promise
for any future, and so for any hope of fulfilling the poet's sense of
self-identity and destiny. "The Dump," with its crowd of wasted
lives, qualifies as a poem of this type as well as a poem of escape
from the past; in effect, it is a record of failed deliverance. The

figures of "Make Up," originally depicted in details recalling their bodily, even erotic natures, drift away from living and harden into "Ghost/stone, and the stone/daughter" at the end. The woman of "Sew" busily stitches from her "church of scraps" an image of a man suited to her ideals and in her myopic fashion endows it with life, "until it stands up like a person/made out of whole cloth"; but the short closing stanza, spoken by the poet, reveals how far she has missed knowing what he is. Frustrated from rising into the amplitude of existence, he remains solitary, neglected if unharmed, among the untested possibilities of his dreams:

> Still, I lie folded
> on the bolt in the dark warehouse,
> dreaming my shapes.

Like Roethke's "Dolor" and Karl Shapiro's "Office love . . ." from *The Bourgeois Poet*, poems of the same bleak but oddly humorous spirit, "The Repeated Shapes" focuses on the emotional depression Hall associates with modern technical efficiency—in this case, the shiny emptiness of public sanitation. The line-up of urinals, to Hall's slightly hallucinated eye, appears as a uniform row of old men with whom, in his own despairing mood, he acknowledges family ties. Here, as elsewhere in these poems, the awareness of waste and futility is nearly overwhelming:

> They are my uncles,
> these old men
> who are only plumbing,
> who throb with tears all night
> and doze in the morning.

On a note of historical authenticity the smashed airplane returns in "The Man in the Dead Machine," this time as a Grumman Hellcat fighter plane "High on a slope in New Guinea," where its pilot brought it to rest undiscovered "among bright vines/as thick as arms." While the human remains in "The Blue Wing" seem plainly those of a woman, these are, of course, as indicated by both title and details, a man's, and Hall devotes an entire stanza of close description to "the helmeted/skeleton" still strapped rigidly upright in the pilot's seat decades later. Then, as we have had occasion to note before, the poet without warning completes the poem in a stanza that changes direction and casts on the figure of the pilot and his fate quite different meanings:

> Or say that the shrapnel
> missed him, he flew
> back to the carrier, and every
> morning takes his chair, his pale
> hands on the black arms, and sits
> upright, held
> by the firm webbing.

The first two-thirds of the poem simply provides a grim, matter-of-fact piece of reportage from which there can be no issue but the unvarnished account of what is observed. But with the reversal of actual death and the assertion of a daily reenactment of another sort of death, we are no longer in the realm of inanimate external objects like fallen airplanes and skeletal figures; instead, a monstrous ritual of inner existence, confined by the structure of its habitual gear, has been disclosed. The reader cannot help but feel that, in some ways, this fate is far worse than the one of the poem's opening, for the living pilot of the last stanza does not really live but each day endures a death, while life itself waits . . . elsewhere, beyond. Not surprisingly, Hall's most frighteningly graphic poem of imprisonment, self-torment, and utter despair, "The Corner," is printed immediately after "The Man in the Dead Machine." In this piece the self has succumbed to anonymity and descended to the condition of a maddened animal, but in the manner in which only a human can. The horror of the situation is compounded by the concluding revelation of the impossibility of relief, even through death:

> It does not know
> its name. It sits
> in a damp corner,
> spit hanging

from its chin, odor of urine
puddled around.
Huge, hairless, grunting,
it plays with itself,
sleeps, stares for hours,
and leaps
to smash itself on the wall.
Limping, bloody, falling back
into the corner, it
will not die.

"The Alligator Bride" shares with the poems we have been discussing manifest elements of guilt, separation, destructive energy,
and death, but it weaves more completely the fabric of an irrational
or surrealist fable, with a group of characters which includes a
sinister cat, the bride herself, and the speaker. Hall's BBC notes
disclose how the poem began as "fragments" he had written down
which finally were drawn together by the introduction of "the
strange figure of a dead stuffed alligator in a bride costume," and
it developed until it became "a macabre little story," containing, as
he realizes, materials from his own life. Knowledge of his biography is not important, however; for, as he says,

> The story, and the characters, are there, and the story is one that,
> if you leave yourself open to the language of dreams, is available
> to everyone. That is, it has the same sort of general availability that
> a story like Beauty and the Beast has. You have to listen to a poem
> like this, or read it, as if you were dreaming but keeping your eyes
> wide open. You have to be alert, but you musn't be inquisitive. You
> may not *translate* anything in the poem, you have to *float* on it. At
> the same time you have to receive every detail. Perhaps this is more
> demanding than any other kind of poem.

With this advice and admonition in mind we can try to approach
the poem on its own terms and stay within the range of allusiveness
it establishes. The initial lines of the first two stanzas are connected
by a preoccupation with the passage of time, thus reminding us of

the poet's obsessive linking of temporal perceptions with his constant awareness of mortality:

> The clock of my days winds down.

> *   *   *   *

> Now the beard on my clock turns white.

In the stanzas which these lines respectively begin, Hall creates a domestic scene, a relationship between the speaker and his cat, who "eats sparrows outside" the window, that leads toward intimacy through the latter's seemingly generous impulse; but at the moment of their communion the cat is losing an enigmatic object she cherishes:

> Once, she brought me a small rabbit
> which we devoured together, under
> the Empire Table
> while the men shrieked
> repossessing the gold umbrella.

We cannot gauge much of the significance of this umbrella beyond the most obvious reasons for its value: it is gold and provides shade, hence perhaps a circle of comfort and security. It appears to be valued as well by the anonymous men who in "repossessing" it are presumably claiming what once was theirs. In any event, this action disrupts the commerce between speaker and cat in the second stanza, where the image of the snowy-bearded clock indicates a rapid flow of time and existence. Now the cat, to all appearances estranged from the speaker (though he can refer to her as "My cat"), continues in a despondent state, not only over her lost umbrella but also for love of the Alligator Bride, who enters the poem in the next stanza, a grotesque, mocking figure that would do credit to a child's nightmare:

> Ah, the tiny fine white
> teeth! The Bride, propped on her tail
> in white lace
> stares from the holes

of her eyes. Her stuck-open mouth
laughs at minister and people.

Following a catalogue of food and wine—which also includes the
cat and Bride—assembled for the wedding festivities, there comes
a swift change of direction as the poem turns toward the speaker
as its focal point and as the source of subsequent events. The speaker
begins a disclosure of his own malice, in which the cat enjoys a
voluntary complicity—apparently as her love shifts into hatred—
finding release and termination only in the death of the Alligator
Bride. This will to harm or destroy shows itself in images of two
very different artificial products of a highly technical age:

> The color of bubble gum,
> the consistency of petroleum jelly,
> wickedness oozes
> from the palm of my left hand.
> My cat licks it.
> I watch the Alligator Bride.

And the stanza after, in its own puzzling fashion, starts off with
similar details of imagery, though now they are more widely applied. The odd, inert houses sealed together in "gelatin"—and the
speaker's house we learn from the closing stanza is one of these—
suggest the same confinement and exclusion of the world that we
observed in Hall's criticism of middle-class living in the early poem
"Christmas Eve in Whitneyville." In the present instance as well
the restrictive conditions of "Big houses like shabby boulders" that
"hold themselves tight in gelatin" seem to exert unendurable pressures on those inhabitants who, like the speaker, refuse to be imprisoned in this manner and desire a freedom which is associated
with the powers of imagination. The speaker's declaration that he
is "unable to daydream," then, makes sufficiently obvious how
claustrophobic the atmosphere of this life has become. Need we
add what should here be plain: that the cause of this decidedly unpleasant condition is the Alligator Bride, or better perhaps, that it
results from the relationship between the Bride and the speaker,

who is, after all, the Groom. The inability to "daydream" under
these circumstances leads to the violent climax of the poem and to
the unsettling aftermath which brings no particular relief:

> The sky is a gun aimed at me.
> I pull the trigger.
> The skull of my promises
> leans in a black closet, gapes
> with its good mouth
> for a teat to suck.
>
> A bird flies back and forth
> in my house that is covered by gelatin
> and the cat leaps at it
> missing. Under the Empire Table
> the Alligator Bride
> lies in her bridal shroud.
> My left hand
> leaks on the Chinese carpet.

However confusing and distressing these events may be, and difficult to unravel with any degree of certainty (and it is in this very
respect that their riddling irrationality closely reflects the inextri-
cable mass of motives, thoughts, and acts involved in much more
ordinary occurrences), we can readily comprehend how the speaker
in pulling the trigger has destroyed himself, or some aspect of his
existence, at the same time that he has murdered the Bride. The
poem's end does not, however, see him liberated; but in a setting
which might even be taken as a dream parody of a murder scene
in some Agatha Christie or Ellery Queen detective novel we discover the ravenous cat in vain pursuit of a new prey, the corpse of
the Bride, and the guilty speaker, whose "wickedness" (with sexual
suggestion?) flows like an open wound to stain the exotic carpet.
The air of this situation is one of bewilderment and irresolution;
any final impression of the poem's conclusion must also incorporate
the fact that the trio of cat, Bride, and speaker remain imprisoned
in the latter's "house that is covered by gelatin." Whatever the underlying problems might be, the speaker's impulsive course of ac-

tion has left damages but no satisfactory achievements, except the release of violent energy. The poem itself, carefully and subtly composed, effective in its resonances and its use of detail, is satisfying and stages an intricate drama of relationships which proves endlessly engaging to the reader's imagination.

"Swan," "Apples," and "This Room" share elements of dream, fantasy, and narrative with "The Alligator Bride," though the incidents are apt to seem more disjunct, to comprise less of what could be termed a "story" of any sort than the latter poem contains. In addition, these three poems point in affirmative ways, especially through their associations with the world of nature, toward a new level of life, which is gained, at least momentarily, in certain love poems such as "The Coal Fire," "Lovers in Middle Age," and "Gold." Two other poems, "The Table" and "Mount Kearsarge," deserve mention here because both of them return to the New Hampshire farm of Hall's youthful experience and manage to accomplish, in distinctive and quite moving ways, a recovery of the past which confirms it as an essential ingredient of the poet's existence in the present. The last lines of "Mount Kearsarge" reveal that Hall no longer needs to live on his grandparents' farm to be aware of the haunting spectral shape of the mountain; its form has been absorbed in consciousness and cannot be lost:

> I will not rock on this porch
> when I am old. I turn my back on you,
> Kearsarge, I close
> my eyes, and you rise inside me,
> blue ghost.

Similarly, in "The Table" Hall spends almost the entire poem on recollections of days shared with his grandfather on the farm, and each detail is lovingly recalled; the finish of the poem, however, is in the present, where the poet revisits the farmhouse. In an instant of strange, Proustian communication the life which he knew and is not past, the life which the previous part of the poem has re-created, comes suddenly alive to his mind and senses as he touches a table in the familiar bedroom and receives a startling perception of his grandfather's dead horse and the busy, humming summer landscape, long gone but existing unchanged. Through the agency of this old piece of furniture, in which it mysteriously resides, a time that was lived and felt to the fullest extent has been resurrected in the poet:

> This morning
> I walk to the shaded bedroom and lean
> on the drop-leaf table.
> > The table hums
> a song to itself without sense
> and I hear the voice of the heaving
> ribs of Riley
> and grasshoppers
> haying the fields of the air.

Divided into five separate sections, though apparently concentrated on scenes and events within one geographical area, "Swan" explores relationships between man and the earth or nature's hidden energies; it also renders the absence or dissolution of such relationships. In its theme, then, the poem has close ties with many of Hall's pieces from *A Roof of Tiger Lilies* discussed previously. At the outset it is winter, a darkening afternoon, as the poet, climbing "Mill Hill," observes a fire in the fields burning off the stubble in preparation for another season's planting:

> Smoke blows
> from the orange edges of fire
> working the wheat
> stubble. "Putting
> the goodness back
> into the soil."

These details complete the first section and set the precedent for the whole poem: each part, of varying length, is devoted to an individual experience, whether it is almost pure, immediate observation, as in sections one, two, and five; an amalgam of perceivings and inward vision, as in part three; or a mingling of desire and memory into quite specific description, as in part four. Whatever differences exist among these distinct moments of experience, in one way or another each touches the thematic currents we have mentioned, and the reader must draw them together by allowing them to move freely together in his mind. In the passage above the setting at once lends itself to a capacious sense of nature in its entirety, of its cycles, and so of its preparations for renewed fertility to which man contributes here. Such regenerative powers of nature, and the feeling of fundamental, enduring realities that proximity to earth can arouse in a person lead Hall through this poem toward his own physical contact and discovery in the natural realm.

The account of a separate incident, strange and dramatic in character, constitutes the second section and contains one of the two specific references to the bird which gives the poem its title:

> Driving; the fog
> matted around the headlights;
> suddenly, a thudding
> white shape in the whiteness,
> running huge and frightened, lost
> from its slow stream . . .

Seemingly, these lines give us the entire experience, and the stanza trails off inconclusively. The passage recalls perhaps two famous swans in exile in French Symbolist poetry: the swan escaped from its cage and bathing its wings in the dust of Parisian streets in Baudelaire's "Le Cygne," and the swan trapped in ice but desirous of the infinite azure of the skies in Mallarmé's sonnet "Le vierge, le vivace et le bel aujourd'hui." In both poems the bird is, to one degree or another, emblematic of the poet tormented by exile and unfulfillment. While I do not wish to imply that Hall had these previous poetic instances in mind, he certainly knows the poems in question, and the present passage may be illuminated somewhat by recalling them. Here, too, it is difficult not to view the significance of the incident, the sudden appearance of a swan out of the thick fog—in which the poet must likewise find it troublesome to make his way—and the details selected to describe it ("running huge and frightened, lost/from its slow stream . . ."), as somehow related to the poet's own condition, a condition that can only be called one of uprootedness, for he is portrayed throughout the poem as always in movement, a kind of wanderer. The stanza's indecisive ending leaves open the possibilities still available for the swan to discover the route back to the stream; the poet is left, like the bird, to maneuver as best he can through the fog toward an unspecified—and probably as yet unknown—destination.

The third section not only stands in the middle of the poem but holds the thematic center as well, tying together important particulars of imagery and providing in its use of the windmill image a focus of the poet's quest for an existence in harmony with nature's rhythms and energies. The mill appears as if seen in reverie or dream; like an agency of nature it channels and lifts the hidden forces of the subterranean world, transforming them in the process. The "dark" on which it draws as a source again recollects the black waters and pools of earlier poems also associated with primal forces or the covert origins of life. Beneath the mill, the network of "tunnels" it taps embraces the world, reaching "to the poles/and down to the center of the earth"; and so this queer edifice seems almost a temple of natural religion through the activity of which great chthonic powers achieve release. The next stanza, of merely two lines, returns to the fire of section one, only then to disclose the mill halted in its operations:

> Fire breaks out in the fields.
> The wheel of the mill does not turn.

The sterility of winter is implied here, for the fire in the initial stanza was witnessed by the poet in December burning "the wheat/stubble"; the mill, too, must remain idle during this period. Now

the fog reappears as well, and unexpectedly the section closes with
a startling flourish of surrealist images:

> The windmill
> flies, clattering its huge wings, to the swamp.
> I make out cliffs of the Church,
> houses drifting like glaciers.

Surely, though the poet does not specify it, the swan somehow
merges with the mill as it takes flight—enigmatically, not toward
the stream but toward a swamp. It is difficult to determine all this
journey may suggest, but in any event it prepares the way for the
desolate, frozen, infertile images of church and houses, which replace the natural life and energy symbolized by the windmill with
the supernaturalism or abstract theology represented by the church
and, following the pejorative connotations of the dwellings in
"Christmas Eve in Whitneyville" and "The Alligator Bride," the
seclusion from full existence of the bourgeois. The movement of
this section traces the abdication of natural modes of being and
their replacement by artificial and ideological ones.

The dreamlike qualities of the third part vanish entirely in the
next section, to be exchanged for the poet's open declaration of desire for an existence lived in proximity to earth, drawing sustenance
of both a spiritual and physical kind from a close working relationship with the soil. He envisages in the daily and seasonal routines
of another, ideal individual the life he wishes for himself:

> I envy the man hedging and ditching,
> trimming the hawthorn, burning branches
> while wasps circle in the smoke of their nest,
> clearing a mile of lane, patches of soot
> like closed holes to a cave of fire,
> the man in his cottage
> who smokes his pipe in the winter, in summer
> digging his garden in ten o'clock light,
> the man grafted entirely to rain and air,
> stained dark
> by years of hedging and ditching.

These lines terminate the feeling of restless movement that pervades previous sections, and, of course, the type of living presented here contrasts decisively with what was observed at the close of part three with its glacial houses and cliff-like church, thus marking a return to harmony with creation. The "cave of fire" may hint at buried forms of natural energy, not unlike those the mill reaches, to which the anonymous man, who has blended with his environment, has access. His identification with nature is so complete that, in addition to fire, he is associated with the other elements of water, air, and earth as well: "grafted entirely to rain and air,/stained dark/by years of hedging and ditching."

The final section, like the second, is brief and inconclusive, but where the latter offered the desolate, helpless image of the swan lost from its stream in the fog, this stanza evokes the swan by analogy and now in an affirmative way:

> The close-packed surface of the roots
> of a root-bound plant
> when I break the pot away,
> the edges white
> and sleek as a swan . . .

By some means, in the transition from the fourth part of the poem to this last one, the poet has progressed from "envy" of the man whose life revolves about contact with the soil and what grows there to his own direct physical relationship with nature or natural process, suggested quite plainly by his handling of the plant. In thematic and symbolic terms the breaking of the pot surrounding the plant and the discovery of "the edges white/and sleek as a swan . . ." is comparable to a moment of rebirth for the poet, who is, as we noticed, linked to the figure of this bird. The fact that Hall refuses to complete his poem with a period can only be understood to reinforce the idea of potentiality which the experience has made manifest. In like fashion "This Room," which is simultaneously the actual dwelling of the poet, his body, and the metaphorical space of the self's living context, concludes on an ecstatic note of acceptance by the natural cosmos in the form of flowers; the sexual overtones of the imagery broaden the implications here and also look toward the love poems mentioned before and to a volume of love poetry, *The Yellow Room: Love Poems*, unpublished at the time of this writing:

> Climbing the brown stairs
> of the air, I enter
> my place. I am welcomed
> by pots of geraniums, green stems
> thick as a thumb, uprushing
> leaves! I live
> in your exhalations, sweet
> tongued flowers!

Of the poem "Apples" Hall says in his BBC remarks, "When I started it, I thought it was about old dead poets. A number of friends of mine who were poets had died all in a year or so, and I wanted to make up a place for them to be. By the time I'd finished the poem, I saw that it was really about other things." The poem is certainly about death, entrance into the underworld or kingdom of the dead, and the beginning of a new paradisaical form of being which consists largely of earthly delights;[3] but poets are not specified as participants, the dead might be anybody. Though ritual elements appear in the circular movement of the dancers at the poem's end, no religious intentions except those implied by the subjective fantasy of acceptance by and habitation within the earth itself can be discerned. The recurrent and resonant image of the apple, together with other particulars drawn from nature, such as grapes, grass, a marigold, and a peacock's feather, keep this poem consistent with those pieces which, like "Swan," seek out an order of harmony with creation. That kind of natural correspondence Hall projects in a vision of the conditions of life after death:

3. The apple here carries very old ties to the traditional paradisaical image of Avalon or Land of Apples. On this island, by some accounts, King Arthur lies buried See Robert Graves's comments in *The White Goddess* (New York, 1959) and in his edition, *English and Scottish Ballads* (London, 1957).

> They have gone
> into the green hill, by doors without hinges,
> or lifting city
> manhole covers to tunnels
> lined with grass,
> their skin soft as grapes, their faces like apples.

The disappearing dead who, in fairy-tale fashion, vanish into the verdant passageways of earth already possess the aspect of renewal, as the analogy between their skin and faces and the fruit specifies. By means of the magical transformations of sight which the "round eye" of a peacock feather—introduced in the second stanza—permits, giving the "curved spot" on the apple's surface the appearance of a "fat camel" and synesthetically changing a "fly's shadow" into "the cry of a marigold," the poet approaches, "looking hard," the world the dead have entered, then swiftly moves into it himself:

> I am caught in the web of a gray apple,
> I struggle inside
> an immense apple of blowing sand,
> I blossom
> quietly from a window-box of apples.

Proceeding through conditions of storm and turbulence seems necessary as a preparation for entrance into the underworld, and the journey is followed by the unmistakable imagery of rebirth within the precincts of this natural paradise, the activities and pleasures of which occupy the last two stanzas of the poem. "Seven beautiful ladies" are provided "each man" and serve him "whiskey"; mysteriously, stories are told by the "rungs of a ladder"; and, not surprisingly, the analogy with apples is announced once more, leading the poem toward its climactic dance about the hill, whose shape derives from that fruit but whose qualities are likewise those of the powerful peacock feather. Within the boundaries of reverie, the poet participates in this ideal cosmos of his imagining:

> Their voices like apples brighten in the wind.
> Now they are dancing

with fiddles and ladies and trumpets
in the round
hill of the peacock, in the resounding hill.

Another note of intense revitalization is struck by the love poems
in *The Alligator Bride*, which include "The Coal Fire," "Lovers in
Middle Age," and "Gold." The last two poems, together with "Waters," which carries oblique hints of sexual fulfillment, and "The
Dump," discussed previously, Hall places, with minor changes, in
the context of his new book, *The Yellow Room*, a sequence of
"poems and fragments" that chronicle a love affair, its complexities
and complications, the depths of emotion and awareness it reveals,
its rhythm of communion, withdrawal, and reunion, and its painful conclusion in a final separation. The poems of this sequence
vary considerably in style, tone, and feeling; certainly they demonstrate a further development in Hall's work, a new delicacy and
fineness in many instances that brings his art close in quality to
Chinese poetry—or at least to what we apprehend of such poetry
in the versions, say, of Ezra Pound and Kenneth Rexroth. And, of
course, these poems form a unity among themselves, plotting points
along the route of an extraordinarily intimate relationship which,
even though it must conclude unhappily, impels the poet to a self-
renewal that, one imagines, cannot be destroyed entirely even with
the final parting of the persons involved. Obviously then, the poems
from *The Alligator Bride* which Hall also uses in the sequence will
assume different implications in accord with their various positions
there; so, for example, "Waters" becomes much more explicitly
sexual in terms of its changed context. "Gold" continues the spatial
metaphors noted before in "This Room" and apparent in *The Yellow Room*, but its color symbolism, effective enough in isolation in
this beautiful poem, is enlarged by the extension of that symbolism
throughout the sequence. In "Red, Orange, Yellow," which appears
near the close of *The Yellow Room*, we discover some important
explanations:

For five years of my life, or ten,
I lived no-color.

> In a beige room I talked
> clipped whispers
> with a lady who faded while I looked at her.
> Even our voices were oyster-white.

This opening easily reminds us of earlier poems of domestic disharmony, but a second stanza provides explicit statements of the warm, vibrant colors the poet associates with the woman he does love and now has lost:

> So I looked for the color yellow.
> I drank yellow for breakfast,
> orange at lunch, gold for dinner.
> Red was the color of pain.
> Now I eat red
> all day. The sky is her yellow.
> Sometimes no-color years
> rise in slow motion,
> like Mozart on drums. Their name is Chumble.
> They smile
> like pale grass, looking downward.
> But red sticks
> needles in my eyes.
> Yellow
> dozes on the beach at Big Sur
> or in the center of my new room
> like a cactus
> that lives without water, for a year.

Even the rending agony of loss receives a bright, burning color and takes its share in a momentous revivification of the self that promises to leave behind certain negative phases of the past. Undoubtedly, torment and despair will recur, but the experience which a poem like "Gold" realizes must, as its brief and stunning last stanza proclaims, inaugurate enduring alterations in the inner life of the psyche and the emotions of both lover and beloved:

> Pale gold of the walls, gold
> of the centers of daisies, yellow roses

pressing from a clear bowl. All day
we lay on the bed, my hand
stroking the deep
gold of your thighs and your back.
We slept and woke
entering the golden room together,
lay down in it breathing
quickly, then
slowly again,
caressing and dozing, your hand sleepily
touching my hair now.

We made in those days
tiny identical rooms inside our bodies
which the men who uncover our graves
will find in a thousand years
shining and whole.

Without entering into further detail about an as yet unpublished book,[4] which may undergo considerable revision, we can still affirm that the fundamental patterns of descent and ascent, death and rebirth, positive and negative polarities are perceptible in these love poems. They also, as previous poems do, find completion in images of stoical suffering and harsh conditions of solitude; one may, however, await beyond them another stage of growth, a new opening out to the possibilities of existence. As the reader looks back over Donald Hall's career, the remarkable strides of his development which follow upon his abandonment of the supposedly correct poetic modes of the 1950's and his subsequent freedom to explore his experience honestly, to say what he needed to say in a voice tested and found to be truly his own, rather than one imposed from without and legislated by alien theoretical criteria, become quite evident. From *A Roof of Tiger Lilies* through *The Yellow Room* his work displays that high level of imaginative power and technical accomplishment which has secured him an enviable place among the American poets of his generation.

4. *The Yellow Room: Love Poems* was published (New York, 1971) after the present collection of essays had been completed.

6   "The True and Earthy Prayer": Philip Levine's Poetry

We live
the way we are
   —P.L., "The Sadness of Lemons"

The poetry of Philip Levine, from *On the Edge* (1963) to his two latest collections, *Red Dust* (1971) and *They Feed They Lion* (1972), has always displayed technical skill, a dexterous handling of both formal and, more recently, informal modes, and a command of the resources of diction and rhythm. Yet these aspects of technique seem in a way secondary, absorbed as they are by a central, driving intensity peculiar to this poet's approach. Such intensity leads him to a relentless searching through the events of his life and the lives of others, through the particulars of nature as these signify something about the processes of living, the states of existence, in order to arrive not at Eliot's transcendence, Roethke's "condition of joy," or Whitman's ideal of progress and brotherhood (though the sharing of suffering and the common ties of humanity are basic to Levine's attitude) but to the sort of awareness suggested by Yeats's phrase, "the desolation of reality": an unflinching acquaintance with the harsh facts of most men's situation which still confirms rather than denies its validity. If this is a difficult prospect, we must acknowledge how familiar it has become of late through the poems of Robert Lowell, David Ignatow, James Wright, Allen Ginsberg, and Galway Kinnell, to mention a few obvious names. In the writing of these poets, as in Levine's, the range of human sympathies, the frankness, perseverance, and

sensitivity create of themselves an affirmative, life-sustaining balance to the bleak recognition of religious deprivation, war, social
injustice, moral and spiritual confusion.

Levine's early poetry is taut, sharp, formal but gradually alters to
accommodate his desire for greater freedom in line length and
overall construction. A prominent theme of his first book is the
reversal or defeat of expectations. Put another way, it motivates a
struggle on the poet's part to view life stripped of the vestiges of
illusory hope or promise, a type of hard spiritual conditioning
which helps to engender his fundamental responsiveness to the
dilemmas of the poor, embittered, failed lives of the "submerged
population" (the late Frank O'Connor's term) in modern society,
a responsiveness that accounts for much of both the energy and the
deep humaneness of all his work. A firm grip on existence itself
takes priority for Levine from the start, though with it necessarily
comes an acceptance of pain and the admission that failure, defeat,
and imperfection—but not surrender!—are unavoidable in men's
affairs. The penetrating look he gives himself in "The Turning"
from *On the Edge* points the direction he follows to maturity,
which depends on the realization of flaws as well as the capacity to
exist, to continue, made sturdier by this self-knowledge:

> . . . . . no more a child,
> Only a man,—one who has
> Looked upon his own nakedness
> Without shame, and in defeat
> Has seen nothing to bless.
> Touched once, like a plum, I turned
> Rotten in the meat, or like
> The plum blossom I never
> Saw, hard at the edges, burned
> At the first entrance of life,
> And so endured, unreckoned,
> Untaken, with nothing to give.
> The first Jew was God; the second
> Denied him; I am alive.

Committed to a fallen, unredeemable world, finding no metaphysical consolations, Levine embraces it with an ardor, anguish, and fury that are themselves religious emotions. In a brief comment on his work contributed to *Contemporary Poets of the English Language* (1970) he lists among his "obsessions" "Detroit" (where he was born, did factory labor, and studied), "the dying of America" (a recurrent theme in various guises), and "communion with others," which incorporates its predecessors as well as specifying what is for him a primary poetic impulse. Writing frequently of persons whose lives are distinct yet touch his own, he increases his consciousness and imaginative powers, and a chord of compassion and understanding reverberates within and beyond the boundaries of his poems. This is not to say that Levine puts himself out of the picture or chooses a mask of impersonality, but that his presence in a poem, whether overt or concealed, constitutes an enlargement of personality, a stepping out of the ego-bound "I" into the surrounding life. Paradoxically, he reaches inward, far into the recesses of the psyche, at the same time he reaches outward, thus fulfilling a pattern of movement Robert Bly has long advocated as essential to a modern poetry rich in imaginative potentialities.

Among the poems of Levine's initial volume, this self-extension appears most complete when he adopts the voices of different persons—the Sierra Kid, four French Army deserters in North Africa, the unnamed officer of "The Distant Winter"—to replace his own. Another sort of identification, of a crucial kind for the line of development his work pursues, occurs in the title poem "On the Edge," and also in "My Poets" and "Gangrene." In these instances he does not assume the role of another speaker but takes up the question of a poetic vocation and the destiny of poets in society today. In one shape or another, each of these poems really considers the problem of speechlessness, the lacerating irony of the mute poet imprisoned by circumstances which thwart or oppose his art, making its practice unlikely or impossible. So Levine sorts through the probabilities of his own future. The poet/speaker of "On the Edge" describes himself as the insane, alcoholic Poe of

the twentieth century, born, as Levine was, "in 1928 in Michigan."
This latter-day Poe plays the part of an observer who doesn't write,
only watches the actions and prevarications of nameless people. In
the last stanza he repeats a refusal of his art, though we are provided
in its statement of alienation, perceptiveness, and silence with a
poetry of angry eloquence:

> I did not write, for I am Edgar Poe,
> Edgar the mad one, silly, drunk, unwise,
> But Edgar waiting on the edge of laughter,
> And there is nothing that he does not know
> Whose page is blanker than the raining skies.

This abstention from writing, or persecution for telling the truth
by means of it, occupies the other poems mentioned. Levine's effort
here is to indicate the need for honest speech, the conditions which
militate against it, and the frustrating atmosphere of separateness
the poet faces. Thematically, the poem "Silent in America" from
Not This Pig (1968), Levine's second collection, brings such matters to a critical climax and to a moment of transformation and
decision. Though it is not the first poem in the book, dramatically
speaking it should be thought of as a pivotal piece, for its procedure
and resolution make possible what Levine is doing elsewhere in
the same volume: breaking down those barriers which prevent him
from entering areas of otherwise lost or unapprehended experience
requisite to the poetry he wants to write. At the outset the poet announces his silence, which fashions for him a state of remoteness
and solitude that border on anonymity. Watching ordinary things
—a sprinkler wetting a lawn—stirs him toward utterance, but he
stays quiet. A doctor's examination uncovers no defect. Details of
nature engage him with the elusive tracery of their being; still, the
animate *something* he notices in trees, water, and flowers defies his
wish to name it, and thus his muteness persists. Locked in isolation,
Levine now falls victim to inner torments, to his "squat demon,/my
little Bobby," a splintered apparition of the self who plagues him
with insatiable sexual demands. The poem develops rapidly toward

hysteria and derangement until the poet bursts out with a negative cry of resistance. A section ensues in which he articulates the aims of his writing—to give voice to the varied experience of lost, unknown, or forgotten individuals he has met, speaking with and for them—but he is likewise forced to assent to the fact that each person remains finally impervious to total comprehension and communion. The following passage handsomely summarizes Levine's intentions and concerns:

> For a black man whose
> name I have forgotten who danced
>   all night at Chevy
>   Gear & Axle,
>   for that great stunned Pole
> who laughed when he called me Jew
>   Boy, for the ugly
>   who had no chance,
>
>   the beautiful in
> body, the used and the unused,
>   those who had courage
>   and those who quit—
> Rousek and Ficklin
> numbed by their own self-praise
>   who ate their own shit
>   in their own rage;
>
>   for these and myself
> whom I had loved and hated, I
>   had presumed to speak
>   in measure.
> The great night is half
> over, and the stage is dark;
>   all my energy,
>   all my care for
>
>   those I cannot touch
> runs on my breath like a sigh;
>   surely I have failed.

My own wife
and my children reach
in their sleep for some sure sign,
but each has his life
private and sealed.

Levine's anxiety arises from the profoundly felt impulse to put his language, as poetry, in the service of others' lives, in addition to his own. The walls of privacy and individuality he cannot traverse cause him regret and a feeling of loss. Yet, just as surely, he *does* speak for others to the very limit of his abilities, not only here but also in the rest of this book, as well as in his subsequent poetry. If he is unable to appropriate the entirety of another life, like a second skin, it is still possible for him to go with others, moving to the rhythms of their existence and assimilating the details which his imagination requires. This kind of correspondence and kinship receives treatment in the closing section of the poem, where Levine meets a friend, H., in a Los Angeles bar and talks with him. H. is perhaps a writer too; in any event, he is described as doing essentially what an artist does: he creates a world composed of half-real, observed figures and half-fictitious ones who fit in with their actual counterparts, and he lives with them in imagination and sympathy. In the tavern Levine senses the presence of a person of fabulous name, apparently a wholly fictive man, conjured by his mind, who imposes himself no less strongly on the poet's awareness and emotions because of that:

Archimbault is here—
I do not have to be drunk
to feel him come near,

and he touches me with his
life, and I could cry,
though I don't know who he is
or why I should care
about the mad ones, imagined
and real, H. places

in his cherished underground,
  their wounded faces
glowing in the half-light of
  their last days alive,
  as his glows here.

Whatever his self-questioning, Levine clearly cares, and his expressed wish in the next lines merges his own existence with that of such persons as fill the bar, until all seems to become part of poetry itself: "Let me have/the courage to live/as fictions live, proud, careless,/unwilling to die." So he would have his life speak itself as poems do, tenacious of their being. At the conclusion Levine and H. leave the bar and "enter the city." The poet urges his readers to join him, to blend into the mass of humanity thronging the streets in their restlessness, at last to go "beyond the false lights/ of Pasadena/where the living are silent/in America." This invitation is as much a definition of his own poetic pursuits as it is a gesture by which the poet makes his reader a partner to what he sees. Levine will invade those areas of the unspoken life and lend them words.

Rich and complex though they usually are, the poems of Levine's first two collections are relatively direct, proceeding by certain logical, sequential, narrative, or other means which provide the reader with support and guidance. Levine never altogether abandons poems of this sort, but even in *Not This Pig* he begins to widen his fields of exploration to include experiences which manifest themselves in irrational, dreamlike, fantastic, or visionary forms, doing so variously in such poems as "The Rats," "The Business Man of Alicante," "The Cartridges," "The One-Eyed King," "Animals Are Passing from Our Lives," "Baby Villon," "Waking an Angel," "The Second Angel," and "The Lost Angel." These pieces prepare the way for the surrealist atmosphere of *Red Dust*, the elliptical, disjunctive composition evident there, and further visible in portions of *They Feed They Lion*. Levine has cited the Spanish and

Latin American poets Hernandez, Alberti, Neruda, and Vallejo, in addition to postwar Polish poetry, as having presented new possibilities available to him. The freedom, vigorousness, metaphorical and imagistic daring of these poets plainly has had a tonic effect on Levine's more recent writing, releasing him to new boldness and strength.

So, by any but a narrow or restrictive view, Levine's latest books must be judged extraordinarily successful, exhibiting an access of inventiveness and vision. In *Red Dust* the elements of experience move into different focus; they are less "distanced," talked about, or pointed to than rendered dramatically as the very substance of language and image in the poems. The general character of these poems is also freer, more intuitive, and thus occasionally more difficult, unyielding to logical analysis. From the beginning we find an openness in the structure of poems, in the sense that they are not brought to a tidy conclusion but often end in a startling, seemingly irrational—yet, on consideration, perfectly apt—statement. Here is the final section of "Clouds," a poem which gathers considerable momentum by associative leaping among apparently random details whose disconnectedness actually pulls together a grim portrait of the contemporary world. Over the shifting scenes and figures the aloof clouds travel, absorb, and spill out their rain, giving the poem coherence while at the same time implying a universal indifference to which the poet responds with vehemence in the striking lines at the close:

> You cut an apple in two pieces
> and ate them both. In the rain
> the door knocked and you dreamed it.
> On bad roads the poor walked under cardboard boxes.
>
> The houses are angry because they're watched.
> A soldier wants to talk with God
> but his mouth fills with lost tags.
>
> The clouds have seen it all, in the dark
> they pass over the graves of the forgotten
> and they don't cry or whisper.

> They should be punished every morning,
> they should be bitten and boiled like spoons.

In poems of this sort the components are set down in combinations which resist or contradict ordinary rational expectations for them. The reader, thus perceptually thrown off balance, has the option either to give up or give in, and so to see and feel the particulars of experience fused in vivid, evocative ways. Gradually, the shifting shapes, the elisions and abrupt juxtapositions will disclose their significance, if the reader will only accept them on their own terms. As indicated previously, Levine's social and moral preoccupations retain their urgency, but, as in the work of the Spanish-speaking poets he admires, such interests tend at times to be integral with the immediate, elliptical, or surreal orderings of imagery and statement. Frequently now, the poems seek out specific details of landscape, cityscape, even vegetation and animal life, though these directly or obliquely correspond with aspects of human existence. Sensitivity to place—whether Detroit, California, or Spain (where Levine lived for two years recently)—the imagination exercised on what is perceived there, leads readily into poems of large expressive force. The figures inhabiting these pieces may be quite separate and distinct, with Levine himself only a transparent or invisible speaker (though, of course, an indirect commentator, sometimes a savage one), as in "The End of Your Life" or "Where We Live Now"; or they may involve the poet openly, as he tries to define himself and his life, or when he captures a moment's affective resonance, a mood charged with implications, of the kind we observe in "A Sleepless Night," "Told," "Holding On," and "Fist." In "Noon" he draws self and others together beautifully within the frame of a landscape:

> I bend to the ground
> to catch
> something whispered,
> urgent, drifting
> across the ditches.
> The heaviness of

flies stuttering
in orbit, dirt
ripening, the sweat
of eggs.
        There are
small streams
the width of a thumb
running in the villages
of sheaves, whole
eras of grain
wakening on
the stalks, a roof
that breathes over
my head.
                Behind me
the tracks creaking
like a harness,
an abandoned bicycle
that cries and cries,
a bottle of common
wine that won't
pour.
At such times
I expect the earth
to pronounce. I say,
"I have been waiting
so long."
                Up ahead
a stand of eucalyptus
guards the river,
the river moving
east, the heavy light
sifts down driving
the sparrows for
cover, and the women
bow as they slap
the life out

of sheets and pants
and worn hands.

In this poem, as in many of Levine's newest, man's common attachments with earth, his relationship with objects, the hard, painful climate in which most lives are lived, are evoked through a skilled interweaving of images, the particulars of the world suddenly caught up to view, suffused with the "reek of the human," to borrow a phrase from Donald Davie. "How much earth is a man," Levine asks in another poem; his answer indicates an indissoluble, fateful bond: "a hand is planted/and the grave blooms upward/in sunlight and walks the roads." In the three angel poems from *Not This Pig*, which create a little sequence among themselves, the realm of transcendence, of the spiritual ideal, dissolves or collapses before the spectacle of flawed earthly reality. What aspects of the spiritual can become evident belong not to a hidden or remote sphere but radiate, if possible, from the ingredients of day-to-day mundane affairs. So, in Levine's work, life is circumscribed by the finality of death, but this inevitability is countenanced with toughness, stoicism, staying power. As he says of his fist in the final stanza of the poem bearing that title:

It opens and is no longer.
Bud of anger, kinked
tendril of my life, here
in the forged morning
fill with anything—water,
light, blood—but fill.

Between the poems of *Red Dust* and those of *They Feed They Lion* no alterations occur in Levine's attitude toward such matters; two poems, "The Space We Live" and "How Much Can It Hurt?", are even reprinted from the earlier book. In general, however, Levine employs less of the dense irrational or associative manner so prominent in *Red Dust*, though with no loss of concentrated force. The opening poems, "Renaming the Kings" and "The Cutting Edge," for instance, dramatize personal incidents in a direct, sequential way quite appropriate to the experiences. These pieces, along with several others, examine the poet's encounters in the midst of natural settings, with each occasion revealing some facet of a relation between the things of earth and a man—a relation sometimes assuring and harmonious, sometimes disturbing or painful. In "The Cutting Edge" a stone under water gashes the poet's foot; he casts it out of the stream and hobbles away. Later he returns, discovers it, and pauses to wonder before deciding what to do with it:

> I could take it home
> and plant it in a box;
> I could talk about
> what it did to me
> and what I did to it,
> or how in its element
> it lives like you or me.
> But it stops me, here
> on my open hand,
> by being a stone, and I send
> it flying over the heads
> of the fishing children,
> arching alone above
> the dialogue of reeds,
> falling and falling toward water,
> somewhere in water to strike
> a conversation of stone.

A very different type of "conversation" takes place in "To a Fish Head Found on the Beach Near Málaga," where Levine, walking alone, comes upon the ravaged body and head, hanging by its shred of bone, then confides his "loneliness," "fears," and torments to it. The result of his strange speech makes him sense the contours and characteristics of his own face and head, and, at last, "throw the fish head to the sea./Let it be fish once more." The poem's concluding lines assert the speaker's comprehension of the unalterable cyclicism of existence, the ironic necessity of destruction for renewal:

> I sniff my fingers
> and catch the burned essential oil
> seeping out of death. Out of the beginning,
> I hear, under the sea roar, the bone words
> of teeth tearing earth and sea,
> anointing the tongues with stone and sand,
> water eating fish, fish water,
> head eating head to let us be.

This volume also includes sequences of varying length, as well as groups of obviously connected poems. "Thistles," the longest of them, dedicated to the poet George Oppen, is composed of discrete pieces each of which focuses on a singular occasion, perception, or ambiance of feeling. The same may be said for the shorter sequence, "Dark Rings." These poems are not bound tightly together, though the thistle appears in the first and last pieces of that sequence, and the "dark rings" refer not only to a specific detail in one poem but also to images in most and the mood of all of them. Yet their swift, free, occasionally abbreviated notation and arrangement give an impression of accuracy, deftness, and assurance in the handling of experience. The poems are full of nuances and overtones which linger on. One must place with these sequences most of the poems in the book's second section, dealing with Levine's Detroit life among the automotive workers and the abandoned, hopeless, silent figures we have seen him desirous to know and to speak for. The angels return in this section in shifting but always earthly forms, evanescent protective spirits hovering about the poet, presences in his closet, or incarnate in someone of his acquaintance, as in the fourth poem of "The Angels of Detroit" group. Here "the angel Bernard," trapped and frustrated by the massive industrial system for which he labors and cannot escape, writing poems no one will read, aching for love, release, even death, awakens as always to find himself surrounded by the debris of manufacture, our

values and lives rupturing from the shapes of steel and rubber in
which we have conceived them:

> At the end of the mud road
> in the false dawn of the slag heap
> the hut of the angel Bernard.
> His brothers are factories and
> bowling teams, his mother is the
> power to blight, his father
> moves in all men like a threat,
> a closing of hands, an unkept
> promise to return.
>   We talk
> for years; everything we
> say comes to nothing. We drink
> bad beer and never lie. From
> his bed he pulls fists
> of poems and scatters them
> like snow. "Children are guilty,"
> he whispers, and the soft mouth
> puffs like a wound.
>
> He wants it all tonight.
> The long hard arms of a black woman,
> he wants tenderness, he wants
> the power to die in the
> chalice of God's tears.
>
> True dawn through the soaped window.
> The plastic storm-wrap swallows wind.
> '37 Chevie hoodless, black burst
> lung of inner tube, pot metal
> trees buckling under sheets.
> He cries to sleep.

Such a poem gives notice of the incredible strength, the economy
and muscle with which Levine endows the majority of his poems.
Two of the most amazing and powerful pieces, "Angel Butcher"
and "They Feed They Lion," bring the book's second section to a

climactic level of prophetic vision; the latter poem is dazzling in its syntactic, linguistic, and dramatic invention, its use of idiomatic effect. But both poems need to be read in their entirety and are too long for quotation here. It remains now simply to say for the purposes of this brief commentary that Levine's poetry, praiseworthy at the start, has developed by momentous strides in the past decade. His new poems make it impossible for him to be ignored or put aside. He stands out as one of the most solid and independent poets of his generation—one of the best poets, I think, anywhere at work in the language. It is time to begin listening.

> Can you hear me?
> the air says. I hold
> my breath and listen
> and a finger of dirt thaws,
> a river drains
> from a snow drop
> and rages down
> my cheeks, our father
> the wind hums
> a prayer through my mouth
> and answers in the oat,
> and now the tight rows of seed
> bow to the earth
> and hold on and hold on.

Selected Bibliography

This bibliography contains a selective listing of volumes by most of the poets mentioned in "Creation's Very Self," as well as those to whom the other individual essays are devoted.

Ammons, A. R. *Selected Poems*. Ithaca, N.Y., 1967.
———. *Tape for the Turning of the Year*. New York, 1972.
———. *Collected Poems 1951–1971*. New York, 1972.
Ashbery, John. *Some Trees*. New Haven, Conn., 1956.
———. *The Tennis Court Oath*. Middletown, Conn., 1962.
———. *Rivers and Mountains*. New York, 1966.
———. *Selected Poems*. London, 1967.
———. *The Double Dream of Spring*. New York, 1970.
———. *Three Poems*. New York, 1972.
Belitt, Ben. *The Enemy Joy: New and Selected Poems*. Chicago, 1964.
———. *Nowhere but Light*. Chicago, 1970.
Benedikt, Michael. *The Body*. Middletown, Conn., 1968.
———. *Sky*. Middletown, Conn., 1970.
———. *Mole Notes*. Middletown, Conn., 1971.
Berg, Stephen. *The Daughters*. Indianapolis, 1971.
Berryman, John. *Homage to Mistress Bradstreet*. New York, 1956.
———. *Short Poems*. New York, 1967.
———. *Berryman's Sonnets*. New York, 1967.
———. *The Dream Songs*. New York, 1969.
———. *Love & Fame*. New York, 1970.
———. *Delusions, Etc*. New York, 1972.
Blackburn, Paul. *The Cities*. New York, 1967.
———. *In. On. or About the Premises*. New York, 1968.
———. *Early Selected Y Mas. Poems 1949–1966*. Los Angeles, 1972.
Bly, Robert. *Silence in the Snowy Fields*. Middletown, Conn., 1962.
———. *The Light around the Body*. New York, 1967.
———. *The Morning Glory*. Santa Cruz, Calif., 1970.

————. *Jumping out of Bed*. Barre, Mass., 1973.

————. *Sleepers Joining Hands*. New York, 1973.

Creeley, Robert. *For Love: Poems 1950–1960*. New York, 1962.

————. *Words*. New York, 1967.

————. *Pieces*. New York, 1969.

————. *A Day Book*. New York, 1972.

Dickey, James. *Poems 1957–1967*. Middletown, Conn., 1967.

————. *The Eye-Beaters, Blood, Victory, Madness, Buckhead and Mercy*. New York, 1970.

————. *Babel to Byzantium* (prose). New York, 1968.

H. D. (Doolittle, Hilda). *Selected Poems*. New York, 1957.

————. *Hermetic Definitions*. New York, 1972.

————. *Trilogy*. New York, 1973.

Dorn, Edward. *The Newly-Fallen*. New York, 1961.

————. *Geography*. New York, 1966.

————. *The North Atlantic Turbine*. New York, 1967.

————. *Gunslinger, Part I*. Los Angeles, 1968.

————. *Gunslinger, Part II*. Los Angeles, 1969.

Duncan, Robert. *The Opening of the Field*. New York, 1960.

————. *Roots and Branches*. New York, 1964.

————. *The Years as Catches*. Berkeley, Calif., 1966.

————. *The First Decade*. London, 1968.

————. *Derivations*. London, 1968.

————. *Bending the Bow*. New York, 1968.

Eberhart, Richard. *Collected Poems 1930–1960*. New York, 1960.

————. *The Quarry*. New York, 1964.

————. *Selected Poems 1930–1965*. New York, 1965.

————. *Shifts of Being*. New York, 1968.

————. *Fields of Grace*. New York, 1972.

Eigner, Larry. *On My Eyes*. Highlands, N.C., 1960.

————. *Another Time in Fragments*. New York, 1967.

————. *Selected Poems*. Berkeley, Calif., 1972.

Hall, Donald. *Exiles and Marriages*. New York, 1955.

————. *The Dark Houses*. New York, 1958.

————. *A Roof of Tiger Lilies*. New York, 1964.

————. *The Alligator Bride: New and Selected Poems*. New York, 1968.

————. *The Yellow Room: Love Poems*. New York, 1971.

―――. *String Too Short to Be Saved* (prose). New York, 1961.

Ignatow, David. *Poems*. Prairie City, Ill., 1948.

―――. *The Gentle Weightlifter*. New York, 1955.

―――. *Say Pardon*. Middletown, Conn., 1961.

―――. *Figures of the Human*. Middletown, Conn., 1964.

―――. *Rescue the Dead*. Middletown, Conn., 1968.

―――. *Poems 1934–1969*. Middletown, Conn., 1970.

―――*Notebooks*. Ed. R. J. Mills, Jr. Chicago, 1973.

Justice, Donald. *The Summer Anniversaries*. Middletown, Conn., 1959.

―――. *Night Light*. Middletown, Conn., 1967.

―――. *Departures*. New York, 1973.

Kees, Weldon. *Collected Poems*. Ed. D. Justice. Lincoln, Nebr., 1962.

Kinnell, Galway. *What a Kingdom It Was*. Boston, 1960.

―――. *Flower Herding on Mount Monadnock*. Boston, 1964.

―――. *Body Rags*. Boston, 1968.

―――. *The Book of Nightmares*. Boston, 1971.

Koch, Kenneth. *Ko, or A Season on Earth*. New York, 1959.

―――. *Thank You*. New York, 1962.

―――. *The Pleasures of Peace*. New York, 1969.

Kunitz, Stanley. *Selected Poems 1928–1958*. Boston, 1958.

―――. *The Testing-Tree*. Boston, 1971.

Levertov, Denise. *The Double Image*. London, 1946.

―――. *Here and Now*. San Francisco, 1957.

―――. *Overland to the Islands*. Highlands, N.C., 1958.

―――. *With Eyes at the Back of Our Heads*. New York, 1960.

―――. *The Jacob's Ladder*. New York, 1962.

―――. *O Taste and See*. New York, 1964.

―――. *The Sorrow Dance*. New York, 1967.

―――. *Relearning the Alphabet*. New York, 1970.

―――. *To Stay Alive*. New York, 1971.

―――. *Footprints*. New York, 1972.

―――. *The Poet in the World* (prose). New York, 1973.

Levine, Philip. *On the Edge*. Iowa City, 1963.

―――. *Not This Pig*. Middletown, Conn., 1968.

―――. *Pili's Wall*. Santa Barbara, Calif., 1971.

―――. *Red Dust*. Santa Cruz, Calif., 1971.

―――. *They Feed They Lion*. New York, 1972.

―――. *1933*. New York, 1974.

Logan, John. *Cycle for Mother Cabrini*. New York, 1955.

————. *Ghosts of the Heart*. Chicago, 1960.

————. *Spring of the Thief*. New York, 1963.

————. *The Zig-Zag Walk*. New York, 1969.

————. *The Anonymous Lover*. New York, 1973.

Lowell, Robert. *Lord Weary's Castle*. New York, 1946.

————. *The Mills of the Kavanaughs*. New York, 1951.

————. *Life Studies*. New York, 1959.

————. *Imitations*. New York, 1961.

————. *For the Union Dead*. New York, 1964.

————. *Near the Ocean*. New York, 1967.

————. *Notebooks 1967–1968*. New York, 1969.

————. *Notebook*. New York, 1970.

————. *History*. New York, 1973.

————. *For Lizzie and Harriet*. New York, 1973.

————. *The Dolphin*. New York, 1973.

Merwin, W. S. *A Mask for Janus*. New Haven, Conn., 1952.

————. *The Dancing Bears*. New Haven, Conn., 1954.

————. *Green with Beasts*. New York, 1956.

————. *The Drunk in the Furnace*. New York, 1960.

————. *The Moving Target*. New York, 1963.

————. *The Lice*. New York, 1967.

————. *The Carrier of Ladders*. New York, 1970.

————. *Writings to an Unfinished Accompaniment*. New York, 1973.

————. *The Miner's Pale Children* (prose). New York, 1970.

O'Hara, Frank. *Meditations in an Emergency*. New York, 1957.

————. *Second Avenue*. New York, 1960.

————. *Lunch Poems*. San Francisco, 1964.

————. *Collected Poems*. Ed. D. M. Allen. New York, 1971.

————. *Selected Poems*. Ed. D. M. Allen. New York, 1974.

Olson, Charles. *The Maximus Poems*. New York, 1960.

————. *The Distances*. New York, 1960.

————. *Selected Writings*. Ed. R. Creeley. New York, 1968.

————. *The Maximus Poems, IV, V, VI*. New York, 1968.

————. *Archaeologist of Morning*. New York, 1973.

Patchen, Kenneth. *Collected Poems*. New York, 1968.

Plath, Sylvia. *The Colossus*. New York, 1960.

————. *Ariel*. New York, 1966.

————. *Crossing the Water*. New York, 1971.

————. *Winter Trees*. New York, 1972.

Rakosi, Carl. *Amulet*. New York, 1967.

————. *Ere-Voice*. New York, 1971.

Rexroth, Kenneth. *Collected Shorter Poems*. New York, 1966.

————. *Collected Longer Poems*. New York, 1968.

Reznikoff, Charles. *By the Waters of Manhattan*. New York, 1962.

Roethke, Theodore. *Open House*. New York, 1941.

————. *The Lost Son*. New York, 1948.

————. *Praise to the End!* New York, 1951.

————. *The Waking: Poems 1933–1953*. New York, 1953.

————. *Words for the Wind*. New York, 1958.

————. *The Far Field*. New York, 1964.

————. *Collected Poems*. New York, 1966.

————. *On the Poet and His Craft: Selected Prose*. Ed. R. J. Mills, Jr. Seattle, 1965.

————. *Selected Letters*. Ed. R. J. Mills, Jr. Seattle, 1968.

————. *Straw for the Fire* (notebooks). Ed. D. Wagoner. New York, 1972.

Schuyler, James. *Freely Espousing*. New York, 1969.

————. *The Crystal Lithium*. New York, 1972.

————. *Hymn to Life*. New York, 1974.

Sexton, Anne. *To Bedlam and Part Way Back*. Boston, 1960.

————. *All My Pretty Ones*. Boston, 1962.

————. *Live or Die*. Boston, 1966.

————. *Love Poems*. Boston, 1969.

————. *Transformations*. Boston, 1971.

————. *The Book of Folly*. Boston, 1972.

————. *The Death Notebooks*. New York, 1974.

Shapiro, Karl. *Poems 1940–1953*. New York, 1953.

————. *Poems of a Jew*. New York, 1958.

————. *In Defense of Ignorance* (prose). New York, 1960.

————. *The Bourgeois Poet*. New York, 1964.

————. *Selected Poems*. New York, 1968.

————. *White-Haired Lover*. New York, 1968.

Simic, Charles. *What the Grass Says*. San Francisco, n.d.

————. *Somewhere among Us a Stone Is Taking Notes*. San Francisco, 1969.

————. *Dismantling the Silence.* New York, 1971.

————. *White.* New York, 1972.

Simpson, Louis. *Good News of Death (Poets of Today III).* New York, 1955.

————. *A Dream of Governors.* Middletown, Conn., 1959.

————. *At the End of the Open Road.* Middletown, Conn., 1963.

————. *Selected Poems.* New York, 1965.

————. *Adventures of the Letter I.* New York, 1971.

————. *North of Jamaica* (prose). New York, 1972.

Snodgrass, W. D. *Heart's Needle.* New York, 1959.

————. *After Experience.* New York, 1968.

Snyder, Gary. *Rip-Rap.* Ashland, Mass., 1959.

————. *Myths and Texts.* New York, 1960.

————. *A Range of Poems.* London, 1966.

————. *The Back Country.* New York, 1968.

————. *Regarding Wave.* New York, 1970.

————. *Earth House Hold* (prose). New York, 1969.

Stafford, William. *West of Your City.* Los Altos, Calif., 1960.

————. *Travelling through the Dark.* New York, 1962.

————. *The Rescued Year.* New York, 1966.

————. *Allegiances.* New York, 1970.

————. *Someday, Maybe.* New York, 1973.

Strand, Mark. *Reasons for Moving.* New York, 1968.

————. *Darker.* New York, 1970.

————. *The Story of Our Lives.* New York, 1973.

Wright, James. *The Green Wall.* New Haven, Conn., 1957.

————. *Saint Judas.* Middletown, Conn., 1959.

————. *The Branch Will Not Break.* Middletown, Conn., 1963.

————. *Shall We Gather at the River.* Middletown, Conn., 1968.

————. *Collected Poems.* Middletown, Conn., 1971.

————. *Two Citizens.* New York, 1973.

Zukofsky, Louis. *All: The Collected Short Poems 1923–1958.* New York, 1965.

————. *All: The Collected Short Poems 1956–1964.* New York, 1966.

————. *'A' 1–12.* New York, 1967.

————. *'A' 13–21.* New York, 1969.

————. *'A' 24.* New York, 1972.

Index